The Death Penalty

Beyond the Smoke and Mirrors

Alfred B. Heilbrun Jr.

UNIVERSITY PRESS OF AMERICA,® INC.
Lanham • Boulder • New York • Toronto • Oxford

Copyright © 2006 by
University Press of America,® Inc.
4501 Forbes Boulevard
Suite 200
Lanham, Maryland 20706
UPA Acquisitions Department (301) 459-3366

PO Box 317
Oxford
OX2 9RU, UK

British Library Cataloging in Publication Information Available

Library of Congress Control Number: 2006922136
ISBN-13: 978-0-7618-3472-4 (paperback : alk. paper)
ISBN-10: 0-7618-3472-9 (paperback : alk. paper)

∞™ The paper used in this publication meets the minimum
requirements of American National Standard for Information
Sciences—Permanence of Paper for Printed Library Materials,
ANSI Z39.48—1984

To Marian and our children

Contents

Tables

Preface

You may wonder why a clinical psychologist would become involved in research on capital punishment and choose to suggest more constructive ways to understand the topic than currently exist. I am not a constitutional scholar and the controversies over the death penalty that show no sign of waning have much to do with the amendments included in the Bill of Rights and their interpretation by the United States Supreme Court. Nor am I a criminal lawyer versed in legal jurisprudence and courtroom litigation. I am a social scientist who has pursued a research and professional interest in violent crime as a form of social deviance for several decades. What I do bring to the table is a belief that efforts to explain any complicated human social phenomenon, and the death penalty is certainly mired in complications, should be free of personal values and efforts to persuade rather than inform. That is what a research psychologist committed to the rule of evidence should be prepared to do.

The pro and con positions in the debate over capital punishment are likely to share the problem common to all controversies bearing upon the intentional killing of one person by another. The death penalty, despite efforts to protect its fairness by legal revision and despite its general public acceptance, is despised by those at one pole of the controversy. By taking the life of someone as punishment, the oppositionist believes that the state simply joins company with the criminal who has intentionally killed another person under especially grievous circumstances. This moral conviction leads oppositionists to seek problems in systems of capital punishment and to magnify these limitations in order to establish their inherent flaws. For examples, executing a criminal for his crime is said to make it impossible to rectify a mistake by the police or the courts; execution by the state simply reinforces the appropriateness of taking a life; capital punishment cases are economically prohibitive.

At the other pole of moral conviction is the view that executing a person guilty of a heinous murder is justified as a punishment because it matches the seriousness of the criminal act. Support for this view can be gained from the Bible, but unfortunately for the sake of conciliation, those opposed to the death penalty can quote Biblical proscription of killing as well. An "eye for an eye . . ." does not rest comfortably with "thou shall not kill" should religion be introduced into the debate. Those who strongly support the execution of those who murder under grievous circumstances also have generated their own list of gains from capital punishment to match in number the limitations proposed by those who oppose it. Murderers who are executed will never kill again; families and friends of the victims will experience a "sense of closure"; a state with capital punishment demonstrates its commitment to being "tough on crime." As it turns out, there is no more reason to accept these retentionist arguments for the death penalty as critical than there is to credit the liabilities posted by those favoring abolition.

There is only one consideration that should tip the scales in favor of or in opposition to capital punishment in my way of thinking. Does the death penalty serve as a deterrent to willful killing? If it does, then opposing the death penalty as a punishment because it requires taking a human life must be questioned as a moral position, since opposition on humanistic grounds would then suggest that it is better to forsake killing a few people convicted of murder in order to save many people who would otherwise die as victims. On the other hand, if the death penalty is not at all effective as a deterrent to willful killing, as many have contended, then there is no legitimate reason to retain that form of punishment. Without a deterrence effect and its social benefit, accusations that state-sanctioned execution is nothing more than revenge against those who violate society's most basic standards of conduct must be taken seriously.

Unfortunately, scientists and scholars who have addressed the issue of the death penalty and deterrence have not distinguished themselves as far as I have reviewed the literature. Of course, I have not examined everything ever written on the subject of capital punishment and the deterrence of homicide and I apologize to anyone whose work has gone unnoticed and which deserves more favorable comment. Enough work has been reviewed though to recognize some commonplace assumptions to which I take serious exception and to note a tendency to limit discussion on the death penalty to yes-or-no considerations without moving on to specific questions that remain unanswered. Evidence on these more focused questions is sorely needed to better understand how we can limit crimes of lethal violence. However, the fact that there is precious little evidence reported in the literature to suggest that capital punishment does work as a deterrent has probably discouraged interest in exploring specific questions relating to why the death penalty might inhibit killing and how the inhibitory mechanism works.

A second type of controversy regarding the death penalty will be considered after the deterrence issue has received our attention; has the death penalty been fairly adjudicated? Even if the evidence points to the deterrence value of capital punishment, retention by the states requires that an equitable assignment of the death penalty is possible within our courts. Three possible sources of bias will be examined. One will involve race and whether racial minorities have been treated fairly as far as assignment of capital punishment goes. Consideration of gender as a second source of possible bias will contend with the question of why so few women are executed? Finally, I will address the knotty problem of mental incompetence that awaits any state that has death-penalty statutes. Should you hold people responsible for their violence when they have limited mental ability brought about by intellectual retardation or mental disorder? Should mental incompetence influence the extent of punishment for violent conduct even if the offender is held responsible?

This book, then, will seek to clarify two straightforward issues by means of evidence and reasoning. Does the presence of death-penalty statutes provide a social benefit by limiting homicidal behavior? Can the death penalty be adjudicated fairly and in a manner consistent with contemporary values? It is difficult to anticipate how persuasive the evidence to be presented will prove to be for those with strong moral convictions regarding capital punishment that are unresponsive to the verdict of evidence. Emotions are not necessarily responsive to facts or reason, and I would be the first to admit that the broad legal issues to be discussed are not readily investigated in ways that generate "hard data," interpretable in only one way. I am not too concerned, however, since my goal in writing this book is not to convert those who are resolute in their convictions but rather to encourage consideration of the death-penalty controversy in a more reasonable light by those still open to choice.

The final point to be mentioned before we begin examining controversial aspects of capital punishment has to do with my own convictions on the subject. I know that scientists are not supposed to be emotionally involved in the topics they are investigating and that goes especially for social scientists who invest themselves in studying human behavior. My own position on the death penalty before I began investigating any of the topics to be considered in this book was "middle-of-the-road." I neither abhorred the thought of executing a human being as punishment for killing an innocent victim, nor did I condone the idea that it should be retribution in kind. However, I did believe that any system of punishment within our nonsuppressive society that helped constrain intentional killing would be beneficial as long as we showed ourselves capable of administering it without bias. Depending upon what the evidence demonstrated, it certainly remained possible that I could be persuaded that capital punishment was a social asset or an indefensible liability.

Section One

DOES THE DEATH PENALTY DETER WILLFUL KILLING?

Chapter One

The Interminable Debate Regarding the Death Penalty

The death penalty as a punishment for specified crimes has been with us since the 1600s when the Massachusetts Bay Colony published its capital laws specifying execution for any of 12 types of misconduct ranging from murder down to blasphemy or witchcraft (Vila and Morris, 1997). Even this code could be considered lenient compared to that left behind by the Puritans in Great Britain that listed 55 violations that were punishable by death. Given the long history of capital punishment in this country and the passionate interest that the topic can generate, it is somewhat puzzling that more progress has not been made regarding whether it has a legitimate place in the criminal justice system. Very likely the passion that it attracts is part of the problem. Public debate lends itself to positioning at the extremes of such an emotional issue with the death penalty cast as justifiable retribution by staunch supporters and unacceptable vengeance by the state among oppositionists. Such polar commitments are not likely to be responsive to more contemplative views even if backed by evidence. Foremost among these views is that of social pragmatism which stipulates capital punishment should be judged by whether it serves a useful purpose for society as a whole.

The social utility of the death penalty is most readily demonstrated by whether it diminishes the likelihood of the crime for which it is almost exclusively reserved in today's society—the intentional killing of an innocent victim. The deterrence question should be one that attracts the interest of even those at the extremes of the death-penalty controversy, since it is probably the only aspect of the issue upon which they might reach agreement. However, the evidence upon which judgments are based regarding capital punishment as a deterrent is seriously flawed in my opinion even when debate rises above anecdote and moral conviction to cite the results of social science. That state

death-penalty statutes serve as a deterrent to willful killing has either remained unproven or, even more devastating for proponents of capital punishment, it even has been proposed as a source of increased violence (Bowers,
1988) in which the state serves as a model for intentional killing.

Although the clear trend of opinion found in the literature on the deterrence
value of the death penalty has been negative, there have been exceptions; perhaps most notably, Ehrlich's (1975) econometric model for predicting executions in a state anticipated a positive restraining effect. However, such theoretical efforts can be greeted with skepticism by scientific colleagues if they
happen to predict a positive deterrence effect. Ehrlich's work, for example, attracted many attempts at replication, some failing and others successful. Included among these was a negative verdict from a study commissioned by the
National Academy of Sciences (Klein, Forst, & Filatov, 1978) and headed by
a Nobel prize winner. Heavy guns, indeed, given the kind of soft data featured
by the Ehrlich model.

That the same skepticism regarding the deterrence value of capital punishment found in scientific journals and scholarly publications could invade public discourse became obvious to me when a guest editorial appeared in the Atlanta newspaper written by Richard Cohen, a well-known columnist for *The
Washington Post*. This November, 2004, opinion-piece offered an unequivocal verdict on the death-penalty for public consumption:

> "Politicians are too afraid to say what they really think about capital punishment—
> or, worse, they sincerely endorse it, almost never citing the only reason that makes
> any sense at all (for retaining the death penalty), vengeance. All the rest—closure,
> proportionality, finality, and especially deterrence—have been disproved, sloppy
> thinking or junk science that cannot withstand examination . . ."

If this represents current public opinion of capital punishment, that all it ac-
complishes is to place an unfortunate power to exact lethal vengeance in the
hands of government, it is indeed time to examine new evidence on the subject generated by credible research procedures and rational interpretation of
the data. This evidence will lend itself to a very different conclusion.

Given the lengthy opportunity to reach some credible conclusions about
the deterrence value of capital punishment in this country, why has social science not done a better job of resolving the issue? There are several problems
facing social scientists who concern themselves with this topic that often go
unmentioned, possibly unnoticed, by those who conduct the research. Certainly, they should prove to be even less apparent to consumers of research
evidence. A review of these problems will precede a description of how I
chose to study the deterrence question without courting accusations of engaging in "junk science."

PROBLEMS IN CONDUCTING RESEARCH CONCERNING THE DETERRENCE VALUE OF THE DEATH PENALTY

The Death Penalty as a Moral Issue

I already have touched upon the morality issue in capital punishment as a problem in reaching an objective judgment, pro or con. Since the deterrence question is one of the few, perhaps the only aspect of this divisive topic that allows for objectivity, the failure to satisfy this requirement of the scientific method is especially troubling.

How would preconceived moral convictions regarding the death penalty affect the scientist's work? We probably are not talking about anything sinister here but rather about what determines the topic scientists choose to study and how they choose to study it. Motivation for studying a topic can properly be influenced by personal convictions about what is important and what is not, but the choice of methodology may introduce a bias that will go undetected and favor a particular result. In my own case, I chose to endorse the death penalty on the condition that it can be shown to have social value—a lifesaving deterrence effect. That certainly encouraged my study of the topic in light of the opinions challenging its deterrence value. Since the methodology of my deterrence investigation involved an analysis of murder rates in this country over time, special concern was shown so as not to introduce bias into the study by arbitrary choices of when and where to focus my research attention. The period of study was long enough to provide a reliable time sample of rate fluctuations and recent enough to be currently relevant; the murder rates were generated by every state in the country. I was well aware that if you pick the right years and the right states, you could probably demonstrate whatever you wished.

Even greater caution is required regarding the encroachment of moral values in capital-punishment investigations when it comes to interpreting the data collected whatever the method of collection might be. However, the meaning of a result is often a matter of interpretation—a judgment. Even though a result may be confirmed by statistical procedures, explaining that result is open to influence by personal convictions if the scientist is not careful.

Criterion Choice in Deterrence Research—the Problem of Availability

To deter, according to the dictionary, means "to discourage or restrain from acting or proceeding": "to prevent, check, arrest." In the present investigation deterrence will refer to the discouragement or restraint of actions by the individual that would intentionally result in the death of another person—murder. (Warranted killing, such as in self-defense or military combat, and accidental

killing are not at issue.) So if something deters, it simply reduces the probability that an individual will act upon the impulse to hurt/kill some victim.
Deterrence, if it occurs, is a psychological state experienced by the person
alone and not open to outside scrutiny. The particular deterrent in the research
to be discussed is the individual's awareness of risk that the death penalty
may be imposed if a victim is killed.

The reason for this exercise in semantics is that it allows me to make an
interesting point. Deterrence per se has probably never been the subject of
investigation in studies of whether the death penalty has a deterrent effect
upon willful killing. It is next-to-impossible to imagine a research design that
would allow investigation of psychological deterrence, a private event, in a
scientifically rigorous way. I suppose people could be asked by the scientist
whether they had used the threat of capital punishment to curb homicidal impulses, but such excursions into subjective experience would be seriously
flawed by limitations of candor, self-awareness, or memory.

Even if a strategy of investigating private experience had some promise of
success, the problem of definition would not be over for deterrence researchers; what is going to represent the gauge of deterrence? The reality of
psychological deterrence may be that one person, given to anger and low on
values, is constrained any number of times over a lifetime by the risk of lethal
punishment but capitulates to impulse on one occasion and commits a homicidal act. Should this be considered a single failure of deterrence, multiple
successes at restraint, or both? The focus on a unitary failure of deterrence at
a particular point in time would be arbitrary; the attempt to establish the person's cumulative record of successful deterrence would be an absurd quest.

What can be done by the researcher or scholar if actual psychological deterrence is not accessible as a source of evidence? The first thing you might
do is ignore the fact that nobody studies actual deterrence, and this has been
a universal strategy. Then, hopefully, some correlate of deterrence will be
available that can be measured and subjected to investigation—something
that should happen or not happen if the death penalty actually did deter willful killing. Murder rate represents an objective criterion for gauging the deterrence value of capital punishment, although using it in a study means that
it is nondeterrence that is being investigated. The research question then becomes: Does the existence of the death penalty limit the occasions when
homicidal impulses lead to acts of murder?

Even using murder rate as a legitimate and available criterion of psychological deterrence does not guarantee meaningful results, since it all depends
upon whether this statistic is employed in a sensible way. I am afraid that
logic and common sense have often been neglected when capital punishment
is under scrutiny. We will return to this assertion on the pages ahead.

Other criteria of deterrence value for the death penalty besides murder rate have been introduced but without much promise of success. For example, polling the presidents of organizations concerned with crime or questioning chiefs of police have been used even though it is not altogether clear why holding these positions should provide special insight into something as complicated as the deterrence issue. Another example of dubious choices is employing the number of executions in a state as a criterion of deterrence—the more executions, the poorer the deterrence. One problem in using the number of executions in a state as a criterion of deterrence is that numbers may have as much to do with criminal justice dynamics and political considerations as with actual constraint. Having death-penalty statutes has not meant that states will choose to make use of them for capital prosecution or that they will execute those sentenced to die. Some states will execute many prisoners, whereas other death-penalty states may go for a number of years without an execution. The second problem is that evidence to be considered later in the book will show that the presumption of more executions meaning poorer deterrence is erroneous. The opposite is actually the case.

Criterion Choice in Deterrence Research—
the Problem of Comprehensiveness

We already have considered one aspect of the criterion problem in deterrence investigations—that we are required to ignore actual deterrence from acting upon homicidal impulse because it is a private and largely inaccessible psychological event for scientific purposes. This means that we must look for what is available in way of correlates. There seems to be general agreement that the number of willful killings per unit of population represents a useful gauge of whether the death penalty for especially egregious homicides has a constraining effect or not upon all homicidal behavior. I agree with that consensus as long as it is understood that murder rates can vary by locale and time for reasons other than whether death-penalty statutes are in place or not. For example, there is the matter of how seriously a state takes its own system of capital punishment, a perception readily available to those who live in that state.

Having agreed with other empirical researchers who have examined the pragmatic value of capital punishment, let me quickly add that, taken alone, murder rate does not provide a sufficiently comprehensive picture to make this judgment. It is easier to explain why if we start with what the murder rate represents and the reason it is used by the Criminal Justice Department in its annual crime reports for the 50 states. The annual number of murder/nonnegligent manslaughter crimes reported by the police are combined by the Justice Department into a "murder" or willful-killing category. This number of murders each year is reported per 100,000 population in a given state to provide the rate figure; a national rate also is given. Using a rate index allows comparison of the homicide risk across states from the smallest in population (Wyoming with 485,000) to the largest (California with 32,000,000). Murder rate proves to be a useful statistic if comparisons are to be made in terms of deterrence effectiveness from one state to the next, since it factors out increases in lethal violence that would be expected based upon sheer population size.

Taken alone murder rate as a risk metric does not provide a complete enough picture to judge the deterrence value of capital punishment though. In order to achieve a more comprehensive idea regarding the pragmatic value of deterrence, it becomes necessary at some point to reintroduce population size as a parameter so that an estimate can be made of the actual number of victim lives that have been spared by bringing the murder rate down or that have been lost because the murder rate goes up. A hypothetical example might help. If establishing the death penalty resulted in a 10% decrease in the murder rate of a highly populated state but no decrease in the murder rate of a state with little population, the changes could be heralded as evidence for a deterrent effect tallied in terms of individual lives. Considering these two states alone, a substantial number of victim lives were spared because the rate drop occurred within a highly populated state. However, those who choose not to consider population size could cite this pair of results as evidence of the equivocal effect of capital punishment upon willful killing; in one state it was associated with a decreased murder rate but in another state it was not. It seems reasonable to me that if we want to reach a national verdict on the merits of capital punishment, it is necessary to reintroduce population size at some point in a cost/benefit analysis.

It is difficult to understand how controversy with regard to the death penalty could have largely ignored population counts and cost/benefit analysis of changes in murder rate in trying to make the case for or against capital punishment. The death-penalty controversy hinges upon the critical importance of human life—the value of the victim's life for those invested in retribution and the value of the perpetrator's life for those strongly opposed to the death penalty. A controversy anchored in a reverence for human life should be especially sensitive to the importance of just how many lives are at stake when a deterrent to murder is being considered.

Death-penalty States Versus Abolitionist States— the Problem of Distinction

It is difficult to imagine how deterrence value could be evaluated with any degree of precision without some type of comparison between jurisdictions that retain capital punishment as a possibility for egregious homicides and other jurisdictions that do not have the death penalty. Whether it is the capital punishment system that is responsible for a seeming deterrence effect or there is some other reason for a drop in murder rate is difficult to judge unless comparison is made to the murder rate in another jurisdiction that does not have the death penalty. Even that kind of comparison falls short of being critical. Ideally the murder rate in a state with the death penalty should be compared with the same state's rate at a time when it did not have the death penalty. Then the difference in murder rate can be put alongside the rate change in an abolitionist state for the same period. This more complex methodology helps to minimize differences in place and time that would otherwise blur the murder rate comparisons and any conclusions about deterrence value.

Even though the states that retain capital punishment as a possible sentence and those that do not is made apparent by state law, another important distinction is generally ignored in deterrence research. Having death-penalty statutes in place has not meant that capital punishment systems were necessarily being effectively implemented; this disparity could introduce differences in the value of the death penalty as a deterrent to murder. The disinclination to prosecute murder as a capital offense or to decide upon the death penalty in a capital case could attenuate the perception of risk. This reluctance might not be readily conceded because it sounds too "soft on crime," but the attenuation of risk still could keep the murder rate higher than necessary. Alternatively, prosecution and sentencing might proceed in a death-penalty state but execution as the culmination of a capital sentence be delayed to the point that inmates backed up on death-row. This sign of diminished commitment also could decrease the threat conveyed by the death penalty. One implication of this reasoning regarding system effectiveness would be that any serious investigation of the death penalty as a deterrent should involve not only comparison between retentionist and abolitionist states but should also take a multi-tier approach to evaluating capital punishment in this country among states having the death-penalty. States with death-penalty statutes that are rigorously implemented should be compared to states with death-penalty statutes that are reluctantly invoked in order to more precisely explore the deterrence value of capital punishment.

The distinction between states having some system of capital punishment and others that do not provide for the death penalty is a matter of record, and keeping them separate does not pose a major problem as long as one remains cognizant of occasional changes in criminal justice code that switch a state from or to the death penalty. These few changes in capital punishment and their timing were taken into consideration when I compiled the evidence to be considered in the next chapter. The more formidable concern came in attempting to establish differences in system effectiveness—how seriously states took their capital punishment statutes. It was necessary to distinguish between one category of states that have the death penalty and more rigorously apply these statutes and other categories that also have the death penalty as a legal option but seem to pursue that option with less enthusiasm. The question became how does one discern the degree to which a state is committed to its death-penalty statutes.

The state's commitment to its death-penalty system could be judged by the number of capital cases that are prosecuted, death sentences that are imposed, or executions that follow conviction. Among these possible markers, only the number who are put to death reflects commitment to satisfying all of the conditions set down in the statutes—prosecution, sentencing, and execution—and was adopted as the criterion of system effectiveness. It might seem a matter of concern that number of executions was criticized as a criterion of deterrence on earlier pages but selected as a criterion of system effectiveness in my research. The difference is that effectiveness, as I am defining it, must still be examined in terms of changes in murder rate in order to establish its impact upon deterrence. A more cogent concern regarding execution numbers would be that this count merely reflects differences in population density among the death-penalty states. Those with more people should have more murders; more murders should result in more cases that merit capital prosecution and the death penalty. If true, states with large populations would automatically qualify as more committed to their systems. However, it did not turn out that way. An analysis of executions over a 25-year period that will be considered as part of the evidence ahead suggests that the number of executions from one death-penalty state to the next has little to do with the population density parameter. For example, Tennessee over this quarter-century span executed only one prisoner; Missouri, a state with equal population, put 53 prisoners to death. Nevada, a small-population state executed nine prisoners during the quarter century, whereas heavily-populated Ohio and Pennsylvania exacted the death penalty in only two and three cases, respectively. Among high-population states Texas put 313 prisoners to death, whereas California, with more than a 50% greater population, executed but 10. Execution numbers go well beyond population size to reveal attitude toward implementing the death penalty.

THE RESEARCH PLAN FOR INVESTIGATING
THE DETERRENCE VALUE OF CAPITAL PUNISHMENT

Given the several research problems that have been considered in the previous section along with others that could be added, the reader might wonder how a study could produce evidence convincing enough to shape opinion regarding whether capital punishment does or does not deter intentional killing. I would only urge patience at this point until research methodology has been described more completely on the pages that follow and the evidence has been presented in the next chapter.

The Indicators of Deterrence

The Two Markers of Deterrence

Sellin (1959), an early and well-respected opponent of capital punishment, was among the first to stipulate that in order to prove that murder has been deterred by the death penalty a number of propositions would have to be confirmed. The most important of these propositions from a psychological perspective is that two effects must be observed in order to demonstrate deterrence; murder rate should *increase* when the death penalty is abolished and should *decrease* when the death penalty is restored. Sellin interpreted his findings as showing that capital punishment had no recognizable effect upon the rate of homicides in selected states, hardly the only social scientist to reach that conclusion. The requirement that deterrence must be tested by verifying the specified opposite effects of abolition and reinstatement of the death penalty upon murder rate was satisfied in the methodology of the present study.

Graduated Deterrence Effects

A third possibility for showing deterrence effects of capital punishment, besides an increase in killing when the death penalty is abolished and a decrease when the death penalty is reinstated, was included in the methodology. As I have discussed at some length, death-penalty statutes are part of the criminal code in the majority of states, although capital punishment systems may be more or less effective. Effectiveness as used here, means that heinous murders are vigorously prosecuted as capital cases, attract the death penalty if criminal circumstances warrant, and result in execution without exceedingly long periods on death row. The more effective the capital punishment system in a state, the better the death penalty should serve as a warning of risk involved in the act of murder and as a deterrent; the less effective the system, the more limited the deterrent value of the death penalty. In the event that the death penalty is found to deter homicides in the comparison of retentionist and abolitionist states, analysis by system effectiveness should offer an even more refined look at the deterrence question. The reasoning here is straightforward; if a system works as a deterrent, that system functioning more effectively should be an even better deterrent. An effect of system commitment, then, in the wake of verified abolition and reinstatement effects would suggest that capital punishment not only deters willful killing in general but that this is most apparent when the state is committed to its system.

Murder Rate as A Criterion of Deterrent Effect

The question of what criteria are to be used to identify changes in deterrence effects given abolishment or reinstatement of capital punishment has received our attention previously. The murder rate in each state is probably the most widely applied statistic in deterrence research for two reasons. By adopting the number of homicides for some standard number of inhabitants in any given state as the metric, the researcher is able to directly compare one state with another or to combine groups of states without being concerned about whether the variable number of people in more and less populous states is biasing the results. The more highly populated the state, the greater the crime totals tend to be; states like California, New York, Texas, and Florida will not have any more weight in an analysis of murder rate than Wyoming and the Dakotas.

A practical reason for using murder rate in considering deterrence effects is that the Department of Justice publishes an annual summary of crimes in each state and in the United States as a nation. This publication, *Crime in the United States*, reports on "murder and nonnegligent manslaughter" as a rate, state by state, using 100,000 as the standard population unit. This index of "willful killing of one human by another" represents a readily accessible indicator of murder rate, as restricted to one-on-one perpetrator/victim circumstances. Investigating deterrence by state jurisdictions is critical to the death-penalty controversy. Whether capital punishment exists at all is up to state government and how effectively the statutes are implemented can be traced to influences at the state level.

The inclusion of one-on-one murder/nonnegligent manslaughter cases in the Justice Department's murder-rate statistic is based solely on the results of police investigation as opposed to findings of the medical examiner, coroner, jury, or other judicial body.

Social Cost/Benefit as A Criterion of Deterrent Effect

Although murder rate represents an important basis for determining whether capital punishment has social value, one of its strengths is also its weakness. Counting the number of murders in a given year per 100,000 inhabitants allows you to compare each state with any other state, even large-population California with small-population Wyoming. The fact that many more crimes occur in California is not allowed to bias the comparison. However, eliminating the number of people residing in a state from the index of willful killing also eliminates the actual number of murder victims from consideration when the social cost of the homicide rate is being gauged.

To illustrate the importance of social cost/benefit analysis based upon actual numbers of victims, say that a state having 10,000,000 people and a state having 1,000,000 both demonstrated a murder rate of 5.0 for a given year. That would mean that the risk of being murdered under one-on-one circumstances was the same in both states—5 in 100,000. However, looking at it in absolute terms, 500 people were homicide victims in the larger state and 50 were victims in the smaller state. The social cost of lethal violence in the larger state is ten times larger in terms of lives lost. Cost/benefit analysis as conducted in my study involved determination of projected victim lives lost by an increase in murder rate (social cost) or victim lives spared by a decrease in murder rate (social benefit) when comparisons by time and state were made.

Three Criteria of Deterrence Value

Three ways of determining deterrence value have been described and were employed in the investigation. Two criteria will satisfy the requirements of a deterrent. Does relinquishing the death penalty result in increased murder rate (disinhibition), and does the restoration of the death penalty bring about a decrease in murder rate (inhibition)? A third criterion will serve as an added basis for weighing the deterrence value of this form of punishment among states that have death-penalty statutes. Given that capital punishment systems generally deter willful killing, it should be possible to show that more effective systems constrain killing better than less effective systems.

It would be wise at this point to emphasize that when I use the term "effective" to describe a state's system of capital punishment that it does not automatically qualify as admiration for putting a lot of people to death for their crimes. Effective is meant to describe the status of a system that is supposed to prosecute the violation of death-penalty statutes, to extend the death penalty if warranted, and to consummate that prescribed sentence. If a state cannot take its own laws seriously, as evidenced by infrequent cases that pass completely through the system, then it should change them. Admiration for an effective system of capital punishment should await the confirmation of deterrent value, demonstrating that taking a relatively few lives after due process can save a far greater number of innocent victims.

The Mirage of Nondeterrence

No discussion of the procedures that were used to investigate the deterrent value of capital punishment would be complete without considering one type of comparison that has obvious but misleading implications which could have been used. If you examine the murder rates for states that do not have death-penalty statutes and states that do, it is apparent that states without capital punishment provide rates that tend to fall below the rates of death-penalty states. As an example, for the most recent period studied in the forthcoming investigation, 1995–2002, the average murder rate for the 12 states without capital punishment was 3.3 per 100,000 people; the average rate for the 38 death-penalty states was 6.1 per 100,000.

A superficial look at those figures might lead someone to question why the deterrence controversy still persists, since jurisdictions that have the death penalty suffer almost twice the murder rate than those that do not provide this punishment option. Demonstrating that states with capital punishment do not bring their murder rates down below states without the death penalty would appear to argue against any deterrent value for the death penalty. In fact, the rate discrepancy could imply to some that execution of murderers serves as a model of lethal conduct or otherwise serves to encourage homicidal behavior—that capital punishment not only fails to deter murder but makes the problem worse.

Misunderstanding the implications for deterrence of the differential murder rate between retentionist and abolitionist states results from the failure to accurately identify cause and effect. If you accept the thesis that this particular difference in murder rate follows from having or not having a death penalty, that the presence or absence of capital punishment is of causal significance, a crucial argument against the deterrence value of capital punishment is available. However, further thought on the matter reveals serious problems with the conclusion that the presence/absence of the death penalty were responsible for the differential murder rate and suggests just the opposite—that differences in murder rates resulted from social factors and led states to adopt death-penalty statutes or choose to ignore them. Adopting the death penalty is an effect of these differences and not the cause. Let us examine these cause/effect alternatives from a logical perspective and then entertain some evidence bearing upon why certain states would adopt the death penalty and others would not.

Logical Considerations

If the absence or presence of capital punishment were responsible for causing the murder-rate difference between abolitionist and retentionist states, then logic would dictate that one or both of the following deductions would be true. Either the absence of capital punishment would have to be responsible for lowering the rate of homicide, or the presence of capital punishment would have to instigate an increase in the rate. Either effect, given comparable murder rates to begin with, would result in the rate disparity noted in the 1995–2002 data. However, neither possibility makes much sense in my opinion.

It is difficult to logically defend the notion that the absence of a proposed deterrent will have a constraining effect—that the failure to feature the death penalty for heinous murder will reduce the incidence of murder. Even if the death penalty were worthless as a deterrent, what is the argument for expecting the absence of capital punishment to serve a restraining function? Is constraint being shown by a potential murderer as a display of gratitude for the state's humane values? Actually, the position opposing the death penalty would have been better off if no difference in murder rate existed between retentionist and abolitionist states. In that case it could be more readily assumed that capital punishment had simply failed as a deterrent. The death penalty, given no difference in murder rate, could then be regarded as a cruel excess without social benefit and abolition as a humane choice without social cost.

The alternative approach to logically explaining the differential murder rate between states with and without the death penalty in causal terms fares little better than the conundrum we have just considered. Could having the death penalty in a state cause an increase in the homicide rate? It has been proposed that such an effect indeed occurs, a phenomenon called "brutalization," so it was not illogical in someone's opinion (Bowers, 1988). In theory brutalization proposes that capital punishment leads potential offenders to identify with the state as "enforcer" and "executioner," empowered to exact lethal vengeance. An execution, according to this theory, may remove inhibitions against killing or strengthen justifications for killing in those who have arrived at a readiness to kill. Other research on executions and murder rate has failed to find either a deterrent or facilitation effect upon individual behavior (Bailey 1990).

The logical impasse that I see in a proposal that stipulates an increase in murder rate as a consequence of having capital punishment is that "identification with the state" as an executioner wreaking lethal vengeance represents such a stretch of reality when it comes to explaining why people simulate the behavior of others. The kind of vicarious reinforcement that is required for identification, such as when a child models after an admired parent or someone assimilates the values of a favored social institution, would be a commodity in short supply for most potential murderers. Inclined toward antisociality, they will be lacking in a sense of bonding with the state. Accordingly, they will tend to be short of the cognitive and emotional resources required to engage in identification learning. There may be an occasional resentfulness expressed as "If they can do it, why not me?" That is not identification with the state though; that is rationalization in the service of antisocial inclinations.

The death penalty, then, may not serve as a deterrent to murder; the evidence remains to be reported. However, there is no logical or psychological basis for assuming that sponsoring execution as punishment in a state could bring about a systematic increase in the murder rate.

Empirical Considerations

If the murder-rate differential between abolitionist and death-penalty states is not to be understood as an effect of having or not having the system, how then are we to explain almost twice the murder rate in death-penalty jurisdictions? A hint at how I would answer this question already has appeared. Logic and common sense suggest that the discussion to this point has put the cart before the horse. Serious problems with criminal violence, especially with willful killing, are what would lead a state to adopt the death penalty in the first place and to remain committed to this extreme punishment option in the hope of deterrence. States that experience fewer crimes of lethal violence are less likely to institute capital punishment statutes, since concern about deterrence would be less of a priority. By this line of reasoning, murder rate is the causal factor and the presence/absence of the death penalty becomes the effect. It would not be surprising if a "tough-on-crime" political stance were sometimes involved in decisions at the state level favoring capital punishment. However, I assume that decisions regarding adoption or maintenance of capital punishment are guided primarily by a critical social concern regarding the safeguard of the populace from lethal violence and the hope that this option will serve as a deterrent.

One way to test the idea that states featuring the death penalty tend to be those that experience lethal violence as a more significant social problem is to consider the parameters of population that would contribute to a high homicide rate. Information on two such parameters was available from the United States Census Report. The total population of a state (density) determines to a significant extent whether inhabitants are likely to live in close proximity to each other within urban areas rather than spread out and separated from each other in rural settings. Social access would be expected to increase the chance of one-on-one violence.

The second parameter that may escalate the likelihood of lethal violence and create a significant social problem is minority representation in states in which a white majority exists (all but Hawaii). The fact that minorities are overrepresented in the crime statistics of this country, including those for murder, is hardly a new revelation, although there is still debate regarding how much this can be explained by prejudice within a white-dominated criminal justice system. We will consider racial bias later in the book when fairness of sentencing is discussed. At this point I will make only the minimal assumption that discord between the white racial majority and whatever minorities exist in each state, along with the frustrations of minority membership, can contribute to the rate of lethal violence. The higher the minority representation, the greater the opportunity for such violence to erupt.

The question of whether murder-rate differences between states could be explained by either of two population parameters conducive to violence, density and minority representation, was considered within two time periods. One period was chosen at the early end of the 45-year deterrence investigation (1958–1967) and the other at the late end (1995–2002) so as to avoid results relevant only to a particular time in our social and criminal history. Each analysis by period proceeded by splitting the states into three levels of murder rate—the third having the highest average rate over the multi-year period in question, an intermediate level, and the third with the lowest murder rate. The average population and minority representation for these tiers of states for the 1958–1967 and the 1995–2002 time periods, based upon 1960 or 2000 census figures, were then determined. (Hawaii was included in the population analysis but omitted from the minority representation calculations, since a white majority was not reported.)

Table 1 summarizes the population-parameter results for the two time periods. The clearest data pattern on this table is provided by the minority-representation figures. Whether it is early or late, mid-twentieth century or into the Twenty-First century, a linear relationship can be found between homicide rate and percentage of minority residents in the state. Higher murder rates are associated with higher percentages of minorities within state populations, and the percentage differences are substantial.

Table 1. Comparison of Population Density and Minority Representation for States at Three Levels of Murder Rate (Per 100,000) for Two Periods of Time (1958–1967 and 1995–2002)

| | Periods of Time | | | |
| | 1958–1967 | | 1995–2002 | |
Murder Rate Level	Average Population Density	Average Minority Representation	Average Population Density	Average Minority Representation
High Rate	3,230,000	20%	6,709,000	27%
Intermediate Rate	6,173,000	9%	8,095,000	17%
Low Rate	1,777,000	3%	1,861,000	9%

NOTE: Statistics for the three murder rate groupings are as follows: 1958–1967—high rate, range = 6.0–11.5, average = 8.5; intermediate rate, range = 2.9–5.8, average = 4.3; low rate, range = 1.1–2.8, average = 1.8. 1995–2002—high rate, range = 7.0–13.8, average = 8.6; intermediate rate, range = 3.6–6.9, average = 5.2; low rate, range = 1.2–3.3, average = 1.5.

The importance of total state population as a correlate of murder rate is less clear. The relationship shows the same curvilinearity in both time periods. The highest murder rate is not found in states with the most dense populations; intermediate density is associated with the greatest homicide risk. The most striking feature of the density figures, however, is that states that have relatively low homicide rates are sparsely populated for the most part. Population figures fall below 2,000,000 in 65–69% of these states in the two time periods. Accordingly, while it is possible to make only a qualified statement regarding how very dense populations might contribute to escalated murder rates, the relationship between density and rate can be more confidently stated at the other extreme. Sparsely populated states are likely to experience fewer problems associated with lethal one-on-one violence.

One more step is necessary in order to complete the empirical consideration of population parameters as explanations for the difference in murder rate between death-penalty states and states without capital punishment. The question remains whether the conclusions from the analysis of population density and minority representation can provide an explanation for the observed murder-rate differential? This would require that death-penalty states with twice the murder rate would not be sparsely populated and would have higher minority representation and that abolitionist states would be more sparsely populated and have lower minority representation.

A simple way to answer this question is to compare the median (middle) values for the distributions of population count and minority representation for abolitionist and retentionist states. The median population for abolitionist states between 1958 and 1967 was under 1,000,000, whereas death-penalty states had a median population of over 3,000,000. Population figures during the 1995–2002 period demonstrated the same difference in medians—under 1,300,000 for states without capital punishment and over 4,400,000 for states with death-penalty statutes. Comparisons of median minority-representation values place minorities at 3% of the population for states without capital punishment during the early period and at 10% for death-penalty jurisdictions. More recent figures point to a 6% minority representation in abolitionist states compared to a median of 20% for retentionist states. Since a higher population figure and a larger minority representation would contribute to a social milieu in which lethal violence is more prominent, the difference in murder rate between states with and without capital punishment finds ready explanation. Death-penalty states are more socially vulnerable to the problem of willful killing.

One subtle research implication of finding capital punishment in effect for retentionist states that are generally more densely populated with a much higher minority cross-section is that the deterrence value of the death penalty is being evaluated under a different set of social conditions than exist in abolitionist states. Capital punishment generally is being asked to serve as a deterrent to murder under social conditions that are more conducive to homicide than found in states without the death penalty. Comparing murder rates in retentionist and abolitionist states directly would represent a biased research procedure, since it would involve pitting two categories of states against each other when one faces more formidable obstacles to restraint. That would be akin to comparing the speed of two sprinters in a track meet when one runs on an unfinished surface and the other runs in an improved lane.

You will have the opportunity to consider how much this potential bias was circumvented when the actual research design is discussed. I am not certain whether it was eliminated completely, so it is important to remember that whatever bias remained worked against finding a deterrence effect for the death penalty. If deterrence is demonstrated, it would be despite the fact that the death-penalty states had to contend with a more difficult challenge to suppression of homicide than the less volatile abolitionist states throughout the period of investigation.

The Importance of Timing in Collecting Evidence

The timing of research probes in investigating the deterrent value of the death penalty assumes importance because of the variable effects upon criminal justice procedures introduced by court decisions and political remonstrations. If you want the clearest proof that capital punishment works in deterring willful killing, periods of time can be identified that will allow you to make the strongest case. If a negative verdict on the death penalty as a deterrent is your preference, there are other times when evidence will seem to prove your point. That is why a judgment concerning the value of capital punishment should be based upon a substantial time period, one that will prevent being swayed by unreliable glimpses at the impact of criminal law. In fact, the timing of an investigation should take significant legal and political decisions into explicit consideration along with the circumstances they create; these decisions may demarcate periods of time in which research questions regarding deterrence can receive only short-term answers.

Both research and legal/ political considerations entered into the timing for my analyses. Reliability of observation was satisfied by a 45-year sample of murder rates in the United States. The period of observation, 1958–2002, provided enough time to allow stable results even when broken down into component periods. (All states were included in the analyses as independent entries as well in order to guarantee reliability of results from a geographic perspective.) Component periods within the 45-year period of investigation were selected with both research and legal consideration in mind. The strategy underlying the selection of periods hinged upon identifying times in the legal history of our country since 1958 when capital punishment was diminished as a system or vacated entirely for comparison with other times when capital punishment had been a viable punishment alternative or was restored to legal status. These types of comparison were required in order to establish whether deterrence by capital punishment would demonstrate both predicted effects of a psychological inhibitor—increased murder rate when the death-penalty threat is diminished or removed entirely and decreased murder rate when the death penalty is reintroduced as a threat.

Six periods within the 45-year time sample were identified. They were long enough to satisfy reliability requirements and also took cognizance of changing legal circumstances within which capital punishment systems functioned. Each will be briefly described from the perspective of research method and significant legal determinants.

Period 1 (1958–1967)

This initial ten-year span was chosen as the *baseline* period for gauging the subsequent effects upon murder rate of diminished status for capital punishment and the social benefit/cost of these changes. Comparisons of the crime figures obtained from the baseline period with those found for the two periods that follow will generate evidence regarding whether capital punishment satisfies the disinhibition requirement of a deterrent—the increase in murder rate that should accompany the reduction or removal of threat.

Although 1958 to 1967 represented a reasonably quiescent time as far as momentous legal decisions regarding the death penalty were concerned, Vila and Morris (1997) identified a shift in the United States during that period away from social commentary on capital punishment to legal debate, especially regarding its constitutionality. The early Supreme Court actions bearing upon this issue were not even concerned with the death penalty per se. *Trop versus Dulles* in 1958 considered court penalties for a World War II soldier convicted of desertion and ruled that the loss of citizenship was in violation of the Eighth Amendment as "cruel and unusual punishment." This is said to have encouraged opponents of the death penalty to believe that it might be abolished by applying a new standard, being "cruel and unusual." *Rudolph versus Alabama* was a rape case brought to the Supreme Court in 1963 but not even heard. It still opened the way for constitutional challenges to capital punishment, since one Justice was spurred by this case to announce he was prepared to raise the constitutionality issue with regard to capital punishment; specifically, what circumstances forbid use of the death penalty because of the Eighth and Fourteenth ("due process") Amendments. Two other

Justices indicated their willingness to entertain challenges to the constitutionality of the death penalty as well. The door was open.

Despite these early constitutional concerns expressed by the Supreme Court, the 1958–1967 baseline period was fairly free of major challenges to capital punishment. Most states chose to have death-penalty statutes; about a third of the states chose not to legalize capital punishment. Stability of the murder rate for this legally quiescent ten-year period was subjected to preliminary test by comparing the average rate for each state over the first five years to its average rate for the second five years. States having capital punishment as an option showed an average increase in homicide rate of 8% from one five-year period to the next; states without the death penalty experienced a 31% increase in rate. Despite this discrepancy, which offered an early hint of deterrence value for the death penalty, it was decided to use a simple ten-year average for each state as the baseline murder rate for comparisons ahead.

Period 2 (1968–1971)

The next span of years in the investigation was a time when significant Supreme Court decisions regarding juries in death-penalty trials led to a halt in executions throughout the country as states awaited some clearer perspective on the constitutionality of sentences in capital cases. The Sixth Amendment ("impartial jury") rights of prisoners attracted special constitutional concern. *Witherspoon versus Illinois* in 1968 challenged the practice of excluding prospective jurors from capital trials if they held reservations about the death penalty. Exclusion was ruled by the Court to be a source of bias in jury selection. Many believed that this would lead to virtual abandonment of capital punishment; addition of those opposing the death penalty to jury pools and re-sentencing promised to be too burdensome in case of reversal. Jury procedures were implicated again during the same year in *U.S. versus Jackson* in which requiring the death penalty to be reached only by a jury was ruled unconstitutional. The Court was concerned that this requirement would encourage defendants to waive the right to an impartial jury trial as a way of avoiding the death penalty.

Two Supreme Court cases in 1971 *(McGautha versus California and Crampton versus Ohio)* raised jury issues regarding uniform standards for assigning the death penalty and the need for separate guilt and penalty phases in capital trials. Neither decision favored the petitioner, but they did encourage challenges to be directed toward the nature of the death penalty itself rather than the sentencing procedures by which it was assigned (Vila & Morris, 1997).

The hold on executions in every death-penalty state along with a growing concern over seeking the death penalty in court because of increasing restrictions on the prosecution provided a four-year period in which this form of punishment showed clearcut signs of weakening as a system. It would be expected, then, that the death penalty would deteriorate as a potential deterrent to willful killing. This *moratorium period*, 1968–1971, as it is compared with baseline, will serve as one test of whether capital punishment qualifies as a psychological deterrent to willful killing. Will the diminished status of death-penalty systems result in a disinhibition effect as shown by increased murder rate and escalating social cost?

Period 3 (1972–1976)

The *Furman versus Georgia* decision by the Supreme Court in 1972 found capital punishment in the United States to be unconstitutional, in violation of the Eighth and Fourteenth Amendments rights of convicted criminals. The telling argument asserted that juries lacked sufficient standards for assigning the death penalty and that "arbitrary and capricious" death sentences resulted. Given the view that capital punishment represented cruel and unusual punishment and a violation of due process, some 600 prisoners on death row across the country had their sentences commuted to life in prison. Although the Supreme Court verdict rendered the death penalty unconstitutional, the way was left open for states to propose statutes that could be considered by the Court regarding their constitutional merit.

The five-year *abolishment period* found interested states beginning to assemble new death-penalty statutes that had to eventually be approved by the Supreme Court on a state-by-state basis. In the meantime, capital punishment was deemed to be unlawful until the charge of "arbitrary and capricious" could be lifted following procedural changes by each state. From a research perspective these abolishment years represent the clearest repudiation of capital punishment, at least since 1958, and offer a basis for comparison with the baseline period that should optimally demonstrate what happens when deterrence effects upon killing are lifted. The 1972–1976 period is a span of time when either abolitionists or retentionists should be best able to support their view about the merit of capital punishment as a deterrent.

The abolishment period ended in 1976 when five capital punishment cases were heard by the Supreme Court. The Court upheld the revised statutes for three states (*Gregg versus Georgia, Proffitt versus Florida*, and *Jurek versus Texas*) but rejected revision efforts by two others (*Woodson versus North Carolina* and *Roberts versus Louisiana*). These decisions were expected to resolve remaining issues regarding death-penalty statutes for other states including the need for separate guilt and penalty trials, automatic appellate review, and review protecting against sentencing disparities.

Period 4 (1977–2002)

Rather than judicial calm, the resumption of capital punishment in 1977 simply opened a new era of debate over the death penalty in which the Supreme Court was taxed with innumerable challenges to the new laws. Issues abounded including the kind of offenders that should be eligible for the death sentence and execution, the types of crime that should merit the death penalty, the forms of execution that should be considered unduly cruel, and the kind of evidence that could be properly considered in the penalty phase of capital trials. All of these issues served to increase court appeals and extend stays on death row. Other tactics expressing opposition to the death penalty such as clemency petitions, public demonstrations, and legislative lobbying also increased in tempo.

Given the uncertainties regarding the continuing legal and political status of the new death-penalty statutes and the possibility that these uncertainties might hamper the prosecution of capital cases, it was not clear to me how well deterrence could be reinstituted during the post-abolishment era or, if so, what its pace would prove to be. There seemed to be no landmark legal decisions to serve as demarcations following the beginning of the 26-year span of study in 1977, the *post-abolishment period*, so the separation into shorter periods was made on research grounds in order to identify changes in deterrence if they appeared. The 26 years were sectioned into three roughly equivalent time spans from which trends in the evidence could be deduced — 1977–1985 (nine years), 1986–1994 (nine years), and 1995–2002 (eight years).

The *initial post-abolishment period* (1977–1985) would seem to be one in which newly restored systems of capital punishment would be the least viable and their ability to deter lethal violence the most curtailed within the 26-year span. Comparison with the abolishment-period statistics will provide an answer to whether this legally chaotic period at least witnessed a drop in murder rate among death-penalty states from the preceding five years in which there were no death-penalty laws. This and the subsequent two post-abolishment periods will provide tests of whether capital punishment qualifies as an inhibitor of lethal violence. Will the restoration of the death-penalty threat reduce murder rate in states with capital punishment and satisfy the inhibition criterion of deterrence?

Three Supreme Court decisions during this initial post-abolishment period seem especially important as far as limiting the prosecution of capital cases in the short- or long-term. *Coker versus Georgia* in 1977 narrowed the scope of violence that could attract the death penalty when this punishment was judged to be excessive and disproportionate for rape. In 1978 *Lockett versus Ohio* broadened the range of mitigating factors that the defense could introduce into a capital trial. The right of the defendant to present all pertinent mitigating circumstances to the jury, factors that argue against the seriousness of the crime, would be expected to reduce the chances of receiving the death penalty. The 1982 *Edmund versus Florida* Supreme Court decision ruled that the death penalty was excessive punishment for someone whose participation in felony murder was minor and who neither killed nor displayed an intent to kill.

The *intermediate post-abolishment period (1986–1994)* continued the trend of limiting prosecution of capital cases through Supreme Court decisions found in the nine years of the initial post-abolishment period. However, the Court's rulings added a new note—some decisions sided with the prosecution in capital cases or at least attracted significant minority dissent from the Justices favoring the prosecution. Whether this represented a pendulum effect in legal decision-making or not is hard for me to say, although it is noteworthy that despite the judicial opposition to capital punishment apparent since the late 1960s, popular polls had consistently reported a majority sentiment favoring the death penalty. Supreme Court opinion had previously cited evolving moral standards of society as a determinant of restrictions on the death penalty. It is possible that majority social acceptance of capital punishment began to register as a moral imperative for the Court by this time. In any case, the drift of Supreme Court decisions between 1986 and 1994 seemed to favor some improvement in the viability of capital punishment systems to the extent that capital prosecution was made less arduous. The escalation of total executions in the country from an average of six per year between 1977 and 1985 to an average annual count of 23 between 1986–1994 also suggested that death-penalty statutes were being more strongly enforced. To the extent that the death penalty serves as a deterrent to murder, increased viability of capital punishment systems should result in a reduced murder rate relative to the initial post-abolishment period.

Some specific Supreme Court actions in the intermediate period that would be expected to complicate the prosecution of capital cases begin with *Ford versus Wainwright* in 1986 that found the execution of the insane to be unconstitutional under the nation's common-law heritage, since doing so would be "savage and inhuman." Three years later a related ruling of the Supreme Court in *Penry versus Lynaugh* stipulated that execution of severely retarded persons who are unable to grasp the wrongfulness of their actions would likely violate their Eighth Amendment rights. Between these two rulings, age became the focus of the 1988 *Thompson versus Oklahoma* decision as the Court ruled that the Eighth Amendment prohibits the execution of someone under 16 years of age at the time of the offense because of "contemporary standards of decency."

However, a seeming turnaround in the tenor of Supreme Court decisions is represented in the 1989 *Stanford versus Kentucky* case in which arguments were rejected that two youths, between 16 and 18 years old when their crimes were committed, should be protected by age from execution because of the

Eighth Amendment. In this case societal consensus was viewed as permitting the imposition of the death penalty. However, like so many Court decisions, this was a 5-4 verdict; the four dissenting Justices concurred that anyone under 18 years should be protected from execution by the Eighth Amendment. *Booth versus Maryland* in 1987 ruled against the prosecution's right to present evidence of victim impact at the penalty hearing as a way of emphasizing the harm caused by the killing. The Court majority reasoned that this information regarding victim impact might elicit arbitrary death-penalty verdicts from the jury. Although this decision would seemingly hamper capital prosecution, the *Payne versus Tennessee* ruling in 1991, only four years later, amounted to a reversal of this previous decision when the Supreme Court decided that the prosecution was put at an unfair disadvantage in capital cases when victim-impact evidence had to be withheld.

The *final post-abolishment period (1995–2002)* in this study began amid numerous signs that capital punishment in the United States had assumed greater popularity not only for the general public but also in the courts. Polls reported an increase to 80% approval of the death penalty by 1994, and total executions in the United States in the years between 1995 and 2001 rose to an average of 70 from previous figures of 6 and 23 per year during the prior post-abolishment periods. States had universally settled upon lethal injection as the least inhumane form of execution, thereby limiting challenges to the death penalty as a violation of the Eighth Amendment right to freedom from cruel and unusual punishment. Procedural delays that might discourage prosecution of capital cases were curtailed by the *Antiterrorism and Effective Death Penalty Act of 1996* that followed the bombing of the Federal Building in Oklahoma City. The momentum of support for capital punishment was building.

Restoration of the death penalty would be expected to lower the murder rate in death-penalty states to the extent that capital punishment provides a deterrent to homicide. This review of legal events in successive post-abolishment periods would lead you to expect an increasing deterrence value for capital punishment and a decreasing murder rate as states proceeded from initial approval of their new death-penalty statutes but increasing restriction on their use to a current era in which a more congenial legal attitude toward capital punishment seems to have arrived.

The Research Plan in Brief

A brief summary of the preceding pages that describe the research methodology may be helpful before we move on in the next chapter to the deterrence study itself and its results. The research question is whether having a system of capital punishment deters people from killing others in one-on-one confrontations. This is to be answered in part by determining whether the risk of being executed for a lethal act satisfies the two required features of a psychological deterrent. Murder rate and the social cost in victim lives must go up when the risk is diminished or removed (disinhibition) and must go down when the risk is reinstated (inhibition).

The deterrent value of capital punishment also will be examined from a third perspective—effectiveness. The states that have made a greater commitment to their systems will be compared to other death-penalty states that have made a lesser commitment with regard to murder rate and social cost/benefit in victim lives. Commitment, as determined by number and timing of executions, would be expected to enhance awareness of the death penalty and perceived risk of engaging in an act of murder. To the extent that the death penalty has a deterrent value, more effective systems of capital punishment should reduce murder rate better than less effective systems.

Analysis from these three perspectives on deterrence will be conducted with several safeguards in mind. The fact that three ways of examining deterrence value of the death penalty will be used is a safeguard in itself against a too-narrow view of what proof of deterrence requires. Analysis of change in murder rate will be based upon every state in the union, each state considered individually before being combined within more general categories—death penalty or abolitionist. Results will be considered in terms of stable multi-year averages. All of these considerations bear on the reliability of evidence.

Finally, the study will focus on a nine-year period, 1968–1976, as the linchpin of the overall analysis. It was during this period that executions were halted nationally (1968–1971) or that capital punishment was ruled unconstitutional by the United States Supreme Court (1972–1976) so that each state wishing to reintroduce the death penalty had to submit revised statutes to be approved by the Court. Since the death penalty was either rendered ineffective or subsequently abolished completely, these periods provide the opportunity to see what happens to willful killing in this country with diminished or no concern about receiving the ultimate punishment and what follows from restoring the threat of capital punishment. If, as many avid abolitionists claim, the death penalty has no deterrence value, there should be no discernible fluctuation in murder rate or social cost in victim lives during these two periods. On the one hand, an increase in lethal violence within the moratorium or abolishment period would suggest that a deterrent to murder has been lost, a disinhibition effect. On the other hand, a drop in lethal violence after capital punishment is restored would be evidence that the death penalty serves as a constraint; the second requirement of a psychological deterrent, inhibition of willful killing, would be met.

Chapter Two

The 45-Year Study of the Death Penalty and Deterrence

REMOVAL OF THE DEATH PENALTY AND FLUCTUATION IN WILLFUL KILLING

The first requisite of a psychological deterrent that we shall consider in this chapter, disinhibition, would be satisfied if its removal increased the probability of the act that it is supposed to deter. In the present case, the deterrent is the risk of being executed for your action, and the act is the intentional slaying of another person. Study of what happened when capital punishment was compromised or removed as a source of deterrence was made possible by Supreme Court decisions that created two contiguous periods in which degrees of abolition were apparent. A "moratorium period" (1968–1971) includes years when executions stopped across all death-penalty states while the constitutionality of capital punishment was being debated; an "abolishment period" (1972–1976) followed when the Supreme Court ruled the death penalty unconstitutional based upon Eighth Amendment considerations. These periods were considered separately in the analysis.

Diminished Death-penalty Threat and Deterrence— Baseline Period (1958–1967) versus Moratorium Period (1968–1971)

Murder Rate

The average number of murders per 100,000 inhabitants of each state having capital punishment was determined for the ten years of the baseline period. This figure was subsequently combined with the murder rates, computed in the same way, for the remaining death-penalty states by further averaging. This provided a mean annual murder rate averaged over all states maintaining

27

capital punishment systems and all years of the period. The same procedure was followed for determining the average annual murder rate in the same states over the four-year moratorium period when the death-penalty systems were diminished in effectiveness. A comparison of these murder-rate averages allows us to determine whether one-on-one killing decreased, remained the same, or increased when capital punishment systems ground to a halt as far as executions were concerned. The same procedures were followed to compare murder rates in states without the death penalty before and after the viability of capital punishment systems abated. The first column of Table 2 includes the percentage change in the murder rate from baseline to moratorium for retentionist and abolitionist states.

As Table 2 makes clear, a substantial increase in murder rate occurred when executions came to a halt within the moratorium period. States with capital punishment statutes saw their murder rates jump by an average of 42% for the four-year period. Surprisingly, however, states that did not have the death penalty also demonstrated an increase in murder rate; in fact, the 54% figure represented a greater increment than shown by the death-penalty states. This was a surprising revelation, since it involved an escalation in murder rate with the changed status of a deterrent that did not even exist. Explanations will be considered in the next chapter. The conclusion regarding deterrence value of the death penalty that can be drawn at this point is that limiting the effectiveness of the systems did have a disinhibiting effect upon murder rate in states featuring the death penalty, but the effect was apparent in almost every state of the Union (48 out of 50).

Social Cost/Benefit in Victim Lives

Whatever the percentage change in murder rate might prove to be for each state in the prior analysis, it could be converted into an estimated social cost/benefit figure by considering the population of the state in question during the four-year moratorium period. If the percentage change represented an

Table 2. Change in Murder Rates and Resulting Cost/Benefit in Victim Lives for Death-penalty and Abolitionist States from Baseline Period (1958–1967) to Moratorium Period (1968–1971)

	Average % Change Per State in Murder Rate	Average Cost/Benefit in Lives Per State Per Year Over the 4-year Moratorium Period[a]
Death-penalty States	+42%	+102
Abolitionist States	+54%	+72

[a]A plus count means that the change in murder rate during the moratorium period cost lives beyond what would have been expected given the previous baseline rate.

increase in murder rate during the moratorium period, the cost in victim lives of having the higher average homicide rate rather than the average rate found in the baseline period could be determined. On the other hand, in the rare case when the murder rate fell in a state during the moratorium period, a benefit in lives spared would be realized. The cost/benefit figure, given that suspending executions had no disinhibiting effect on murder rate and no value as a deterrent, would approach zero. The second column of Table 2 presents the average number of lives lost per state per year over the four-year moratorium period when the changes in murder rate were taken into consideration for states which did and did not have capital punishment.

Examination of the cost/benefit figures for the two categories of states reveals that the more populous death-penalty states suffered a greater projected loss of lives by their rate elevation than the abolitionist states. Each of the states with capital punishment reported an average of 102 more homicides for each of the four years than would have been observed if murder rate had been contained at baseline level; projected homicides for each abolitionist state showed an average increase of 72 for each of the same four years.

The comparison between abolitionist and retentionist states in the estimated total cost of lives associated with increased murder rates during the moratorium on executions is worth reporting; the critical importance of each human life is at the heart of the death-penalty controversy. However, this total must be cautiously considered . There were about three times as many states with capital punishment as without, and death-penalty states are more populous to begin with. These totals of victims lost over the four-year period for death-penalty states and separately for abolitionist states do provide a sense of the seriousness of the victimization problem though. Projected totals based upon increases in murder rate come arithmetically to over 900 additional people claimed as victims in abolitionist states during the moratorium; death-penalty jurisdictions suffered almost 3800 additional murders based upon their increased murder rates over the same four-year period.

Diminished Death-penalty Threat and Deterrence—
Baseline Period (1958–1967) Versus Abolishment Period (1972–1976)

If murder rate and social cost in lives are adversely affected by systemic impairment to capital punishment dealt by court decisions, what would happen if the systems were abolished entirely? To the extent that a viable death-penalty system serves as a deterrent to willful killing, an impaired system should still offer more restraint than no system at all. This logical conclusion found support in the evidence to be considered next. The same type of data analyses were conducted involving comparison between the baseline period and the five-year abolishment period that followed the moratorium on executions.

Murder Rate

The number of murders in each state per 100,000 population during each year of the baseline period (1958–1967) and during each year of the abolishment period (1972–1976) were averaged over the years within each period. These average murder rates for each state during the two periods were then combined into an average for retentionist and abolitionist categories as before. The percentage of change in murder rate from the earlier period when capital punishment systems were intact to the later period when they were abolished was then determined as an indication of altered deterrence value and disinhibition. Table 3 provides the murder-rate evidence along with the social cost/benefit of these changes in terms of victim lives.

Table 3 makes it clear that the average rate of murder across the nation as a whole continued to soar after capital punishment statutes were found to be unconstitutional in 1972. Death-penalty states experienced a 71% escalation in murder rate from baseline levels to the abolishment period, a substantial increase even when compared to the 42% jump when moratorium-period rates were compared to baseline. Only 3 of 37 capital punishment states failed to show this trend of new highs in murder rate as death-penalty systems went from impaired status during the moratorium to nonexistence.

States without capital punishment displayed further decay in control of lethal violence during the abolishment period with murder rate increasing by an average of 99% from baseline figures. Finding a substantially greater murder rate in these states when the death penalty was abolished than was evident in their 54% increase during the moratorium years becomes even more mysterious and needful of explanation. Why would legal jurisdictions that do not allow capital punishment demonstrate an increasing surge of willful killing over a nine-year period in which the death penalty disappeared? It is as

Table 3. Change in Murder Rates and Resulting Cost/Benefit in Victim Lives for Death-penalty and Abolitionist States from Baseline Period (1958–1967) to Abolishment Period (1972–1976)

	Average % Change Per State in Murder Rate	*Average Cost/Benefit in Lives Per State Per Year Over the 5-year Abolishment Period*[a]
Death-penalty States	+71%	+213
Abolitionist States	+99%	+154

[a]A plus count means that the change in murder rate during the abolishment period cost lives beyond what would have been expected given the previous baseline rate.

though they had suffered a loss in containment from the demise of a deterrent they did not have in the first place. Two of the thirteen states without death-penalty statutes defied the trend of increasing murder rate from 1968–71 to 1972–1976.

Social Cost/Benefit in Victim Lives

As murder rate continued to climb in the period during which capital punishment was considered unconstitutional, so did victim cost. Table 3 tells us that more populous death-penalty states suffered a projected average of 213 more killings a year per state than would have been found if the baseline murder rates of 1958–1967 had been maintained. Each abolitionist state attracted an average social cost figure of 154 more murders per year based upon the state's average change in murder rate.

If the social cost problem is considered in terms of totals for retentionist and for abolitionist categories, the cumulative number of victims claimed by the surge in murder rate from baseline to abolishment periods takes on ominous proportions. The toll becomes around 8000 victims over the five-year period in states that had capital punishment ruled unconstitutional, and the cost was about 2000 victims in the abolitionist states. Perhaps it is not necessary to repeat that these victim totals are in excess of what would have been expected if baseline-period murder rates had been sustained through the 1972–1976 period.

RESTORATION OF THE DEATH PENALTY AND FLUCTUATIONS IN WILLFUL KILLING

We have covered the evidence on the first of three criteria that must be satisfied in order to consider capital punishment to be a psychological deterrent to murder; the disinhibition requirement stipulates that the removal of the proposed deterrent must increase the probability of the act in question. The evidence seems clear. Impairment in the effectiveness of capital punishment systems was associated with an escalating murder rate and projected social cost in victim lives. Compete abolishment of these systems had even more serious ramifications as far as increased rate of homicide and social cost were concerned. These releaser effects were evident in almost every state, whether retentionist or abolitionist. This spread-of-effect qualifies as a conundrum now, but explanations will be considered in the next chapter.

At this point the analysis will move to the second criterion of a psychological deterrent; an inhibition effect would require that its restoration must decrease the probability of the act in question. The research plan for this phase of the analysis already has been described, and I will not go into detail again. In broad terms the 26-year span from 1977, when revised death-penalty statutes "kicked in," through 2002 was broken into three roughly equal periods. This allowed a trend analysis of murder rate and social cost/benefit in each state based upon reliable time periods. Serendipity played a role here as the 9-9-8 split in years coincided with what seem to be discernible shifts in Supreme Court and legislative attitudes toward capital punishment. Legal action went from continuing efforts to limit the scope of prosecution for the recently-approved statutes (1977–1985), to mixed signals regarding the legitimacy of death-penalty systems (1986–1994), to a display of support favoring the exercise of capital punishment (1995–2002). The shifting sands of jurisprudence and legislation, polls showing the continuing popular support for the death penalty, and the time required for new systems of capital punishment to be reestablished would lead us to expect retentionist states to show not only a general reduction in homicide over the post-abolishment years as evidence of inhibition and deterrence but also a declining murder rate and an escalating social benefit over these successive post-abolishment periods.

Enhanced Death-penalty Threat and Deterrence—
Abolishment Period (1972–1976) versus the Post-abolishment
Periods (1977–1985, 1986–1994, 1995–2002)

The method of investigation in this phase of the analysis involved comparisons in murder rate between the abolishment period in which no capital punishment existed throughout the country and each of the successive post-abolishment periods. Evidence of deterrence value would require that a decrease in murder rate and a social benefit in victim lives spared would be observed in states with capital punishment as the death penalty was re-instituted by meeting Supreme Court standards. (These were much the same states as had death-penalty statutes before this form of punishment was ruled unconstitutional.) A drop in willful killing from the abolishment period to a subsequent period after the death penalty was restored would be consistent with the inhibition requirement of psychological deterrence. Introducing a true inhibitor must be associated with a decreased likelihood of the act to be inhibited. If my reasoning is correct, not only this general inhibition effect should be observed but also diminishing murder rates over the three successive component periods. The same comparisons were made between abolishment and post-abolishment periods for states that chose not to allow capital punishment. The averaging procedures employed in inhibition analyses were those described previously in analyzing disinhibition.

Murder Rate

Table 4 includes the average percentage changes in murder rate from the abolishment period to each of the post-abolishment periods for death-penalty states following reinstatement of capital punishment and for states that eschewed the death penalty (Table 4, left column); the social cost/benefit in victim lives projected from these rate changes is also found (Table 4, right column).

Examination of murder rate over the three periods following the legal reestablishment of capital punishment reveals a systematic decrease in average homicide rates for death-penalty states. This begins with a 7% average drop in murder rate during the initial post-abolishment period, is followed by a 13% average decline during the next period, and reaches an average 30% reduction in rate for each retentionist state relative to the abolishment period within the most recent period.

Average murder rates for the states without the death penalty followed the same trend downward but declined less and in a more erratic pattern. Very little decrease in lethal violence was observed in the first two post-abolishment periods, a span of 18 years; no drop from the peak homicide rates of the abolishment years was found for the first nine years and only a 4% decrease in the nine years following. It was not until the final time span, 1995–2002, that an appreciable decline of 23% in murder rate was detected for abolitionist states relative to the abolishment period.

Table 4. Change in Murder Rates and Resulting Cost/Benefit in Victim Lives for Death-penalty and Abolitionist States from Abolishment Period (1972–1976) to Post-abolishment Periods

	Average Percentage Change Per State in Murder Rate	Average Cost/Benefit in Lives Per State Per Year Over the Post-abolishment Periods[a]
Initial Post-abolishment Period (1977–1985)		
Death-penalty States	−7%	−16
Abolitionist States	0%	−14
Intermediate Post-abolishment Period (1986–1994)		
Death-penalty States	−13%	−42
Abolitionist States	−4%	+11
Final Post-abolishment Period (1995–2002)		
Death-penalty States	−30%	−213
Abolitionist States	−23%	−54

[a]A minus count means that the change in murder rate during the period proved a social benefit in that fewer victims lives were claimed than would have been expected based upon the previous baseline rate.

Direct comparison of percentage changes in homicide rate over the post-abolishment years shows even more clearly that the inhibition effect of the death penalty surpassed the drop in murder rate observed in the abolitionist states. Jurisdictions that had renewed the death penalty demonstrated the greater decline in murder rate in each of the three post-abolishment periods with the difference ranging from 7%-9%. If these single-digit figures seem unimpressive, consider two things. For one, decreases in murder rate during the post-abolishment era came much more gradually and were more moderate in magnitude than the radical increases of the moratorium/abolishment years. It was more difficult, then, to reestablish an inhibition effect for capital punishment than to lose containment through disinhibition. Also consider the point made earlier; retentionist states were facing more serious obstacles to reestablishing inhibition because of their population characteristics—higher density and greater minority representation. Restoring the death penalty provided an advantage to retentionist states in suppressing homicide despite having more formidable problems with willful killing than abolitionist states.

Social Cost/Benefit

The projected numbers of homicide victims that were spared or lost by state per year when murder rate changed to post-abolishment levels are presented in the right column of Table 4. The social benefit of capital punishment is seen in the diminishing figures for the death-penalty states—an average of 16 fewer victims each year in each state initially, then 42 less victims, and then an average of 213 lives saved per year per state by 1995–2002.

An average of 14 fewer victims per state per year were reported in the initial post-abolishment period for states without the death penalty, but this figure reverted to a plus in the ensuing nine years—11 more lives lost to homicide each year as a state average. The abolitionist states, then, showed essentially no evidence of a social benefit over the first 18 years following restoration of capital punishment, but by 1995–2002 their substantial decrease in homicide rate projected an appreciable drop of 54 in victim lives.

Again the comparison in state categories is quite revealing. There was very little difference in social benefit between death-penalty and abolitionist states between 1977 and 1985, but by the succeeding two periods the presence of the death penalty provided a far greater social benefit. It is when you no longer use averaging by year and state and divisioning by periods and report totals for retentionist and abolitionist states over the post-abolitionist era that the comparison becomes startling. The erratic but receding murder rates over the 26-year period relative to 1972–1976 levels for states without the death penalty would be projected to have spared about 700 individuals from becoming homicide statistics, a commendable outcome. Yet the states allowing capital punishment would have accumulated a social benefit of over 10,000 people spared during the same 26-year span. The deterrence effect of the death penalty since it was reinstated in 1977 not only registers scientifically in terms of murder-rate percentages but has been of considerable social value in terms of human lives.

INEFFECTIVE APPLICATION OF THE DEATH PENALTY AND FLUCTUATIONS IN WILLFUL KILLING

The third criterion of deterrence that was considered in this investigation goes beyond what is required to happen in order to demonstrate psychological disinhibition or inhibition of willful killing given specified changes in the status of the death penalty. A correlated expectation of capital punishment, if it is to be considered a true deterrent, would be that the more effectively the state system demonstrates features required for constraint, the less likely that willful killing will occur. This third criterion of the deterrence value associated with capital punishment assumed increasing importance as the other results became available. Not only are three tests of some proposal more convincing than two, but the appearance of disinhibition and inhibition effects in abolitionist states was proving to be an interpretive paradox—deterrence effects without the deterrent. Even though the death penalty had demonstrated both the disinhibition and inhibition requirements of a deterrent to homicide, vexing "shadow effects" were apparent in the elevated murder rates between 1968 and 1976 for the abolitionist states and to a lesser extent in the eventual reduction in murder rates of the post-abolishment era.

Capital punishment has been referred to as a system, one based upon a sequence of interactive factors that allow it to function. It starts with the investigation of a violent killing by the police and with the apprehension of a suspected perpetrator; has enough evidence been uncovered to sustain a capital prosecution? Then the question becomes whether death-penalty prosecution, if pursued, will be vigorously conducted. If so and guilt is substantiated by trial, will the jury be willing to assign the death penalty during the penalty phase? Finally, if the death penalty is levied, will the courts and elected officials allow execution to be consummated following a reasonable period of time on death row for appeal?

The number and timing of executions in states with capital punishment were chosen as the most accessible and critical of these systemic elements for determining system effectiveness and, by implication, how seriously each death-penalty state is committed to its own system. That system effectiveness, defined by executions in a state, should relate to murder rate is in keeping with the straightforward logic of how the death penalty works in inhibiting willful killing. The potential killer must first be aware that the death penalty exists; given this awareness, the more certain that person is regarding the imposition of the death penalty in a state the greater the perceived risk. The greater the threat conveyed by the perceived risk, the more likely that the impulse to kill will be inhibited. More effective systems of capital punishment, then, are more likely to convey the information required for the awareness-perceived risk-threat progression.

A very low number of executions over an extended period of time in a state that has death-penalty statutes could mean a number of things as far as that state's capital punishment system is concerned. I previously illustrated how population density proves to be a fallible predictor of execution numbers in a state. Although there may be other explanations for very few executions in states that maintain systems of capital punishment, reluctance to exact the ultimate penalty ranks high among the possibilities. On the other hand, relatively frequent executions require that the antecedent stages in the criminal justice progression—investigation/apprehension, prosecution, adjudication—are functioning sufficiently well to allow the system to do what it is devised to do—ensure that proven violation of death-penalty statutes results in the designated punishment. Public awareness that the capital punishment system is functioning effectively within a given state should add to its deterrence value. Awareness that the state is maintaining only a pallid version of capital punishment should do less to deter willful killing.

Commitment to Execution and Deterrence

Examination of the number of executions that have occurred within each death-penalty state following the restoration of capital punishment was made possible by an internet table compiled by Dr. Rick Halperin, Professor of History at Southern Methodist University. His compilation of executions by year covered the post-abolishment period from 1977–2003 for states that maintained capital punishment statutes throughout that period. The assumptions underlying this analysis have already been discussed; a commitment to execution indicates a more effective system of capital punishment, allows a greater public awareness of the state's willingness to punish heinous violence by this extreme measure, and provides better opportunity for deterrence of lethal violence.

Although the number of executions performed in a state over the 1977 to 2003 span of years represents a critical aspect of commitment, it does not exhaust the information available from the Halperin table relevant to system effectiveness and deterrence value. Three aspects of timing bear a logical relationship to deterrence as well. For one, the number of years in which no execution was performed in a given state attests to how continuously awareness of the system is reinforced by public reminder that the death penalty can be exacted. For a second, the longest number of years in a row during which executions were absent in a state offers much the same implication as total years, although a large number of consecutive years introduces a special risk of a gap in public attention when capital punishment is lost from public notice. The third aspect of timing involves earlier versus later comparisons. If the number of executions within a state in the first half of the 1977–2003 period exceeds the number in the second half, it may signal a decreasing interest in pursuing the death penalty. The opposite pattern might suggest an increasing interest in implementing a system of capital punishment statutes. The difference in number of executions during the first and second halves served as the determinant of decreasing or increasing interest.

The Halperin table, accordingly, provided the basis for determining the *pattern of execution* for each of 32 states with capital punishment systems between 1977 and 2003 rather than just the sheer number. For a state to demonstrate a strong system across the board it would have had to perform many executions, shown few years in which no execution was performed, not displayed a lengthy sequence of years without executions, and indicated an increasing commitment to this form of punishment. Execution-pattern analysis proceeded by ranking the states from 1 to 32 on each of these four markers of commitment to capital punishment with each set of ranks in order of decreasing commitment. Ranks on the four markers were added for each state with lower sums describing a pattern of commitment in which the jurisdiction has more rigorously pursued the death penalty for especially heinous murders.

Murder Rate

The procedure chosen to evaluate the relationship between post-restoration effectiveness of capital punishment systems and deterrence value of the death penalty involved comparison of the murder rate found in the baseline period (1958–1967) for each death-penalty state with the rate for the same state during the final post-abolishment period (1995–2002). This beginning comparison tells us how well each death-penalty state was able to approximate the relatively low murder rates preceding the upsurge in homicide between 1968–1976 by the end of the post-abolishment era.

A tripartite division of the 32 states by their execution-patterning score defined groupings with high, medium, and low effectiveness of their capital punishment systems. The average murder rate across states within each tier for the 1958–1967 and 1995–2002 periods was determined. The average percentage difference in the 1995–2002 murder rates from the 1958–1967 standards can be found in Table 5 (left column). It can be seen that murder-rate changes did not fall in a systematic order according to effectiveness level, although there seems to be no doubt that the ten states which were the most committed to their capital-punishment systems between 1977 and 2002 also demonstrated the greatest containment of murder relative to pre-1968 baselines. Frequency of one-on-one lethal violence per 100,000 population was actually brought below baseline levels of the 1958–1967 period for the tier of states that most rigorously consummated the death penalty in capital convictions.

In contrast, the remaining two tiers of death-penalty states with less commitment to their systems failed to regain their relatively low murder-rate baselines, falling 20% to 45% above this earlier standard on average. In general terms, then, states that made a greater commitment to their capital punishment systems by consummating the sentence were better able to reduce their homicide rates, although this was evident only at the high-commitment end. I will offer an explanation for the irregularity in relationship between lesser levels of system effectiveness and return to baseline murder rates on the pages ahead. As it stands, the tier of states showing intermediate commitment to their systems of capital punishment were less able to bring their murder rates down to 1958–1967 levels than the states that seemed to have little commitment at all, rarely executing a prisoner.

The states without the death penalty were included in this analysis to provide an all-or-nothing comparison with the three tiers of death-penalty states. The 12 states that stayed free of the death penalty between 1977 and 2003 ended up with murder rates that remained an average of 53% above their baseline levels. Reference back to Table 5 confirms this record of containment as the worst in the nation. As shall become apparent in the next section,

Table 5.   Change in Murder Rates and Resulting Cost/Benefit in Victim Lives for Death-penalty States at Three levels of Effectiveness from Baseline (1958–1967) to Final Post-abolishment (1995–2002) Period

Level of Effectiveness	Average Percentage Change Per State in Murder Rate	Average Cost/Benefit in Lives Per State Per Year Between 1995–2002[a]
High[b]	−14%	−194
Medium[b]	+45%	+217
Low[b]	+20%	+58

[a]A plus count means that the change in murder rate during the final post-abolishment period cost lives beyond what would have been expected given the previous baseline rate; a minus count indicates a savings in lives because of a decreased murder rate.
[b]The average number of executions over the entire 27-year period within these effectiveness groupings offers the most recognizable indicator of commitment. These averages are 64 for the highly effective states, 11 for the medium effective, and 2 for the low effective.

the best comparison of this 53% figure is with the 20% above baseline for the low-effective group. Having no death penalty compared quite unfavorably to maintaining even a weak capital punishment system as far as suppressing homicides was concerned .

Cost/Benefit Analysis

Table 5 (right column) includes the cost or benefit in projected lives lost or spared per state per year by the discrepancy in murder rates found in 1958–1967 and in 1995–2002 when tiers of states are considered by system effectiveness. This translation into victim lives, as a reminder, requires consideration of percentage difference in state murder rate from one time period to the next and population of that state in the later period. If the murder rate stays above baseline, victim lives have been lost; if the rate drops below baseline, victim lives have been spared. The death-penalty systems that proved most effective in terms of executions also were most successful in deterring murder; rates were brought below baseline by 1995–2002, achieving a projected savings in lives with an average of 194 fewer victims per state per year. This would translate into more than 15,000 fewer victims during that eight-year period. Intermediate effectiveness as far as execution pattern was concerned brought the opposite result—a projected 217 additional victims on average and more than 19,000 additional murders over the final post-abolishment period than would have been realized if these states could have reestablished their earlier homicide rates. Low-effective states with very few executions fell in-between these extremes; the average 58 extra victims claimed by each state per year summed to over 5000 during the final post-abolishment period.

States that did not allow the death penalty between 1977–2003 and that demonstrated the poorest performance in returning murder rate to baseline experienced a social cost in lives that projected to 42 added victims per year per state—a cost of just over 4000 extra victims between 1995 and 2002.

It is not difficult to make sense out of these social cost/benefit findings once the state populations are considered. Reference to the 2000 census tells us that states with the greatest commitment to the death penalty had large populations of around 7,900,000 on average. States in the intermediate tier, with much lower execution numbers, averaged 7,700,000 inhabitants—nearly identical in size. Success in bringing the murder rate down below baseline would qualify as especially beneficial in terms of lives saved in a densely populated state; a problem in doing so would show up as being very costly in an equally dense state. This observations does not take us beyond the arithmetic character of the cost/benefit formula; the important psychological significance of this finding will concern me in the next chapter.

The states that rarely used execution as punishment, consequently qualifying as least effective in implementing their capital punishment systems, fell in-between the large-state extremes in their ability to reestablish early and relatively low baseline murder rates. The mean population of these least-effective states was about 3,600,000, only 45%-47% the size of the other tiers of death-penalty states. The combination of more closely approximating baseline rate and having less than half the population brings the social cost figure down far below that projected for the intermediate states.

The introduction of population density into the explanation of how system efficiency influences social cost/benefit of the death penalty may seem contrary to my previous conclusion that number of executions could be used as an indicator of system commitment without considering size of state populations. You may recall that at the outset of this discussion I offered illustrative examples of disproportionality between execution numbers and state populations. The fact that the tier of highly effective states and the tier of states at intermediate effectiveness had much the same high population counts but such discrepant numbers of executions affirms my contention. The states in the high tier averaged executing 64 between 1977 and 2003. This number dropped radically to an average of 11 executions per state over the same period for the intermediate tier—the same average population but only 17% the number of executions. The radical difference between these two tiers in executions shows up in the deterrence results. Large-population states that were highly committed to capital punishment brought their murder rates down to a point 14% below their 1958–1967 baseline figures; the large-population states that were appreciably less committed to their capital punishment systems ended up with murder rates that remained 45% above baseline.

As a point of interest, the least-efficient tier of states averaged only about two executions each over a 27-year span. That these relatively low-population states were able to bring their homicide rates down closer to baseline levels than the intermediate-tier states adds an important complication to the analysis of system effectiveness. Lagging commitment in a high population state to its own capital punishment system provided a far greater obstacle to deterrence than an almost nonexistent commitment in a low-population state. Population density enters into the deterrence value of capital punishment in a way that has not yet been emphasized. That will concern us in the next chapter.

The 12 states without capital punishment throughout the post-abolishment era were the least successful in bringing their murder rates down to baseline relative to death-penalty states at any level of commitment. The abolitionist states were, by and large, the most sparsely populated states in the country according to the 2000 census figures with an average number of inhabitants totaling less than 2,600,000. Five of these states (42%) had populations under 1,000,000

(Alaska, Hawaii, North Dakota, Rhode Island, and Vermont) and two others had populations numbering less than 2,000,000. Even though the abolitionist states demonstrated the clearest failure to return to murder-rate baselines by 1995–2002 relative to retentionist states, this failure did not convert arithmetically into a huge social cost because of their small state populations.

The system-effectiveness analysis based upon the patterning of executions following restoration of capital punishment in 1977 confirmed the conclusions drawn from the prior analyses of disinhibition and inhibition effects — that the death penalty does serve as a deterrent to murder. States that demonstrated the greatest commitment to enforcing death-penalty statutes were far more successful in suppressing homicides than states showing less commitment. All retentionist states, however, without respect to level of commitment, did better in deterring willful killing than states lacking capital punishment. When these system-effectiveness results are added to the positive evidence from the analysis of constraints following restoration of capital punishment, the inhibition of homicide by the death penalty is clearly established. Once we take a more comprehensive look at the complicated effects of disinhibition during the moratorium/abolishment era, I am confident that evidence regarding this third criterion of deterrence will lend itself to the same conclusion. Disinhibition, what happened when capital punishment was compromised or removed as a restraint, simply followed different rules of change than inhibition, what happened when capital punishment was restored.

Chapter Three

Conceptual Lacunae
in the Deterrence Evidence

So after reference to more averages, percentages, and totals than you might otherwise choose to consider, what can now be said about whether the death penalty for heinous murder has a deterrent effect upon lethal violence? The evidence in stark "yes or no" terms supports the conclusion that the death penalty does deter willful killing of the one-on-one variety, but it is equally clear that there are places in the consideration of evidence where gaps in explanation remain or at least some thorny issues have not been sufficiently addressed. I shall use this chapter to examine some of these conceptual gaps and issues. New evidence will be introduced when possible and prior evidence will be reexamined in the course of this examination; sometimes I will simply have to wing it.

QUESTIONS THAT REQUIRE FURTHER ATTENTION

Why Does the Death Penalty Work as a Deterrent?

Perhaps you have noticed that up until this point in the book that I have not considered the obvious psychological question of why having the death penalty as a possible punishment should be expected to translate into behavioral constraint and the deterrence of willful killing? There are so many psychological factors militating against the constraining effect of the death penalty that it is no small wonder deterrence was as clearly demonstrated by the evidence as it was. Let us consider some of these limiting factors. We can begin with the fact that the constraint being studied represents a generalized effect upon all intentional killing, since death-penalty statutes are written with circumscribed conditions of egregious murder in mind. This expected generalization requires that the threat of being put to death for an especially uncivilized act of murder will generalize to a broader array of lethal actions that in most cases will lack these outrageous features. Something must be lost for the potential offender in way of anticipated risk of being executed for anticipating a criminal act that most likely will not warrant capital punishment. The generalization factor is generally ignored as critics complain that having the death penalty does not have an appreciable effect on violence in America. Psychological principles would predict the greatest effect upon premeditated violence so extreme that it could attract capital punishment. Capital punishment should have a generalized effect upon less heinous acts of murder, but it should be less. Whether engagement in forms of nonlethal violence will be influenced by the death penalty remains to be demonstrated. They are rather far out on the generalization gradient that determines how much inhibition should be expected.

There are other sources of limitation for death-penalty deterrence of murder besides requiring a generalization of risk to violent behaviors that most likely would not attract such extreme punishment. Emotionality of the moment or lack of familiarity with the law could make rational analysis of execution risk impossible for the potential perpetrator. The individual's disinterest in whether he or she lives or dies when anticipating the crime could make a threat of the death penalty ineffectual. Any number of rationalizations could diminish concern about the consequences of your actions (will not be caught, will not be convicted, etc.). Such possibilities are frequently cited by those who are convinced that the death penalty does not have a salutary effect upon murder rate in order to explain why putting one's own life at risk does not deter engaging in lethal violence. Of course, such observations are more formidable when deterrence value of the death penalty is dismissed. In light of evidence for deterrence value of the death penalty, they are more reasonably regarded as limitations imposed by idiosyncracies of human thinking and self-governance. Capital punishment works despite these imperfections.

There seems to be little to gain from further exploration of reasons why the death penalty does not function very well as a deterrent to willful killing. I agree that capital punishment does not provide a strong constraint upon murder, but the investigation did show that it does have deterrence effects which, if considered in terms of victim lives contribute an important benefit to society. The debate over capital punishment cannot invoke the sanctity of human life as an argument against execution of convicted murderers without factoring in the far greater number of lives that are spared by the system despite its limitations.

The challenge of explanation for me actually has less to do with why capital punishment does not work any better than it does than with why such an imperfect system still shows demonstrable deterrence value. As I will elaborate on the pages ahead, having a system of capital punishment for especially heinous murders is a reflection of a state's attitude toward willful killing as a social problem and of its general investment in alleviating the problem. However, commitment by the state to its system of capital punishment appears to be a variable asset; the greater the commitment, the better the deterrence. Heightened commitment to death-penalty statutes can be viewed as an aspect of a "climate of concern" about lethal violence in its criminal justice system, media, and other institutions as a state attempts to limit this unacceptable behavior and ameliorate the conditions that are responsible. A state's climate of concern, almost certainly demonstrated by more frequent executions, would be expected to augment the individual awareness that capital punishment statutes are in place and increase the perceived risk that the death penalty is likely to be put into practice if the statues are violated.

Awareness of the death penalty in someone with an instigation to kill along with a fear that being executed might be the price to pay would qualify as the basic determinants of constraint. Anything that makes it more likely that awareness and fear register prior to acting upon a homicidal impulse should enhance deterrence, and that is what a climate of concern should help facilitate. Why does the death penalty work as a deterrent? It works to the extent that (1) people are aware that the penalty exists and will be vigorously pursued if criminal circumstances call for it and (2) the extent to which this awareness represents a threat to the person. However, the psychological basis for deterrence involves more that; the threat must (3) arouse enough fear that the person will be motivated to suppress the impulse. Given that these three conditions are met, the homicidal act is less likely to occur. A failure in awareness, a lack of threat, or the absence of fear would increase the chances of lethal action.

What Evidence Is There that a Climate of Concern Regarding Homicide Is a Viable Concept and Is More Likely to Prevail in Death-penalty States?

Some evidence that states with capital punishment are more likely to be more concerned about lethal violence in their jurisdictions, or at least should be, already has been presented in the first chapter and summarized in Table 1. Two parameters of population, density and minority representation, were considered for states having high, medium and low murder rates. The findings were the same whether the temporal focus was early (1958–1967) or late (1995–2002). Population density had a curvilinear relationship with the number of murders per 100,000 population. High and intermediate rates of murder were found in more populous states; low rates were associated with relatively small populations. Minority representation in a state and murder rate were linearly related; elevated rates coincided with high minority presence and reduced rates with low minority numbers. Putting these demographics together, a high murder rate as a continuing reminder that lethal violence is a problem would more likely be found in states that are densely populated and which include a substantial percentage of minorities. More restricted murder rates would be expected in less populated states with lower minority representation.

It also has been established that abolitionist states would qualify as low in density and low in minority representation, thereby as being less vulnerable to problematic murder rates, whereas death-penalty states, being higher in both, would be expected to confront a more significant problem with murder. Looking at the 1995–2002 period for example, we find that states with no death penalty had an average population under 3,000,000, whereas death-penalty states averaged well over 6,000,000 people. Abolitionist states had a mean minority representation of about 9%, and states with capital punishment revealed a 20% minority figure on average. What these figures affirm is that states with capital punishment are more likely to demonstrate the population characteristics that are associated with higher murder rates; a climate of concern regarding lethal violence would be warranted. Abolitionist states, restricted in population and minority representation, should have lower murder rates and less basis for concern. Examination of the average homicide rate during the 1995–2002 period for these state categories substantiates the supposition that states with capital punishment are those with a greater homicide problem. Death-penalty states experienced a 6% rate over these eight years, whereas murder rates in abolitionist states were only half that severe (3%).

It has been my contention that the prevalence of willful killing and the degree of concern about lethal violence in a state that it generates are responsible in large measure for choosing and maintaining capital punishment as a deterrent to murder. I would also expect degree of concern to determine how seriously the death-penalty system is implemented. At this point I would like to introduce a new way of looking at the evidence on the proposal. Without stronger corroborating evidence these contentions could register as unduly prejudicial, since they suggest that some states fail to generate an expected sense of concern about willful killing. What the data on state population parameters, density and minority representation, suggest is that some states have more reason to be concerned on that score than others. It is imperative that even stronger evidence be made available for this conclusion before it is assumed that some states are misreading their problems of lethal violence.

The most pivotal assumption underlying the climate-of-concern proposal is that the homicide problem will escalate as minority representation increases. Statistics showed that the minority percentage went up linearly and substantially as tiers of states suffering increasing murder rates were considered. Population density was also important, but its positive relationship with murder rate was less direct. What kind of evidence is available that would support the contention that more extensive minority representation in a state is not only associated with increasing homicide problems in a correlational sense but goes beyond correlation to confirming causal significance? Such evidence would suggest that an obvious barometer exists for anticipating and dealing with problems of lethal violence.

Minority representation as a state population parameter that may influence murder rate was reexamined by returning to the Justice Department's annual compilation of crime statistics to note the racial characteristics of murderers — whether they were white or belonged to a minority race. The homicides in question included only one-on-one murder (or voluntary manslaughter) as in our prior analyses of murder rate—"willful killing" to use an inclusive term favored by the Justice Department. The racial characteristics of the perpetrators in these crimes are not always known at the time the results of police investigations are compiled; accordingly, the count of murderers was restricted to those identified as white or identified as belonging to some minority after homicide investigations have been completed. Despite these restrictions, the murderer count by race in the United States between 1976–2002 was based upon substantial pools of murder cases.

The other information necessary to conduct this new analysis were the numbers of white and minority residents (combined) in the United States at a particular point in time, estimated from the ten-year census reports from 1970 to 2000. Given the two types of information—murderer count by race and total racial numbers—it was possible to compute a new statistic modeled after the murder rate used in the original study. The reported number of white murderers in the United States for a given year and the estimated white population of the United States in that year were entered into an index indicating the number of white murderers to be found per each 100,000 of white population in the country—a murderer rate for whites. The same procedure was followed for determining the number of murderers combined across minorities per 100,000 minority population in the United States for any given year. Each of these murderer rates would represent an underestimate of the true rate because of the murder cases in which racial identity of the perpetrators is unknown, but I had no reason to believe that unknown cases would affect one murderer rate more than the other. Murderer rate, then, represented a crime metric that clearly ties intentional killing to race of the murderer, at least as clearly as police investigation allowed.

The murderer rate over the 27-year period presented very different pictures for whites and minorities. This majority rate varied but little, ranging by the year between 2 and 4 murderers per 100,000 of the white population in the United States. In contrast, the rate of murderers found among minorities in this country extended from 8 to 20 per 100,000 over the same years. Minority rate was consistently much higher than the white rate, and it was far more variable over the years. The minority murderer rate at its lowest was still about three times that of the white murderer rate and averaged over five times greater between 1976–2002. Obviously, the chances that some minority group member would engage in one-on-one lethal violence were appreciably greater than was true for those in the white majority. It follows that states with a higher minority representation will more likely be faced with murder as a substantial problem that requires amelioration.

This conclusion is actually over-determined. Since high minority representation is usually found in densely populated states, the combination translates into high minority numbers. The greater number of minority individuals and a national murderer rate five times higher than for whites, in turn, translate into substantial numbers of homicides. It is little wonder that states with high minority representations typically have resorted to capital punishment as a possible constraint upon killing. The analysis of murderer rate offers a partial explanation, and it does so in causal terms.

The appreciable decline in rate of murder from the peak years of death-penalty abolition (1972–1976) to the most recent post-abolishment period studied (1995–2002) came after two post-abolishment periods of more grudging diminishment (1977–1985, 1986–1994). This decline in homicides was accompanied by a similar drop in murder rate for the minorities. In 1977–1985 there was an average of 17 minority members per 100,000 who committed a murder in this country. This dropped to an average rate of 15 per 100,000 in the 1986–1994 years. By 1995–2002 the minority murderer rate had declined to about 10 in 100,000, still well above the stable average white rate of less than 3 in 100,000 but a substantial drop nonetheless. The restoration of capital punishment allowed the nation to get a grip on its homicide problem, but it took many years before that could happen. A drop of over 40% in murderer rate among minorities appears to be a big part of this welcome correction. The declining murderer trend qualifies as critical to the national interest in that minorities are becoming an increasing component of the United States population according to the census: 1960, 13%; 1970, 14%; 1980, 20%; 1990, 24%; 2000, 33%. Moreover, these percentages do not even include the illegal aliens who in increasing numbers would not be represented in the United States census reports.

How Are the Paradoxical Fluctuations in Murder Rate for Abolitionist States to be Explained?

The murder-rate trends are puzzling for the abolitionist states from 1958–1967 to the moratorium years on execution(1968–1971) and then on to the period of total abolishment for the death penalty (1972–1976). To a lesser extent, the same thing could be said about the murder rate for the states without capital punishment from 1972–1976 peaks through post-abolishment periods. The paradox afforded by these results is simply this. Why should states that chose not to have capital punishment as a possible sentence for murder demonstrate an increase in murder rate when death-penalty executions were brought to a halt and an even greater increase when the death penalty was abolished completely in the United States? By the same token, why should murder rate eventually drop in states without the death penalty after capital punishment was restored as a legal option nationally?

These systematic fluctuations in homicide rate are counterintuitive; there seems to be no logical basis for such changes in abolitionist states as long as one thinks only in terms of deterrence associated with the death penalty. How could removal or restoration of the death sentence make a difference in the prevalence of homicide for a state that did not allow that form of punishment? One way to explain this paradox can be found in a concept already discussed — the climate of concern about lethal violence.

It has been suggested that the presence of a death-penalty system, especially if it is implemented effectively, signals a high level of concern about lethal violence. Furthermore, heightened concern is routinely warranted in states having a high minority representation because of the murderer rate among minorities and, most likely, a dense population. This concern would show itself in a variety of ways within the legal and civil communities that make the state populace more cognizant of societal repugnance for willful killing and of the significant risk that the death penalty will be pursued for such crimes. It is this added emphasis upon the unacceptability of murder along with the state's commitment to extreme punishment if warranted that stand to magnify threat when contemplating lethal violence.

What has this supposition to do with the paradoxical fluctuations in murder rate for abolitionist states? It stands to reason that the climate of concern over willful killing in states with capital punishment is shared to some extent with states that do not feature this form of punishment even though abolitionist states usually have fewer social problems associated with lethal violence. When Supreme Court decisions diminish capital punishment as viable systems or remove them altogether, as happened between 1968 and 1976, it may well have had the unintended effect of decreasing the stigma attached to murder. It would be difficult for a death-penalty state to contend that homicide is as objectionable or that it is as serious about constraint when capital crimes become increasingly difficult to prosecute or the death penalty is banished as "cruel and unusual punishment." The Supreme Court decisions may have been judicially sound in light of the Bill of Rights, but the message remained that "murder is bad but not that bad." To the extent that a shift in attitude was conveyed by diminished punishment for murder, the change would not only be expected to appear in states that had lost the death penalty but to influence states that previously had not adopted capital punishment as well. This was a national edict proclaimed by a national court.

The restoration of the death penalty as a legal punishment by the Supreme Court and eventual reduction of obstacles to capital prosecution could have signaled another shift of attitude in the opposite direction. The perception of a decreased tolerance for lethal violence would be reinforced on a national scale. A drop in murder rate would be expected for states that reinstated capital punishment and states that did not, although retentionist states might be expected to more readily restore a climate of concern because they chose to affirm their intolerance for willful killing by reestablishing the death penalty.

What I am proposing here is that decisions regarding the death penalty by the Supreme Court contributed to a national attitude concerning extreme violence. That attitude influenced deterrence of homicide committed in a death-penalty state but also influenced deterrence in states without capital punishment as well. When the Supreme Court halted executions and then abolished capital punishment by their constitutional decisions it may have added to the legal protection of suspected or convicted murderers, but it brought excess baggage—a more tolerant attitude toward willful killing. Restoration of the death penalty sent the opposite message conveying less tolerance for homicide, and that would explain the reduction in murder rate during the post-abolishment years for both retentionist and abolitionist states. If this conjecture is correct, the paradoxical rise and fall of the murder rate in abolitionist states corresponding to High Court decisions on the death penalty finds ready explanation. However, paradox is replaced by irony, since this spread-of-effect would mean that states denying themselves the use of capital punishment on principle gain some constraint upon homicide from the existence of the death penalty elsewhere.

I have proposed that Supreme Court decisions in the 1960s, 1970s, and 1980s bearing upon the constitutionality of capital punishment could have affected attitudes toward the crime of murder anywhere in the United States whether a state featured the death penalty or not. That assigns a great deal of importance to High Court rulings on crime and punishment as far as attitudes toward violence are concerned, perhaps more importance than the reader might expect. Now would be a good time to come up with evidence that a Supreme Court ruling regarding the death penalty for a particular violent crime influenced the rate of that crime in a way best explained as a shift in public attitude. There is a piece of legal history relating to capital punishment and the rate of violent crime that offers rather compelling evidence that a Supreme Court decision can have that kind of effect.

When Georgia reinstated the death penalty following the abolishment period, it was apparently the only state to include the possibility of a death sentence for rape among its statutes. This particular statute was challenged in **Coker versus Georgia** (1977), and the Supreme Court ruled that the death penalty was an excessive and disproportionate punishment for the rape of an adult woman whose life had not been taken. The seemingly unintended but conveyed meaning of the ruling becomes an issue; could this be taken to mean that rape is bad but not that bad? The question of whether the removal of the death penalty in Georgia created a more tolerant climate for the act of rape in that state is open to empirical test in a way comparable to the analysis of murder-rate trends in the moratorium/abolishment periods. Actually, what happened to the rate of rape in Georgia following removal of the death penalty can provide an even more stringent test of High Court influence on attitude toward this form of violent criminal conduct.

There was no capital punishment for rape in Georgia for the five years preceding the 1977 **Coker versus Georgia** decision (1972–1976); in fact, there was no capital punishment anywhere in the United States for any violent crime, since those were the years that the death penalty was abolished as "cruel and unusual punishment." During those five years prior to the 1977 ruling, the rate of rape per 100,000 in Georgia was 1% below the national average. The **Coker versus Georgia** ruling that the death penalty was excessive and disproportionate punishment for rape that did not involve the death of the victim was followed by a five-year period in which there was an immediate and sustained upsurge in sexual assault within the state of Georgia. The rate of rape rose to 23% above the national rate in 1978 and averaged 22% above the national figure during the entire 1978–1982 period. In fact, the increment in rape in Georgia was sustained for eight more years until 1991 with sexual assault remaining almost 20% above the nation's average. At that point rape as a crime was finally brought under better control in Georgia after a 13-year surge.

Let us now review the specifics and consider the implication of this footnote to legal history. The rate of rape in Georgia for two periods of time were compared; neither the 1972–1976 period nor the 1978–1982 period involved capital punishment as a deterrent to this crime. The difference between the two periods, as far as the death penalty is concerned, is that immediately before the 1978–1982 span of years the Supreme Court ruled that this extreme form of punishment was excessive considering the level of violence involved in rape. That could readily translate into "rape is bad but not that bad," and this message and subsequent attitude shift would explain the substantial upsurge of rape within the state. The abrupt escalation in sexual assault cannot be attributed to a change in the risk factor for the rapist, since neither the five-year period preceding the Supreme Court ruling nor the one that followed featured the death penalty for rape.

In order to put this change into proper context, it is important to recall that the increase reported in rate of rape for Georgia was relative to the national average—from 1% below the United States average to 22% above it. The Supreme Court decision abolishing the death penalty for rape concerned only Georgia, the one state with a capital punishment statute covering that crime. The Georgia escalation in sexual assaults relative to the entire nation came at a time when there was an increasing rate of rape nationally—a 36% jump from 1972–1976 to 1978–1982. This substantial increase in sexual assault across the United States puts the Georgia crime statistics into bolder relief. The repositioning of Georgia 22% above the national average for the crime of rape between 1978–1982 from a position below the national average between 1972–1976 took place despite the increasing prevalence of rape across the entire country. If rape was escalating in the nation, it had to be surging in Georgia.

Could the Changes in Murder Rate Simply Be Part of More General Fluctuations in Violence that Are Unrelated to the Status of the Death Penalty?

Asking oneself whether there could be another meaning for scientific findings other than the one that you have laboriously pieced together can be a disquieting experience. It requires that you seek a way of discarding your own assumptions and conclusions in favor of some alternative way of viewing the evidence. It also means that the method of study you have designed fails to provide evidence that allows unequivocal interpretation. However, I have not been reluctant on the pages ahead to criticize interpretation of death-penalty statistics that failed to consider a viable alternative. So, "Live by the sword, die by the sword." It is time to examine a possibility that would prove embarrassing for my conclusion that capital punishment is a deterrent to murder.

An alternative way of explaining the precipitous climb in murder rate nationally that followed the weakening and then abolishment of death-penalty systems would be that these changes were not restricted to willful killing but could be observed in violent crime across the board. If so, the rise in violence generally could not be attributed to the revised status of the death penalty, not directly at least; most violence did not attract capital punishment. Perhaps these changes had their roots in social changes occurring in this country that made engaging in violence more permissible or that made the motivations for violent engagement more compelling. Continuing this line of reasoning, the gradual decline in murder rate that was observed following reinstatement of the death penalty would not be explained as a specific effect of a change in legal policy but instead as a general decrease in violence related to another shift in social conditions.

I am not prepared to say what social changes might have occurred that would bring fluctuations in violence on a national scale; this is not my preferred way of interpreting the evidence. That being so, I am not able to speculate why the social changes would have displayed the timing and patterning required by the trend analysis of murder rate. Changes in social conditions would have to explain a rapid and substantial escalation in general violence that coincided with the demise of the death penalty and a gradual and more restrained decline in violence beginning with the restoration of the death penalty and accelerating in the latter stage of the post-abolishment era. Despite the vagueness with which I pose this alternative, it is clear that if the rates of other forms of violence not associated with capital punishment follow the same trend lines as murder rate, my proposal regarding the deterrence value of the death penalty would have to assume an additional burden. Why should the deterrence afforded by capital punishment for willful killing extend to less serious forms of violence that do not allow for the death penalty?

If this sounds familiar, it is reminiscent of the paradoxical changes in states without the death penalty when their murder rates fluctuated in correspondence with the absence or presence of capital punishment. If murder rate changes, up or down, were found to be part of more general violence trends, it would become necessary for me to propose a comparable generalized effect if I were to stick with the conclusion that the death penalty serves as a deterrent to murder. The conclusion would become that the importance of capital punishment as a deterrent not only extends to states that do not feature the death penalty but to violent crimes that do not allow for the death penalty as well. Depending that much on generalization effects to sustain a proposal could limit its credibility.

Method of Studying Fluctuations in Violence

The Justice Department's annual report on crime in the United States that served as the source of murder-rate data from 1958 until 2002 also includes rate counts over the same years for three other types of violent crime—forcible rape, robbery, and aggravated assault. Murder and voluntary manslaughter represent the two forms of lethal violence included in the Justice Department's version of murder as willful killing. Rape, robbery, and aggravated assault represent the most serious types of nonlethal violence.

The question of whether changes in murder rate were simply part of more general fluctuations in violence would be answered by comparing national trends in the rate of nonlethal violence with those found for the rate of murder. Some of the same periods chosen for analyzing the disinhibitory and in-hibitory effects of murder as a deterrent were reconsidered, but this time na-tional rates of murder and nonlethal violence were compared. (The original analysis did not make use of the countrywide rate index, since it computed change for retentionist and abolitionist states independently.) The current analysis, then, homed in on the comparison between rates during the baseline period (1958–1967) and the period during which the death penalty was abol-ished (1972–1976). Murder rates reached their apex across the country in the latter period; the question being considered was whether nonlethal violence demonstrated the same surge in rate as lethal violence. Of greater importance, as it turned out, a comparison was made between the rate changes from the abolishment period (1972–1976) to the final period studied (1995–2002) fol-lowing restoration of capital punishment. By that time the murder rate had dropped to its lowest level since the death penalty was reinstated; would the rate of nonlethal violence show the same decrement?

Evidence on Fluctuations in Violence

The comparison of lethal and nonlethal violence from baseline to the abol-ishment period was not at all reassuring as far as assuming murder-specific disinhibition when the death penalty was abolished. While it was true that the rate of murder increased radically over baseline by 86% in the United States between 1972–1976, the rate of nonlethal violence surged even more; rape, robbery, and aggravated assault showed an average 175% increase during those five years. Eliminating the death penalty either had a generalized effect upon other serious forms of violence or another social influence had a facili-tating influence on all forms of violence at that particular point in time.

The second step of the violence analysis became critical in determining whether capital punishment as a deterrent to murder had been the object of study in this investigation or whether the possibility of some other social in-fluence had to be conceded. A decrease of 31% in the national murder rate from 1972–1976 highs was observed by 1995–2002; restoration of capital punishment was associated with an appreciable drop in homicides across the country. Comparing the same periods, nonlethal violence demonstrated an in-creased rate of 30%; restoring the death penalty did not bring down nonlethal violence as the counterproposal of a common effect on all forms of violence would require. In short, capital punishment qualifies as a deterrent to willful killing, since the requirements of disinhibition and inhibition were satisfied. On the other hand, the trend lines for nonlethal violence cannot be explained by changes in the status of the death penalty. The required inhibition effect of a deterrent was missing. This means that the trends of nonlethal-violence rates in this country do not compel alternative interpretation of the death-penalty deterrence effect upon murder. The surge in nonlethal violence in the abolishment period coincided with the radical increase in murder, presumably as a strong generalized effect, and simply continued as an increasing "fact of life" in America.

Before moving on from consideration of national trends in violence, let us examine one more comparison—the years prior to judicial compromise of capital punishment in the United states (1958–1967) to the final post-abolishment period (1995–2002). This will give me the opportunity to present some final figures on the deterrence value of capital punishment that offer a particularly striking picture of legal constraint in an increasingly violent society.

The average national murder rate between 1995 and 2002 remained 28% above the average for the baseline period some 35 year earlier; the death penalty was legal during both periods. This figure actually underestimates the constraint imposed within retentionist states that are committed to their systems of capital punishment which, as you may remember, brought their murder rates down below baseline levels. The clearest perspective on this 28% figure comes from a comparison with counterpart figures for the three nonlethal forms of violence. Over the same period of time, forcible rape had escalated to 238% above baseline; robbery rate went up 244%; the rate of aggravated assault climbed 305%. Comparisons emphasize the fact that the restoration of capital punishment not only deterred willful killing, as previous analyses have made clear, but deterrence of murder took place in an era of mushrooming nonlethal violence.

Perhaps you have been exposed to the sophistry implicit in "Whatever does not kill you, makes you stronger." While rarely true that certainly seems to be the case in these analyses of violence trends. They originated in considering the need for a reinterpretation of deterrence as part of a general effect upon all forms of violence of some unidentified social influence. Analysis ended by showing not only that capital punishment alone qualified as a deterrent to murder but that death-penalty constraint upon murder occurred despite a national explosion in nonlethal violence.

Are Disinhibition and Inhibition of Willful Killing Opposite but Otherwise Comparable Criminal Phenomena?

You never know what may surface from empirical search should you choose to go beyond moral conviction and try science in addressing the death-penalty controversy. Unanticipated findings regarding the way that deterrence works can be ignored up to a point since any given study cannot be expected to provide an explanation for every ripple in the data. However, there was one aspect of the deterrence analyses that stood out in the original trend analysis of murder rate in retentionist and abolitionist states considered separately. Not surprisingly, the same "ripple in the data" reappeared when national homicide trends were subjected to analysis. This aspect of deterrence seems important enough to merit discussion, since it has implications for future courtroom litigation bearing upon the status of capital punishment.

Psychological principles were introduced when the death penalty was considered as a deterrent to murder by requiring that this form of punishment satisfy the two basic requirements of an inhibitor. The removal of the death penalty had to increase the likelihood of murder (disinhibition), and the restoration of the death penalty had to decrease the likelihood of murder (inhibition). Since disinhibition and inhibition represent opposite extremes of the same constraint process and I was interested in how they affect the same behavioral act, it might appear that they would show up as opposite but otherwise comparable processes. At least, I anticipated no qualitative difference between disinhibition and inhibition effects relating to the death penalty other than in their contrasting influence on murder rate.

Yet the difference in how disinhibition and inhibition made their appearance as far as timing and generalization of effect were concerned made itself blatantly obvious in the crime-rate data. Disinhibition of murder that followed upon the disruption and then demise of capital punishment systems as deterrents had an almost immediate effect upon rate in both retentionist and abolitionist states—an appreciable increase from 1958–1967 to 1968–1971 and a further increment from 1968–1971 to 1972–1976 before rates crested. An independent analysis of what happened to the rate of rape in Georgia once the Supreme Court struck down the death penalty for this crime revealed the same immediacy and extensity of the disinhibitory effect. Between 1972 and 1976 Georgia ranked slightly below the national rate of rape; between 1978 and 1982, following the 1977 Court decision, this sexual crime climbed to a rate that exceeded the national average by over 20%.

Besides the immediacy and substantial size of the disinhibitory effect, the demise of the death penalty also had the same impact across jurisdictional lines; the same immediacy and extensity of effect was observed whether the state featured capital punishment or not. The disinhibition of lethal violence that followed abolishment of capital punishment even seemed to generalize to other forms of violence that did not involve the death of a victim—forcible rape, robbery, aggravated assault—and to do so across the entire country. At least these three violent crimes demonstrated a radical rate increase that coincided with the abolishment of capital punishment. Everything that this investigation disclosed regarding trends in violent crime traceable to the demise of capital punishment as a deterrent to murder attests to the immediate and extensive impact of disinhibitory release from the threat of execution.

The examination of inhibition effects, on the other hand, reveals a very different picture. Reintroduction of the death penalty was accompanied by the decline in murder rates for retentionist states required to fully qualify capital punishment as a deterrent—an increase in rate when removed and now a decrease when restored. Yet the drop in willful killing was not immediate; in fact, retentionist states had to wait 18 years to get beyond a moderate reduction in homicide to a period when more tangible results were in evidence. Generalized deterrence effects were constrained or disappeared altogether. States without the death penalty experienced a decline over the 26-year post-abolishment period but practically none for the first 18 years. The drop in murder rate for the abolitionist states lagged well behind the retentionist states, and this proved to be true no matter how ineffectively death-penalty systems were implemented. Crime rates for nonlethal violence no longer mimicked the rate changes found for lethal violence; rape, robbery, and aggravated assault continued to increase substantially while the rate of willful killing declined over the post-abolishment years.

There may be many implications of finding disinhibition and inhibition effects of changes in capital punishment status to be qualitatively different, not only in their expected opposite influence but also in their timing and generalization. I am most interested in the implication of these findings for future legal intervention that affects the status of the death penalty. The data make it clear that it is easy to relinquish whatever deterrent value is provided by the death penalty through legal interdiction, whereas it is a formidable challenge to restore deterrent value by subsequent legal changes. Thousands of victim lives may be forfeited by lenient revisionism with regard to the death-penalty code, especially if drastic changes are made. This is not a call for a "hands-off" policy with regard to the death penalty. It is an expression of concern that moral persuasion will be allowed to hold sway over social pragmatism in deciding whether and under what conditions capital punishment should be permitted. This concern extends to the courts as well as to the state policy makers and criminal justice officials who oversee the containment of violence in their respective states.

I should have anticipated that there would be a difference between the immediate, substantial, and generalized effects of disinhibition upon murder rate when the death penalty was removed and the grudging changes over time and specificity of inhibition when it was restored. It was really a matter of common sense. Disinhibition follows from lifting all constraints associated with the threat of possible execution. There are no cognitive demands made upon the individual except whatever it takes to appreciate that the death penalty no longer exists. Inhibition involves the reinstatement of capital punishment and the restoration of constraint. This revision in criminal law must not only become known to the individual, but the reinstatement of deterrence must cut through the cognitive resistances that people show to curtailing any emotionally-driven behavior. Those are more formidable learning requirements.

Is the Conclusion that the Death Penalty Is a Deterrent to Murder Becoming Unduly Complicated?

Three criteria had to be satisfied in the present investigation before it could be concluded that capital punishment deters one-on-one murder. Two of these were obvious given the psychological meaning of deterrence as it would be demonstrated in individual behavior. If something is to qualify as a deterrent to a particular kind of activity, it must be shown that the probability of the activity increases when the factor is removed and the probability of the act decreases when the factor is restored. Reliable evidence that the death penalty has these disinhibition and inhibition effects on murder rate was presented in analyses covering all retentionist states and over extended time periods. States without capital punishment revealed the same disinhibition of homicide but failed to match the changes called for by inhibition.

Besides these fundamental requirements, a third criterion of deterrence was added as a way of "fine tuning" the analysis. Capital punishment within a state represents a system involving a progression of stages beginning with criminal investigation and progressing through prosecution, adjudication, and execution. Some systems work more effectively than others based, presumably, in large measure upon the degree to which lethal violence is perceived as an urgent problem within a state. Effectiveness can be gauged by how well a capital punishment system performs the function for which it was devised—executing those who are convicted of especially repugnant displays of lethal violence. System efficacy qualifies logically as a deterrence criterion because if a system of punishment serves generally as a murder deterrent, it follows that more effective systems should bring the murder rate down further than less effective systems or no capital punishment at all. This third criterion of deterrence value was satisfied as well by independent analysis.

Requiring satisfaction of three criteria of deterrence before concluding that capital punishment constrains willful killing in this country should prove reassuring to some, although it might be perceived as an unnecessary complication by others who are more attuned to categorical pro or con moral verdicts in settling the death penalty controversy. In fact, by the time I finished pursuing the ideas that (1) adoption and maintenance of the death penalty depend on population size and minority representation, (2) disinhibition and inhibition of lethal violence show up not only as opposite but qualitatively different patterns of change in criminal behavior, (3) how well capital punishment serves as a deterrent depends upon the state's commitment to the system as a way of alleviating its homicide problem, and (4) attitudes regarding criminal violence seep into abolitionist states when changes in death-penalty status are legally imposed, (5) etc., understanding the death penalty as a deterrent to murder may appear conceptually burdensome.

Yet I see no advantage to passing off the deterrence issue as a simple one when it is not. Perhaps the luxury of a categorical moral decision about capital punishment which avoids the necessity for elaboration or qualification, that it is invariably wrong to take a life as punishment or invariably just to put someone to death for a heinous killing, is one of the reasons why the death-penalty controversy has persisted over the years. Evidence, and I believe good evidence, that capital punishment deters murder to some extent and results in saving a vast number of lives should encourage interest in detailing the psychological mechanisms and the social circumstances that govern the constraint of lethal violence. Elaboration of these details strike me as an important step in increasing the pragmatic value of this form of punishment.

I have tried to make the case for not only marshaling evidence that addresses the question of whether capital punishment has deterrence value or not but for going beyond simple affirmation or denial to disclose some specifics of the deterrence process and qualifications to the effect. This has resulted in a more complicated set of answers than this controversy often attracts. However, things could have been worse as far as elaboration of death-penalty effects goes. Who knows how many related variables went unstudied because of logistical limitations? Even the variables that were studied offered the opportunity for more complex analysis that was bypassed so as not to obfuscate the exposition of research results. As an example, consider the intertwined relationships between the two parameters of state population that were subject to study and the third criterion of deterrence—effectiveness of the state capital punishment system. The population parameters included the number of people in the state and the percentage of this number that had minority status. The effectiveness standing for capital punishment systems was based upon the number and patterning of executions consummated within a retentionist state over a lengthy period following restoration of the death penalty.

Now, the relationships that were supported by evidence or logically inferred begin with population size and minority representation in that population. More populated states have a more substantial percentage of minority individuals. Minorities, in turn, demonstrate a much higher propensity for willful killing than majority whites. These translate into a greater homicide problem for highly populated states, as shown by their murder rates and especially by the sheer number of homicide victims. If you consider the ten most populated states and the ten least populated according to the 2000 census, you find their respective average murder rates between 1995 and 2002 range from over 6 per 100,000 for the more populated states to under 3 per 100,000 for the least populated. The most populated states experience over twice the rate of willful killing than their least populated counterparts, and when this higher rate is considered in light of the denser population, it is not difficult to see why they have more to be concerned about when it comes to the social factors that augment lethal violence.

There is a complication in specifying the relationship between state population numbers and murder rate, however. The relationship is curvilinear when all states in the union are considered. Two-thirds of the states having the highest and intermediate population numbers look much alike as far as a higher murder rate is concerned; the difference resides in the low-population states that show a diminished rate. It is more accurate to say, then, that a sparse population is conducive to reduced lethal violence than to say that denseness of population fosters lethal violence.

Minority representation offers a more straightforward, thus compelling, picture with respect to issues related to violence and the death penalty. The percentage of the state made up by racial minorities is positively and linearly related to murder rate—the higher the proportion of minority members, the higher the murder rate. A somewhat more direct look at the issue of minorities and murder rate is afforded by a different statistic based upon national rather than state figures. Minorities, considered collectively, presented a substantially higher risk each year of murdering another person than those in the white majority; both probabilities were based upon the total number of either minority members or whites in the country. The difference in murderer rate for combined minority and for white majority populations gradually diminished over the last decades of the 20th century and into the 21st, but it never fell below a ratio of almost three times the risk for the minorities. These minority findings, state or national, leave little doubt that densely-populated states with more sizeable minority populations will experience a more serious problem with lethal violence.

This alignment of population characteristics and problems with willful killing brings us to a ready explanation of why many states have adopted and sustained a capital punishment system, whereas a fewer number have failed to adopt the death-penalty option. Capital punishment is chosen because the need for containment of willful killing is more pressing and the need for an extraordinary deterrent more obvious. Only one of the ten most-populous states with a high minority representation, Michigan, was an abolitionist state as the main study came to a close in the 1995–2002 period; the other nine— California, Texas, New York, Florida, Illinois, Pennsylvania, Ohio, New

Jersey, and Georgia—were death-penalty states. Examination of the states with small populations and low minority representations revealed a trend in the opposite direction. Six of these states—Maine, Rhode Island, Hawaii, North Dakota, Vermont, and Alaska—were abolitionist, and only four—Montana, Delaware, South Dakota, and Wyoming—had adopted death-penalty statutes.

The relationships between population characteristics and the death penalty become more complicated when the focus of interest is shifted from problems of violence that result in adopting this deterrent to the effects upon murder rate that follow the adoption. States with death-penalty statutes in place demonstrated widespread differences in commitment to their own systems of capital punishment. States that made the strongest commitment to their systems over more than a quarter century experienced a decrease in murder rate that brought willful killing 14% below pre-moratorium/abolishment lows. States at the other extreme that made only a halting commitment, rarely executing a prisoner, achieved poorer results; murder rates remained 20% above pre-1968 lows by the end of the period of study. The states that fell between these extremes introduced a mysterious note to this analysis. Intermediate effectiveness of the capital punishment system was associated with the poorest record of deterrence among all death-penalty states—a murder rate still 45% above the pre-1968 standard and an improvement only upon abolitionist states in curtailing homicides.

This irregularity in the relationship between system effectiveness and deterrence found partial explanation when the two population parameters were considered for the three tiers of states. Those with the most effective death-penalty systems based upon execution numbers were highly populated—7,900,000 people on average. The least effective systems were found in states that averaged 3,200,000 people, only 42% the size. States with a dense population (and expected high minority representation) not only needed capital punishment to curtail problems of lethal violence, but the system served them well in achieving this goal when they committed themselves to implementing its statutes. States with much lower density and minority representation had fewer violence-related social problems and afforded less commitment to capital punishment when they chose to adopt such statutes. They paid a price for this choice in terms of a lower reduction in murder rates, but not as great a price as states that made an intermediate degree of commitment or that chose not to adopt capital punishment at all.

The states that demonstrated intermediate commitment to their systems were also highly populated, averaging 7,700,000 people, almost matching the density of the highly-effective states. These intermediate states encountered the greatest resistance to their efforts to bring murder down among the jurisdictions that reinstated the death penalty despite having demonstrated what would seem to be a moderate commitment to implementing their systems.

The explanation for this irregular finding that appeals to me requires further complication, but it does seem to make sense. If a state's population characteristics are conducive to social problems that include excessive lethal violence, it is not enough to initiate a system of capital punishment and then allow it to languish or even to be implemented in a half-hearted fashion. If capital punishment is to be used to deter willful killing in a state that faces excessive violence, it is incumbent upon that state to maintain a system that reflects a firm commitment to prosecution when the death-penalty statutes appear to have been violated and than invoking the full measure of this punishment if that is the court's judgment. States that do not face the murder problems associated with burgeoning populations and high minority representation can get away with pallid capital punishment systems. A populous state that fails to address its more pressing problems with lethal violence in the most effective way possible within the law will pay the price of even more limited deterrence and a heavy forfeiture of victim lives.

If this sounds like a qualification in the research-based verdict that the death penalty does serve as a deterrent to murder, it is. Before those who are adamantly opposed to capital punishment under any circumstances make too much of this qualification, however, let me reiterate that death-penalty states at the intermediate level of effectiveness still performed better relative to deterrence baseline than abolitionist states over the same period. Even death-penalty states in which the systems were not attuned to their pressing homicide problems were better able to bring their murder rates down than states without the death penalty.

Perhaps this review of evidence may suffice as an illustration of how complicated it can get in relating only two parameters of population to the death penalty—to explaining the antecedents to this form of punishment, on the one hand, and its consequences on the other. Imagine how complex explanation could get if focus were expanded to include other violence-related variables associated with social circumstance or individual personality.

Does the Seepage of Effects and Attitudes Related to Capital Punishment Represent a Convenient but Unverified Assumption?

I initiated this investigation of the death penalty as a deterrent to murder in hope of gathering a body of scientific evidence that would prove convincing and help settle a long-standing controversy over the role of capital punishment in the United States. The thrust of the evidence seems clear enough. Fear generated by the threat of being executed for killing another person i ntroduces some degree of constraint beyond that imposed by individual conscience; the added constraint results in the survival of a multitude of people who would otherwise be victims of willful killing.

Even though the investigation found support for three criteria of deterrence —the predicted effects of disinhibition, inhibition, and system effectiveness —there still remained gaps in the evidence that might prove especially glaring to those most committed to opposing the death penalty. While a single study is bound to leave unanswered questions, I chose to address unexpected findings and consider alternative explanations when I could. This consistently involved the examination of crime effects that should not have been observed if capital punishment served as a deterrent for a specific violent crime. The seepage of effects across state jurisdictions or across types of violent crime along with generalized attitudes toward violent crimes were chosen to explain the puzzling evidence. Should these assumptions be considered "convenient but unverified" support for the conclusion that the death penalty deters murder?

Much of the paradoxical evidence appeared during the moratorium/abolishment period (1968–1976) when murder rate escalated across the country as capital punishment was first diminished as a system and then ruled unconstitutional. One thing noted in the explosion of homicides was that it occurred in abolitionist states that had not featured the death penalty as well as in retentionist states that experienced the abolishment of their statutes. A second unexpected aberration in the crime statistics during this period was a radical increase in nonlethal violence across the country; offenses such as rape, robbery, and aggravated assault that did not carry the death penalty became far more prevalent when capital punishment was abolished. Either of these unpredicted effects could be taken as an indication that something other than changes in the status of the death penalty was happening to affect the rate of violence in general within this country. It would follow that the importance of capital punishment as a deterrent to murder had been seriously overstated, since something else was responsible for the release of violence.

These unpredicted changes in violence disappeared as the basis for serious counterexplanation when states were offered the opportunity to reinstate capital punishment and inhibition effects could be studied. Neither the murder rates in abolitionist states nor the rates of nonlethal violence across the United States demonstrated changes that matched the decline in murder rate found in retentionist states, the hallmark of inhibition. Abolitionist states lagged well behind retentionist states in bringing their murder rates down; the nation continued its climb in rates of nonlethal violence despite the renewal of the death penalty. The loss and restoration of capital punishment continued to be the best explanation for the fluctuations in murder rate; these fluctuations satisfy the requirements of disinhibition and inhibition that define a deterrent.

There still remains a need to explain the paradoxical fluctuations in violent crime that appeared between 1968 and 1976, mimicking the disinhibition provided by the loss of the death penalty. I chose to interpret these as generalized effects from the demise of capital punishment rather than as evidence of some unrelated social or legal change in our country. It was proposed that decisions by the courts, especially the Supreme Court, that diminished the status of the death penalty carry an unintended but influential message that registers nationally. "Murder is bad but not bad enough to warrant execution" might be the implied message that seeps across state jurisdictions and affects abolitionist states. The same inferred value judgment could influence the rate of nonlethal violence; if the worst of violent acts is "bad but not that bad," what can be said for violence that does not kill? These suppositions regarding generalization of disinhibition effects remain unproven, although evidence on what happened when the death penalty was abolished for rape in Iowa encourages the view that Supreme Court decisions carry unintended messages regarding crime.

You may have noticed that the surplus meanings that could be associated with legal decisions regarding the death penalty have been discussed in the context of disinhibition and increased violence. The restoration of capital punishment and other decisions that favor these systems should also convey meaning that would cast willful killing as less tolerable. Based upon the evidence we have seen, however, the releasing influences of disinhibition are far more readily generalized than the constraining influences of inhibition.

Has the Importance of Morality Been Neglected in Considering the Value of the Death Penalty Only in Terms of Deterrence?

Beginning this book by rejecting moral conviction as critical to resolving the death-penalty controversy may not satisfy those whose views occupy extreme positions on the issue. Strong moral opposition to intentional killing by the state as a form of punishment even when murder circumstances are deplorable may not capitulate to evidence suggesting the socially pragmatic value of capital punishment as a life-saving legal instrument. The firm belief at the other extreme of the controversy is that capital punishment is justified, even indispensable. This view would be reinforced by the evidence for deterrence value, although it has its own moralistic underpinnings in the fairness of retaliation for taking a life ("an eye for an eye").

I admit that these extreme moral vantage points have been ignored in this investigation. However, despite my conviction that the death-penalty controversy should be decided on pragmatic and not moralistic grounds, it turns out that the two can be only imperfectly separated. Morality has assumed an obvious importance in the method used to study the deterrence value of the death penalty and to convey the meaning of evidence. Morality entered into this investigation in the guise of social cost/benefit figures that allowed me to more fully explore the pragmatic value of capital punishment as a deterrent to willful killing in a more humanistic way. When the value of the death penalty is put in terms of victim lives that are spared or lost, it puts the morality issue in a new light. If the value of human life makes it wrong for the state to execute someone convicted of a heinous murder, what are the moral implications of ignoring the many lives spared by its deterrence effects or lost because the death penalty is diminished as a constraint?

Whatever my intentions in this investigation were at the outset as far as avoiding moral issues, the results that confirmed the socially pragmatic value of capital punishment as a deterrent to lethal violence also raised a strong moral question. Given that it is wrong for the state to intentionally take a human life, is it not far more regrettable for the state to sacrifice a far greater number of lives by not doing so? Evidence of deterrence value is indeed the worst nightmare for those who oppose capital punishment on the grounds that execution is immoral.

Section Two

CAN THE DEATH PENALTY BE FAIRLY IMPLEMENTED?

Chapter 4

Fair Practice in Adjudicating the Death Penalty: The Issue of Race

Having concluded that the death penalty does serve a socially-useful purpose, the next broad question to be considered is whether capital punishment can be administered fairly without allowing irrelevant bias to influence how individuals are to be treated in the courts or elsewhere within the criminal justice system? There are a couple of things that should be kept in mind as we consider the issue of bias.

First, prejudicial inclination can cut either way as far as courtroom treatment is concerned. Racial bias, the subject of this chapter, is usually thought of as working against the individual who is being tried for murder—more likely to be found guilty of the crime, more likely to be given a death sentence if found guilty. However, even if prejudicial courtroom bias exists against members of a given race, such as the black minority in the South, it is possible we also could find that a bias favoring blacks may exist among members of their own minority or that majority whites show greater leniency than the facts merit toward those of their own race. Bias can potentially work either way for the person on trial. However, alternative explanations for seeming prejudice should be explored before reaching a conclusion; appearances may be deceiving as I hope to show in this section of the book.

Second, some would argue that there are types of bias that should be distinguished from irrelevant prejudices such as those based upon race, religion, or social status. In fact, it might be argued that such biases should become the central focus of a murder trial rather than guilt or innocence. The most obvious examples are cases involving cognitive limitation, mental handicaps that can be construed as contributing to lethal violence. Here the emphasis shifts to more humane treatment within the criminal justice systems of our society.

Accordingly, mental disorder and mental retardation could represent sources of positive bias in the courts that work in favor of defendants. Those who are mentally impaired are often held to less rigorous standards of conduct and personal responsibility for their behavior, and this is especially obvious when it comes to crimes for which others might receive a death sentence. Controversies concerning mental competence and capital punishment will be considered later in this section of the book.

Gender issues relating to the death penalty assume an unusual position as far as fair-practice concerns go. The data make it appear that gender bias exists as far as capital punishment is concerned; relative to men, there seems to be a reluctance to execute women in this country for their crimes. A problem exists in getting to the heart of the gender issue, since it could be misleading, not to mention extremely unpopular, to argue that women are "handicapped" as far as constraint of violent impulses is concerned. In this era of female empowerment, implication that they are less capable than males in regulating their own behavior merits a warning label. Yet the chapter on gender bias will consider just such constraint differences as an important basis for distinct capital-sentencing patterns. Violent crimes perpetrated by men and women will be compared in line with earlier efforts to explain female violent conduct in terms of impulsivity (Pollack, 1950; Smart, 1977). This issue is relevant to capital punishment in that impulsive killing is unlikely to attract the death penalty.

Gender differences in execution, however, could just as readily be explained in terms of an equally plausible but far less legitimate rationale—a long-standing reluctance to execute women for murder while men have been considered suitable for this extreme form of punishment. Chivalry, the protective and lenient treatment of women by men, has been noted at all stages of the criminal justice system (Adler, 1975; Armstrong, 1977; Chesney-Lind, 1977; Smart, 1977). Being protective of women would certainly introduce a lenient bias as long as courts are dominated by men; just as certainly, it would be conducive to unfairness in assigning the death penalty.

Some of the material in this adjudication section of the book has been published before as part of my reported research program into criminal behavior. Intent of the writing is clearly different now, however, as the emphasis has narrowed to the death penalty for murder and whether it can be fairly administered. Only one of the studies taken from my program of research was intended to address courtroom bias. Accordingly, the research evidence to be considered will generally require extrapolation and judgment in order to draw conclusions concerning biased assignment of the death penalty and fairness of adjudication.

THE ISSUE OF RACE AND THE DEATH PENALTY

Whether race has entered into capital punishment decisions has received the greatest attention, popular and scholarly, of the bias issues that shall be considered in this section. Much of this notoriety can be attributed to an investigation of sentencing for murder in the state of Georgia (Baldus, Pulaski, & Woodworth, 1983) and subsequent unchallenged reiteration (and elaboration) of the study's conclusions by the media after they were cited in the proceedings of the country's highest court (Supreme Court of the United States, 1987). The issue raised by the Baldus group (hereafter simply "Baldus") was whether a sentencing bias worked against blacks after conviction for murder of a white victim in Georgia, a deep-South state. The bias was thought to substantially increase the risk of receiving the death penalty relative to whites who murdered white victims or blacks who killed other blacks.

The Inferential Nature of Courtroom Bias

Whether conclusions regarding prejudice in the Georgia courts toward blacks can be generalized to other racial minorities in the United States or even in Georgia will not be addressed in this chapter. However, the problems of accurately identifying racial prejudice and the requirements for properly weighing the question as a scientist remain the same whatever the minority in question. The basic thing to be recognized in considering courtroom sentencing bias is that you must contend with an elusive psychological quality that ultimately requires guesswork. Bias in assigning the death penalty can be gauged only by inference and most likely cannot be verified at its source; jury members and officers of the court are unlikely to acknowledge favoring or avoiding an extreme penalty for committing a crime simply because the perpetrator belongs to a particular race.

What is required in the face of such indeterminacy is careful attention to alternative explanations for what may seem to be judicial bias given the psychological attributes of the criminal and the circumstances under which the crime occurred. The facts may seem to suggest prejudicial sentencing for blacks in the South when racial lines are crossed, but are there alternative explanations that may apply? This is not an axiom taken from a social-science 101 textbook that is meant to document the scientific rigor of my thinking. We are dealing with an urgent issue here in that conclusions about bias can go unchallenged by alternatives if they happen to coincide with preexisting personal convictions. Even the brightest among us can be vulnerable to selective verification of preconceived views. We will return to this point when

Supreme Court opinions are considered in a case involving racial prejudice and capital punishment.

Having stated that the assumption of courtroom bias, racial or otherwise, is highly inferential, that bias cannot be verified at its source, and that an assumption of bias should be made only after considering alternative explanations is not the same as saying that individual bias does not sometimes enter into courtroom judgments. If the truth be known, some individuals can be expected to respond prejudicially, whether they are aware of it or not. The issue being weighed in this section is whether **systematic** bias has occurred where bias has been the rule rather than the exception. If systematic bias were found to be the likeliest explanation for the racial disproportionality in death-penalty sentencing in Georgia, the capital punishment system would qualify as unjust. However, the assumption of systematic bias can be disregarded as the explanation for suspicious sentencing patterns if more credible alternative explanations are substantiated.

The Baldus, Pulaski, and Woodworth Investigation of Sentencing in Georgia

The 1983 results and conclusions from the Baldus investigation of Georgia death-penalty rates in murder cases instigated an assumption of bias that still finds its way into the media as an unqualified fact and as a "black eye" for capital punishment in general. Their most compelling finding was the discrepancy in sentencing rates when varying perpetrator-victim racial combinations were considered. In a sample of over 2000 murder cases, death sentences were handed down for 22% of the blacks who killed whites, 8% of the whites who killed whites, 3% of the whites who killed blacks, and 1% of the blacks who killed blacks.

The fact that the study was conducted in a deep-South state with a cultural heritage of white superiority to blacks made conclusions from these discrepant figures seem obvious. White lives, according to the commonplace version of southern cultural heritage, are more valuable than black lives. Accordingly, taking a more valuable life should result in more serious punishment, and that is what the percentages seemed to show. This would hold true for perpetrators of both races who kill a white, and that is implicit in the second-highest 8% death-sentence figure for white intraracial murder. The assumption of more valued loss would be accompanied by a sense of violated racial boundaries when a black steps over the racial line and murders a white, however. The 22% death-penalty rate for blacks killing whites, far out of line among the racial pairings, is what made the most indelible impression on the national psyche as evidence of racial prejudice in Georgia capital punishment proceedings and of the unfairness of the death penalty in general. The apparent leniency of the 1% death-penalty rate when blacks killed blacks or the 3% white-on-black figure could also have been taken as evidence that black lives were less valued and their loss less seriously punished.

The inferred death-penalty bias in the Georgia courts gained impetus nationally in a rather unusual way. The possibility of racial prejudice in Georgia's death-sentencing procedure served as the basis for petition to the U.S. Supreme Court in 1986. It was alleged that Warren McCleskey, a black man who was sentenced to die after murdering a white victim, had been deprived of his Eighth and Fourteenth Amendment rights because of racial discrimination in the Georgia courts. The Baldus investigation data were used as the basis for appeal. The Supreme Court ruled by majority vote against the appeal but not because they challenged the study or the interpretation of its evidence as showing racial bias in Georgia courts. The appeal was rejected because it was uncertain to the majority whether racial considerations played a role in this specific case.

The majority opinion of the Supreme Court reflected some restraint, since no assumption was made that racial prejudice had been responsible for assigning the death penalty to McCleskey. However, those justices who wrote dissenting opinions showed no compunctions at all about regarding courtroom bias as a given in the Georgia courts, citing the Baldus findings; dissenting justices excoriated the state's death-sentencing procedures as misplaced justice. It is the echo of the remarks made by a minority of justices that still is heard when racial injustice in capital cases receives comment. Neglected are the facts that the Supreme Court's decision actually rejected the claim of racial discrimination in the individual case and that alternative explanations for findings of the Baldus investigation have long since been published and available for more considered commentary.

ALTERNATIVE EXPLANATIONS FOR THE APPARENT RACIAL BIAS IN ASSIGNING THE DEATH PENALTY FOUND IN THE BALDUS EVIDENCE

The point has been made that when you are dealing with an inference from evidence that is insulated from verification, care should be taken to consider alternative explanations. Alternatives to the Baldus assumption of prejudicial sentencing that make just as much or even more sense and that depend on independent evidence, not reference to cultural history, have a more compelling quality in my way of thinking. There are two such alternative explanations that occur to me and neither of them is preclusive of the other.

Criminal Dangerousness as an Alternative Explanation

My research interest in criminal dangerousness emerged in the late 1970s (Heilbrun, 1979) and culminated nearly two decades later in a book that summarized the entire program of investigation (Heilbrun, 1996). Criminal dangerousness was considered in terms of the individual's risk of harming others by some behavior contrary to law. This risk was viewed as falling along a continuum. At the low end of the dangerousness continuum the person might be responsible for minor psychological/economic harm to others as would be the case in many misdemeanor or property-crime offenses. The highly dangerous person would be responsible for violent crimes that threaten or inflict serious physical and psychological harm to the victim. In between these extremes of dangerousness we would expect to find those at risk for more damaging nonviolent offenses or for violence in which the victim is exposed to less physical and psychological harm.

Trying to validate this model of dangerousness scientifically required two things. First, the concept of dangerousness had to be made theoretically explicit; how was dangerous potential of the individual to be understood psychologically? My view from the beginning was that dangerousness should be considered a multifactorial trait that depended upon at least two psychological dispositions acting in combination—antisociality (departure from the constructive values of society) and flawed cognition (limitations of the higher mental processes such as reasoning and judgment). A dangerousness index was devised in which scores from both antisociality and cognition measures were entered, providing an estimate of how they might act in concert for any given individual. Greater antisociality and poorer cognition taken together would signal higher risk of criminal behavior in general and increasing harm to the victim if a crime were committed.

The second thing that had to be accomplished was devising a feasible way of measuring criminal dangerousness so that research could be done using a single quantitative score to represent this multifactorial dimension. Without going into detail, I was fortunate enough to hit upon measures of antisociality and cognitive competence level that proved satisfactory from the beginning in a scientifically heuristic sense. That is, the dangerousness score provided results that encouraged new studies and eventually allowed the development of a meaningful theory of criminal risk. Accordingly, it was possible to do research over the years with prisoners in the state of Georgia by the tens of thousands using the same instruments; this allowed the results of earlier and later studies to be readily integrated. (Anyone interested in something more than this cryptic description of concept and measurement procedures might go to my 1996 book on criminal dangerousness.)

There may be skeptics among the readers who wonder whether a single score from a two-factor index could adequately represent something as complicated psychologically as dangerousness seems to be. I will share an observation with you based upon over 50 years of experience as a social scientist that addresses this skepticism. If a program of research involving interrelated studies continues for years and provides results that substantiate a theoretical model, the research procedures that provided the results are validated as well. Serious limitations in measuring instruments or other research procedures will not meet the demands of long-term programmatic investigation, not the least of which is the scrutiny of journal peer review.

The 1996 book presents considerable evidence that the theory of criminal dangerousness has merit and that the index represents a valid indicator of dangerousness as a character flaw that poses risk to the victims of crime. To summarize the major validity findings reported in the book, higher dangerousness scores were found in men who:

1. Commit violent crimes rather than nonviolent crimes,
2. Commit more serious violence in general rather than less serious violence,
3. Perpetrate more severe sex-offenses (rape) rather than less severe sex-offenses,
4. Engage in rapes involving more brutal treatment of the victims,
5. Commit more brutal murders.

You can see a progression in these five categories of evidence. More dangerous men not only tend to engage in violent crime but are further inclined to participate in the more serious types of violence. Even beyond that, high dangerousness is associated with excesses of brutality toward the victim in the conduct of already serious violence like rape and murder.

In addition to this validating progression, the studies of criminal dangerousness also found evidence that more dangerous men were generally less capable of conforming to any code that requires that they constrain their conduct as they:

6. Were a greater problem in prison because of their rule violations than men who were less dangerous,
7. Were less successful on parole in the short-term than their less dangerous counterparts,
8. Were more likely to commit another crime in the community after leaving prison than men lower in dangerousness when social adjustment was followed over a lengthy span of years.

Perhaps that eight-point summary of program evidence will suffice as a prelude to discussing criminal dangerousness as an alternative explanation for seeming racial bias in assigning the death penalty in Georgia. The studies showed rather clearly that men who score high on the dangerousness index demonstrate a greater risk of committing crimes in which serious harm is inflicted upon their victims than is true for men with lower index scores and that they are less likely to conform to rules governing behavior. Confidence in this index will allow us to seek an alternative explanation for the Baldus death-penalty results by reference to empirical evidence, not guesswork.

The Heilbrun, Foster, and Golden (1989) Study of the Death Penalty in Georgia

The Baldus study, published six years earlier, set the stage for this reevaluation of racial disproportionality in assigning the death penalty in Georgia to men who murder a white victim. You may recall the percentages reported by Baldus: the death penalty was imposed for 22% of the blacks who had murdered a white victim, 8% of the whites who had killed a white victim, 3% of the white murderers who had victimized a black, and 1% of the blacks who had murdered a black victim. Race of the perpetrator and of the victim count in the sentencing process, according to these figures, with black murderers attracting capital punishment in disproportionate numbers if the victim was white. The more lenient sentences given to blacks who kill someone of their own race was viewed by an organization of black Baptist ministers as evidence of the same courtroom bias inferred by Baldus. White lives seemed to be considered more worthwhile than black lives (**Atlanta Journal and Constitution**, 1988).

The death penalty in Georgia, as in other states with capital punishment statutes in place, can be sought if the person is accused of willful killing in ways that are deemed unusually cruel or contrary to the public good. The evidence on criminal dangerousness led us to predict that highly dangerous men would more likely be involved in willful killing under circumstances that are especially egregious than less dangerous men. This could involve treatment of the victim in a particularly cruel and inhumane way as part of the crime, selection of multiple or especially vulnerable victims, or targeting public officials for acting in line of duty. General support for dangerousness as an alternative interpretation of the death-penalty sentencing statistics in Georgia would require that murderers, white or black, given a capital sentence, were more dangerous than murderers who received life sentences. Specific and more critical support for this alternative way of interpreting the Baldus data would call for black men who had killed white victims to be exceedingly dangerous even by death-row standards. If this were found, it could be argued that the higher percentage of death sentences among blacks killing white victims resulted from the excessive violence of extremely dangerous men rather than from prejudice in the deep South.

The samples of prisoners included in our study were made up of 109 men convicted of murder in the Georgia courts who had received the death penalty and awaited execution on death row and 134 men who were convicted of murder but received life sentences. Each sentencing group was split evenly by race of the offender; the death-penalty group was 50% black and 50% white, whereas the life-sentence group included 53% black offenders and 47% white. The death-penalty subset represented a complete sample of men on death row at the time of the study, omitting only the few for whom records were unavailable. The life-sentence subset was selected randomly from a larger pool of convicted murderers. When the murderers were broken down by race and sentence, the four groups were quite similar in age, education, and the span of time in the 1970s and 1980s during which the sentences were handed down. Dangerousness-index scores were determined for the death-row and life-sentence murderers from information in prison files.

The first thing to consider is whether death-penalty murderers, black or white, are more dangerous than their life-sentence counterparts. This comparison has more to do with the theoretical model of dangerousness than the issue of alternative meaning for the Baldus data. The question is whether the predicted distinction in dangerousness can be made between groups of men who have committed the most serious of all crimes, murder, but have done so under more and less grievous circumstances. Both theory and index proved up to the test. Death-penalty murderers were the more dangerous criminals, as expected, whether the comparisons with life-sentence murderers involved black or white criminals. Keep in mind that this distinction was achieved despite the high standard of dangerousness set by ordinary murderers.

The critical question for us concerned whether interracial murder by blacks, that so often attracted the death penalty, could be attributed to the extraordinary dangerousness of the criminal and to the excessive violence that would be expected. If no linkage were found, the assumption of prejudicial treatment of the black in the Georgia courts for taking a white life would remain unchallenged. If black men who kill white victims are exceptionally dangerous, even when compared to the broader standard set by male murderers, a viable alternative to prejudice exists to explain the Baldus data. Before we examine the average dangerousness scores in Table 6 for an answer, I should point out that standard norming procedures in my dangerousness research involved statistically setting the average dangerousness score as near 2500 as possible in each study. The meaning of 2500 in terms of criminal risk, then, depends upon what type of criminal is being studied; this average score for a sample of nonviolent criminals would reflect far less criminal risk than the same score for some type of violent criminal. With a score of 2500 (or above) in a sample of murderers, we are getting into the realm of **very** dangerous men.

We will have to work our way toward a conclusion regarding the issue of prejudice versus dangerousness as the source of disproportional assignment of the death penalty by examining the dangerousness scores in Table 6 for intraracial and interracial murderers. The analysis did not turn out to be a simple one, since rate of sentencing required consideration along with level of dangerousness. Start with intraracial murder by blacks who kill black victims. We know that within-race killing by blacks rarely leads to capital punishment; using the Baldus figure, only 1% of black intraracial murderers received a capital punishment sentence. When the death penalty was imposed for black intraracial murder, however, it was to very dangerous men gauged by their average index score (3010). These men, though rare, had index scores averaging over 500 points above the norm for murderers. In theory, then, these few would be capable of the cruel or socially-disruptive excesses that are specified by death-penalty statutes. In contrast, the bulk of the black murderers targeting black victims who received more lenient life sentences gained considerably lower dangerousness scores on average (2470) that would not lead you to anticipate the heinous circumstances of capital offenses. In short, black intraracial murder resulted in sentencing outcomes that were consistent with a dangerousness interpretation even though the highest absolute score for the rare death-sentence case was not predicted.

When we turn to interracial (between-races) killing by blacks in which the death penalty is more commonly found, Table 6 reveals the same direction of difference in dangerousness exists between black murderers of white victims who receive the death penalty (average of 2858) or are sentenced to a life

Table 6. Level of Criminal Dangerousness for Murderers by Race of the Offender, Race of the Victim, and Severity of Sentence

Race of the Offender	Race of the Victim	Severity of Sentence	Level of Dangerousness[a]
Black	Black	Death Penalty	3010
Black	White	Death Penalty	2858
Black	White	Life Term	2627
Black	Black	Life Term	2470
White	White	Death Penalty	2369
White	White	Life Term	2082

[a]Average dangerousness score for the entire sample set near 2500.

term (average of 2627). The difference is not as striking, but the blacks who killed white victims and received the death penalty can still be described as excessively dangerous by murderer standards, the life-sentence murderers less so. This difference in criminal dangerousness would help explain the uneven sentencing of blacks who kill whites. The 22% (again using the Baldus figure) who received the death penalty would have included more dangerous black men whose index scores fell well above the norm for murderers. Men with scores at this level are more likely to engage in a display of violence that would qualify them disproportionately for capital punishment when the victim dies. An even more critical comparison lies ahead.

The third set of circumstances described in Table 6 involve intraracial murder by white offenders. You will note that the data are more restricted for white murderers. So few cases of a white killing a black were found in the samples of death-penalty and life-term prisoners that analysis was not possible. The relative dangerousness scores continue the trend of the previous comparisons. Whites who kill whites and receive the death penalty are on average more dangerous (2369) than those who are given life terms (2082), although both averages are on the low side of the norm. The most important comparison that can be made using the tabled data as far as addressing the Baldus conclusion about biased sentencing is the average dangerousness score for blacks who kill whites (2858) and whites who kill whites (2369) as a prelude to capital punishment. The disproportional percentage of death sentences handed down to blacks who victimize whites (22%) relative to whites who kill whites (8%) is entirely consistent with the more egregious murder circumstances that would be expected for men who are that much more dangerous.

Assignment of the Death Penalty Following Conviction for Murder in the Georgia Courts and Characteristics of the Crime

Let us quickly review where we are in addressing the issue of racial bias in Georgia death-penalty sentencing for murder and the conclusion by the Baldus group that the courts were subject to prejudice when a white victim was killed by a black murderer. Finding that the disproportionate number of black interracial murderers on death row (along with the low number of black intraracial murderers) were especially dangerous by index score when compared to other murderers opened the way to an alternative interpretation of what was thought to be prejudicial sentencing. Black men who killed white victims, being more dangerous, would be more likely to receive the death penalty because their murders were more malicious or were more harmful to the functioning of society than those of whites who killed whites.

As it stands, the dangerousness alternative represents a logical explanation of disproportionate death penalties by race that is at least supported by independent quantitative evidence. The bias proposal by Baldus, while it might seem consistent with the data and southern history, did not involve a quantitative barometer of prejudice in the Georgia courts. Nonetheless, the issue of just sentencing versus bias is not going to be settled without more direct evidence—either proof of racial prejudice that **systematically** influences black-on-white murder trials (good luck in investigating that!) or evidence from the circumstances of lethal violence perpetrated by black men who victimize whites that death-penalty statutes have been routinely violated.

Two studies having a more direct bearing upon the dangerousness alternative to bias will now be considered. Although neither was perfectly aligned methodologically with the issue at hand, both sets of evidence add to the inquiry. I reported the first of these studies in 1990. The same samples of death-row and life-sentence murderers that were discussed in the previous section were considered again except race did not enter into the analysis. Instead, attention was focused exclusively upon the index of criminal dangerousness and its ability to discriminate between men found guilty of murder and given more and less severe sentences in the Georgia courts. The goal of the analysis, then, was to determine whether the greater dangerousness of murderers who received the death penalty was generally associated with the heinous criminal circumstances that would justify a more severe sentence. In the context of the present discussion, this kind of confirmation would lend confidence to the dangerousness alternative in explaining the disproportionality of capital punishment for black interracial murderers who were particularly dangerous. The second study also considered criminal circumstances, severity of sentencing, and criminal dangerousness. Race of the criminal and victim were included in this analysis, but the focus shifted to a different violent crime (rape). The murder evidence will be discussed first, and the rape evidence will be described in the next section.

The male prisoners included in the analysis of dangerousness, criminal circumstances, and sentencing had been convicted of murder and sentenced either to die for their crime or to a life term. As I have said, these were the same criminals that were examined in terms of criminal dangerousness by Heilbrun, Foster, and Golden (1989) when race of perpetrator/victim were considered, although some cases from the earlier study had to be omitted because information critical to the judgments of criminal conduct during the homicide was missing from the files. Judges were asked to rate the degree of cruelty involved in the slaying, inhumane treatment of the victim other than the sheer termination of life. Cruelty toward the victim could be expressed in the situational context for the murder or in the manner of killing itself.

Gender of the victim was introduced as the second aspect of criminal circumstance to be included in the analysis on the assumption that the murder of a woman by a male in our society is considered an even more repugnant act than taking a man's life. The first expectation was that the death penalty would be to an appreciable degree reserved for men who commit the most despicable crimes—the murder of a woman in an excessively cruel manner. If this proved to be correct, the second expectation would be that this killer would be especially dangerous as measured by the index. Given an affirmative answer to that, two things could be concluded: (1) The death penalty in Georgia is being extended to appropriate people based upon circumstances of the crime and independent of race, and (2) these "appropriate people" are those for whom dangerous excesses would be predicted by index score. Table 7 summarizes what was found.

That the death penalty in Georgia murder cases was being assigned appropriately found support in the subject numbers found in the cells of Table 7. About 65% of the convicted murderers responsible for the most reprehensible crimes studied, cruel homicides victimizing women, received the death penalty; some 46% of those who had engaged in the cruel murder of men were sentenced to death; only 21% of the murderers for whom no excessive cruelty toward either female or male victims was reported attracted a death sentence. The dangerousness figures were also as predicted; men, given a capital sentence after committing the most heinous murders, were especially dangerous even by the standards of willful killers. The mean dangerousness score for this group (2902) was distinctively high; the remaining scores were much the same and presented an average well below this figure (2387).

The implications of these findings for the prejudice-versus-dangerousness controversy regarding capital punishment decisions in Georgia seem clear even though race did not enter into the analysis. At the least, the data indicate two things quite clearly about Georgia death-penalty decisions during a period that included the years investigated by Baldus. Sentencing was generally in line with statutes governing capital punishment that stipulate that the most severe punishment should be reserved for the most heinous murders. What

Table 7. Dangerousness of Murderers Considered by Cruelty of Crime, Sex of Victim, and Sentence

	Cruel Murder of a Female Victim		Cruel Murder of a Male Victim		Murder of a Male or Female Victim Without Cruelty	
Sentence	N	Mean	N	Mean	N	Mean
Death Penalty	31	2902	22	2433	22	2490
Life Sentence	17	2400	26	2229	83	2394

should be irrelevant to systematic sentencing procedures, racial status of offender and victim, was not explicitly examined, but the data show that race was not important enough as a variable to compromise the intent of legal guidelines in Georgia.

The other thing coming out of this analysis is a clearcut confirmation of the theory of criminal dangerousness and the measurement of this construct by the index. Men who committed the most serious crime, murder, who did so under especially grievous circumstances, and who were sentenced to death for their actions were singularly dangerous by index score. The especially high measured dangerousness of this group fell at about the same level as was found for black men who murdered white victims and received the death penalty. Accordingly, the lofty dangerousness of black interracial murderers in the prior analysis corresponds to what is expected for any men who receive the death penalty following especially egregious murders. This evidence, based upon actual criminal circumstances, fits the dangerousness alternative better than racial bias.

Race, Characteristics of Rape Crimes, and Severity of Sentencing in the Georgia Courts

The Iowa researchers led by Baldus could just as well have inquired into biased sentencing in the South by directing their attention to the crime of rape and the punishment meted out to black men who victimize white women. This crime not only represents a violation of the woman's right to privacy, but the particular racial pattern of black rapist and white victim as a circumstance of sexual aggression involves a serious breach of the cultural divide between whites and blacks in southern history. Interracial rape by a black represents a violation of past protection afforded the white woman from unsolicited attention of black men, not to even mention their sexual advances. More severe sentencing for rape in black rapist/white victim cases would have been expected if racial prejudice continued to be a telling factor.

The evidence from a study of rapists reported in my 1996 book on criminal dangerousness, taken at face-value, encouraged the same view of "southern justice" in Georgia as Baldus gained from the death-penalty decisions in murder cases. The rape study involved a random sampling of 142 cases selected from Georgia prison files in which sentencing had occurred during much the same period as the two investigations of murder and the death penalty discussed previously. The results of sampling were reminiscent of the Heilbrun, Foster and Golden study of murderers in the Georgia courts as far as racial patterning of offender and victim was concerned. Intraracial rape was amply represented—white rapists and white victims along with black rapists and black victims. Cases of interracial rape by black men victimizing white women were present in sufficient number to analyze, but examples of a black woman being raped by a white man in this sample were so infrequent that this pattern could not be studied. All intraracial rapists were combined into a single category, since the information taken from the files looked to be much the same for both races. The final analyses of race and sentencing severity in Georgia to be reported, then, will compare two rape patterns—intraracial where the male offender and woman victim are of the same race and interracial where the offender is black and the victim is white.

Georgia no longer had the death-penalty option for rape after the 1977 **Coker versus Georgia** decision by the Supreme Court, but severity of sentencing still ranged between a low of five years in prison to a maximum of life. The most common sentence was 20 years. Splitting sentences by severity for purposes of analysis proved unwieldy; the best that could be done was to use a tri-level categorization—low punishment = 5 to 18 years in prison, intermediate punishment = 20 years in prison, high punishment = 25 years to life in prison.

Given this version of severity levels, it turned out that 28% of the black interracial rapists received the harshest sentences, and 28% were extended the most lenient sentences. In contrast, intraracial rapists attracted the most severe penalty in only 13% of the cases, and the most lenient punishment was rendered 47% of the time. These figures invite the assumption of prejudicial sentencing against black men who rape white women.

The next step in the rape analysis paralleled the method of inquiry when dangerousness of the murderer was considered as an alternative to bias. The criminal dangerousness of intraracial and black interracial rapists was determined from prisoner files to see how well this variable could explain the differences in allotted punishment. Support for the dangerousness interpretation of sentencing differences when blacks who have raped white women are compared to intraracial rapists would require the evidence to show two things. First, black men who have engaged in interracial rape would have to demonstrate higher index scores than intraracial rapists. That would position dangerousness as an alternative explanation and was satisfied by the index numbers; black interracial rapists averaged 2631 on the criminal dangerousness index compared to 2377 for intraracial offenders.

A more precise expectation for the dangerousness evidence if it is to serve as an alternative in explaining punishment differences between interracial and intraracial rapists would be a progression of dangerousness scores when interracial rapists were ordered by harshness of sentencing. That is precisely what was found. Black interracial rapists who received the harshest sentences (25 years to life in prison) were the most dangerous

(average = 2920); intermediate sentencing (20 years in prison) was associated with intermediate index scores (average = 2614); the most lenient
punishment (5 to 18 years in prison) was reserved for the least dangerous
men (average = 2368).

The 2368-2614-2920 progression in dangerousness scores with increasing
levels of sentencing severity for black interracial rapists stands in stark contrast to what was found when sentencing of intraracial rapists was examined.
The 2361-2517-2264 dangerousness averages as lenient to harsh sentencing
were considered proved to be uninterpretable. Dangerousness as an alternative to bias in explaining punishment severity for blacks in the Georgia courts
when convicted of rape is restricted to the one criminal circumstance where
racial prejudice would be expected if it played a systematic role in punishing
sexual aggression—when the victim was white. The harsh punishment meted
out to rapists when they were black and convicted of victimizing a white
woman, seeming bias, can also be plausibly explained in terms of the extraordinary dangerousness found in this group of men and the more serious
display of violence that would be expected. These findings do not settle the
bias-versus-dangerousness controversy. However, they do set the stage for
the next kind of evidence that considers the rapists' actual behavior during the
act of rape and bears most directly upon the issue.

The final step in the analysis was to determine whether the variation in
dangerousness found at sentencing severity levels for black interracial rapists
corresponded to the expected variation in harmful behaviors during the actual
sexual aggression; greater dangerousness would lead us to expect greater
harm to the victim, and greater harm should bring a more severe sentence.
Several raters were assigned the task of reviewing the circumstances of each
rape and to make judgments regarding two effects of the act upon the victim—the amount of physical harm inflicted and the degree of psychological
distress suffered. Ratings were made along independent 5-point scales ranging from "none reported" to "extreme." These ratings were subsequently
combined into a single brutality score for each rapist. A third rating considered the degree of victim resistance to being raped that also could range from
"none reported" to "extreme." The final piece of information extracted from
the file regarding the circumstances of sexual aggression was whether the
rapist was not only convicted of rape but also of subjecting the woman to
sodomy (oral or anal sex). It was assumed that sodomy practices under these
circumstances would be especially distressing to the victim and add to the
psychological and physical harm inflicted by the criminal act. The results of
this analysis of rape behaviors, victim resistance, and acts of sodomy are
summarized in Table 8.

Table 8.   Behavioral Characteristics of Rape Perpetrated by Interracial Rapists[a] and Intraracial Rapists[b] Associated with Varying Levels of Sentencing Severity

| | Behavioral Characteristics | | | | | |
| | Brutality of the Rape (0–8 Scale) | | Sodomy Involved? (% of Cases) | | Degree of Victim Resistance (0–5 scale) | |
Severity of Sentence	Interracial Rape	Intraracial Rape	Interracial Rape	Intraracial Rape	Interracial Rape	Intraracial Rape
Low (5–18 yrs.)	5.06	3.83	20%	12%	2.27	1.52
Intermediate (20 yrs.)	5.35	4.77	30%	28%	2.43	1.77
High (25 yrs.–Life)	6.40	6.33	73%	25%	2.27	2.83

[a]Interracial rape = black offender/white victim.
[b]Intraracial rape = black offender/black victim or white offender/white victim.

Beginning with the brutality ratings, we find variation in harm to the victim during the black man's rape of a white woman substantiates prediction from dangerousness theory. The most severe sentences were handed down to the most dangerous men by previous analysis; however, severe sentences were based upon sexual aggression that proved most harmful to the victims. The least punishment was reserved for the least dangerous men; it also was associated with the least harm inflicted upon the victims. Intermediate sentencing of the rapist was associated with intermediate dangerousness and brutality toward the victim. There is no need to look for systematic racial prejudice of the courts in punishing blacks for interracial rape, since the criminals' dangerousness and actual harm of their sexual aggression serve as explanations.

Interestingly, the same correspondence between rape brutality and severity of punishment was found for intraracial rapists as was observed for black interracial rapists. The more brutal the sexual aggression toward a woman of their own race, the greater the punishment. This makes good legal sense, but more to the point it means that black interracial rape was adjudicated on the same terms as any other rape with no implication of bias. There is still the matter of explaining why severity of sentencing for intraracial rape was not associated with increases in dangerousness to match these brutality differences. Why the disconnection of dangerousness and brutality? An answer will be suggested when the resistance findings are examined.

The criminal conduct of the rapist was further considered in terms of whether he required the woman victim to submit to oral or anal copulation as part of his sexual aggression. Sodomy as an added source of humiliation for the woman would render the experience even more devastating to the victim in a psychological sense and increase the risk of physical injury. Black interracial rapists in general were more inclined to force the victim into sodomy; some 40% did compared to a 22% figure for intraracial rapists. The tabled percentages go beyond that to portray an orderly progression of sodomy involvement and punishment severity for black rapists who had victimized a white woman. This culminated in a figure that showed 73% of the black interracial rapists who received the most serious punishment had sodomized their victims. Sodomy, on the other hand, did not qualify as an important factor in determining sentencing differences between intraracial rapists.

What has been disclosed thus far in the rape analysis, then, is that a crime against white women which might be expected to attract prejudicial sentencing for black men based upon racial precedents in the South was in fact associated with more severe punishment. On the face of it, courtroom bias is suggested just as was the case when Baldus examined death sentences for interracial murder. Yet dangerousness emerged as a viable alternative to bias when dangerousness of the black interracial rapist and severity of sentencing proved to be positively correlated—crimes that were more highly punished were committed by more dangerous men. Even more compelling, the harmful behaviors expected of the dangerous criminal were found to an increasing degree in the actual circumstances of the black interracial rapes as they were more harshly punished.

The logic in these findings is straightforward: (1) Exceedingly high dangerousness is found among black interracial rapists who receive long sentences; (2) their crimes involve brutal treatment of their victims, including the likelihood of sodomy, that would be expected of the very dangerous sexual predator; (3) rape that results in greater physical and psychological harm to the woman will attract more serious punishment. There seems little need to invoke racial stereotypes and assumptions of prejudice to explain the greater probability that the Georgia courts would extend more serious punishment to black men who rape white women than to men, black or white, who victimize women of their own race. Black interracial rapists achieved that judicial fate on their own.

The right two columns of figures on Table 8 have not as yet been considered. These figures have to do with the rated amount of resistance displayed by the victim, and they take on special meaning when compared to brutality level of the rapist found elsewhere in the table. Simply scanning the values for both types of ratings makes it clear that the brutality of rapists who target women of their own race is proportional to the amount of resistance offered by the victims. The greatest brutality of these intraracial rapists, men who receive the most severe punishment, is in line with the stronger resistance of the victims; brutality decreases as lesser resistance levels are encountered and sentences become progressively lighter. These findings for intraracial rape suggest that the amount of harmful aggression displayed by the rapist depends upon how much resistance to being raped is shown by the victim. The rapist, by this reasoning, will inflict as much physical and psychological abuse as it takes to subdue the victim and achieve his sexual (or nonsexual) goals. There is doubtless also a reciprocal element as well with the victim increasing her resistance in reaction to more insistent force or escalating distress. This way of understanding the positive relationship between victim resistance and rapist brutality, with an escalating effect upon punishment, would help explain why severity of sentencing did not correspond to distinctions in dangerousness for the man who rapes a woman of the same race. The brutality of the intraracial rapist had more to do with how much the victim resisted than with how dangerous he was.

A dissimilar understanding of dangerousness-brutality-resistance-sentencing alignments is required when we consider the victim-resistance columns for the black interracial rapist. The victim-resistance scores do not correspond to brutality scores in contrast to what was found for intraracial rape. There is little variation in average victim resistance as brutality levels increase. This means that the black men who raped white women and received the most severe sentences for doing so were: (1) identified as extremely dangerous by their index scores, (2) guilty of excessive brutality in their sexual aggression, and (3) responsible for brutalizing their victims without the provocation of heightened resistance to their sexual advances.

It is especially in the brutality of these dangerous interracial rapists as they pursue their sexual aims without systematic regard to how much resistance was offered by the victims that leads me to conclude that their cruel sexual aggressiveness toward white women involved racial attitude and a particularly objectionable way of demonstrating their dangerousness. In any case, the resistance findings, implying brutality beyond that required to achieve sexual goals, offer one more reason why the circumstances of black interracial rape merited the severe punishment that the Georgia courts meted out and that courtroom prejudice was not the prime factor. This inquiry into the circumstances of rape, then, suggests that serious black violence against white victims can be explained in terms of the dangerousness of the perpetrator and the expected display of harmful behavior. The evidence indicates that the strongest punishment possible was justified for both interracial rape and interracial murder by blacks.

Mitigating Factors as Contrary to Receiving the Death Penalty for Murder

The Katz Challenge

The first person to openly challenge the Baldus assumption of bias within the Georgia courts as the explanation of a racial disparity in capital punishment, to my knowledge at least, was J.L. Katz who testified in federal court on the matter in the same year as the findings were published. He had examined the case records of Georgia men convicted of murder with special attention paid to the circumstances of the crime, but his testimony only came to my attention four years later in a newspaper article.

The Katz examination of the prisoner files disclosed that homicide cases in which whites were the victim involved more heinous behavior by the killer, whether white or black, than when blacks were victimized. To quote Katz's (1987) graphic language, cases in which the victims were white:

> ". . . . were more likely to involve other offenses, such as armed robbery, kidnaping, or rape. They were more likely to be brutal, with higher rates of mutilation, torture, and clubbing or stomping the victim to death. And they were more likely to be cold-blooded, with the assailant motivated, for example, by the pursuit of money or the necessity to silence a witness to a crime."

He believed his observations were consistent with the higher rates of death-penalty sentences for murders in which whites were slain reported by Baldus. The excessively brutal and cold-blooded character of the murders along with multiple felonies would explain more severe sentencing without invoking an assumption that greater value was assigned to a white life.

The Katz explanation of the discrepant rate of death-penalty sentences to black and white murderers of white victims placed special emphasis upon the presence or absence of **mitigating** circumstances associated with the crimes. Mitigating factors are those that make a crime less objectionable and more readily understood and that may influence the judgment of guilt or innocence or at least reduce the punishment to be expected. Katz's case examination revealed that the murder of black victims by other blacks were more likely to include mitigating factors than the murder of white victims by blacks. He noted that many of these black-on-black murders resulted from domestic arguments, disagreements over drugs, and quarrels with friends; frequently these fatal confrontations ended up by surrender of the killer to authorities. One explanation proposed by Katz for the higher percentage of death-penalty sentences in crimes where blacks killed white victims took note of the absence of mitigating circumstances in interracial murder. Put simply, the two races do not generally relate to each other closely enough to expect mitigating factors to play an important role in determining how much lethal violence is to be punished.

Katz pointed out that the same reasoning regarding the interpersonal distance between blacks and whites also should apply to adjudicating interracial murder involving a white murderer and a black victim. Lack of mitigating circumstances should lend itself to a higher rate of capital punishment for white interracial murder than for white-on-white homicide. However, his extensive examination of Georgia criminal records revealed the same thing as we found in our death-penalty study; the racial pattern in which a white kills a black was rare. Accordingly, a lack of mitigation in white interracial homicide did not qualify as particularly important as far as contributing to a high death-penalty count. The low 3% figure reported by Baldus for capital sentencing of white interracial murderers would have to be explained in other ways such as their relatively low dangerousness scores.

The role of **aggravating circumstances in** assigning the death penalty, factors that make the murder an even more grievous act, received less emphasis in the Katz testimony. However, I will return to discussing aggravating factors on the pages ahead, since that determinant of the death penalty is more in line with the dangerousness variable. For now, I will concentrate on mitigation and whether absence of familiarity would help explain why black murderers of white victims were most likely to receive the death penalty in the Baldus study. Cases of black interracial murder lacked the mitigating circumstance that might moderate the sentence.

Empirical Documentation of the Katz Verification Proposal

Some supplementary data were collected for the Heilbrun, Foster and Golden (1989) study of criminal dangerousness and the death penalty that went unreported in that publication but were included in my 1996 book on dangerousness. A piece of this evidence is relevant here, since it deals with the main conclusion reached by Katz regarding the role of mitigation in explaining the disproportionally high number of death-penalty sentences given to blacks who had murdered white victims in Georgia. One important mitigating circumstance that would argue against the death penalty for the black murderer would be lacking because of the typical remoteness of association between the two races. Closer relationships between offenders and their victims often provide circumstances that allow a crime to be judged less harshly, domestic murders being a case in point.

Information in the files of black intraracial and interracial murderers from the 1989 study, men who had received the death penalty or a life sentence, was analyzed with respect to closeness of relationship between perpetrator and victim. (This comparison was not possible for white murderers because of the absence of a white interracial group.) Judges rated the killer's closeness of association to the victim along a 4-point scale when sufficient information was available: stranger = 1, acquaintance = 2, friend = 3, and original or marital family = 4. In intraracial murder, when blacks kill blacks, the murderer was fairly familiar with the victim whether it was the rare occasion when the death penalty was invoked (average = 2.61) or the more commonplace circumstance when a life sentence was given (average = 2.79). The overall means for these groups of intraracial murderers were quite similar to each other and placed the average familiarity of the black murderer and black victim closer to friend than to acquaintance. Interracial crime, when blacks murdered white victims, provided a very different picture. This comparison found death-sentence (average = 1.36) and life-sentence (average = 1.25) cases with low and nearly identical ratings of social familiarity. Both averages fell close to depicting a total stranger.

Katz was right. When blacks killed other blacks, a fairly close social relationship was more likely to exist between killer and victim; mitigating circumstances associated with closeness of association could well have moderated their sentences. However, when the black claimed a white victim, lack of familiarity between black offender and white victim would reduce the chances of mitigation and increase the chances of receiving the death penalty.

Aggravating Factors as Conducive to Receiving the Death Penalty for Murder

The emphasis upon mitigating factors in sentencing for murder chosen by Katz does not exhaust the possible circumstances that may influence severity of punishment. Just as mitigating factors may reduce the grievous character of intentional killing and encourage a more lenient sentence, aggravating factors may have the opposite effect—perception of the criminal act as even more objectionable and the justified punishment even more severe. My interest in criminal dangerousness and the risk of victim harm directs special attention to aggravating circumstances and whether they play an important role in severity of sentencing for blacks convicted of murdering white victims. We just covered evidence suggesting that black interracial murderers are likely to be in a poorer position to claim mitigation for their actions. The next question becomes whether aggravating circumstances will more likely be found in black homicide cases involving a white victim. Aggravation without mitigation in a case of murder would represent the strongest case for capital punishment.

The fact is we have previously considered an aggravating circumstance in violent crime earlier in this chapter when evidence on rape brutality was extracted from the files of black rapists who targeted black women and those who victimized white women. (As with homicides, an interracial group involving white offenders could not be constituted; cases in which white men raped black women were rare within our random sample.) You may recall that the predicted correspondence was found between high dangerousness of the black interracial rapist, brutality of his sexual aggression including the likelihood of sodomy, and severity of sentencing for the crime. The brutal behavior of the interracial black rapist and the added finding that these excesses appeared without even being required to overcome strenuous resistance from the victim represent possible aggravating circumstances and help explain the more severe punishment they received. We will now turn to evidence relating to homicide as we consider the possibility that the lethal violence of blacks who killed white victims was more likely to involve circumstances that could be deemed by juries as aggravations of an already grievous act, thereby escalating the risk of receiving the death penalty.

Racial Patterns and Inferred Motivation in Murder Cases across the United States (1977–1996)

The purpose of the analyses to be reported next is to gain a clearer perspective on the dynamics of one-on-one murder in the United States. Although I can go just so far in achieving this goal using national statistics rather than case study, it was possible to develop a hypothesis that could be tested by examining individual cases. This test will be reported as well.

Enough has been said about willful killing by those in racial minorities to make it clear that they present a risk of engaging in homicide that is higher than would be found in the white majority. More specific risk figures that allow a comparison between blacks as a particular minority and whites regarding their chances of engaging in interracial murder, our concern in this discussion, have not been presented, however. Murder information for the nation was collected by race from the annual crime reports published by the Department of Justice and covered a 20-year period, 1977–1996. Sampling, then, began at the time the country returned to capital punishment and the death penalty reappeared as a possible deterrent to lethal violence. It ended when the format of the publication changed, and this particular comparison was no longer possible. The 1977–1996 period included many of the years investigated by Baldus in his study of courtroom prejudice.

The analysis initially focused upon homicide rate by race of offender over the period of study and subsequently introduced the additional consideration of total population numbers for blacks and whites taken from United States census figures. Between 1977 and 1996 about 101,000 white murderers had been identified by police as responsible for intentional one-on-one killings.

During the same years the cumulative number of black murderers reached almost 112,000. In absolute terms, then, the prevalence of murder among whites and blacks was comparable, a bit higher for blacks. Yet when you consider that this rough equivalence over the 20-year span in the cumulative number of murderers by race came about despite the fact that the black population was only 15% as large as the white population in the United States, the disproportionality comes into bold relief. Rate of murder by blacks ran 6–7 times that found for whites.

The next step in the analysis of homicide by race in the United States weighed the more specific question of whether the victims of lethal violence were of the same race as the offenders or were of the other race. (Only black and white racial identities were considered.) The number of black victims killed by white perpetrators across the nation over the 20-year period reached about 5500; white victims killed by blacks totaled 12,800. Comparison of these interracial totals with the overall national murder count makes it clear that intraracial murder is the norm; whites usually kill whites, and blacks usually kill blacks. However, when interracial murder does occur, there is disproportionality; the black murderer targets white victims 2–3 times as often as the white targets a black victim.

It is when these two probability figures are considered together that the racial disparity in interracial murder between whites and blacks comes into sharpest focus. If you consider the rates of interracial homicide, the fact that one racial group only 15% as large as the other engaged in 2–3 times more interracial killings means that over a 20-year span a black individual was 16 times more likely to murder a white victim than were the chances of a white targeting a black victim. The exact factor of 16 is less important at this juncture than is the unchallengeable conclusion that blacks demonstrated a one-sided penchant for interracial murder over a lot of years. Having made that statistical point, the analysis can move on sequentially to the question of what the basis for this lopsided ratio might be.

The annual publication from the Justice Department that generated the evidence on interracial/intraracial murder in the United States also included tabled data over the same 20 years that are relevant to the motivational circumstances of homicide without regard to race of the criminal. By implication, the data allow us to judge the dynamics of murder. These circumstances largely fell into two categories in those cases when situational specifics could be established by the police. The "felonies" category (which I combined with "suspected felonies") describes circumstances in which a murder occurs in the course of perpetrating another felonious act. On average 21% of the lethal violence fell into this category with annual variation between 1977 and 1996 from 18–24%.

The second category was labeled "arguments" and represented a variety of circumstances in which people engage in angry confrontations. A mean of 36% of the homicides evolved out of arguments over the 20 years with the percentage range extending from 31–47%. By 1991 the Justice Department table of circumstances included one more identified category—gangland/juvenile/institutional/sniper killings—which accounted for 6% of the murders over the final six years of the analysis (range 4–7%).

What can be inferred regarding the motivation for murder from these identified circumstances? The common denominator across categories of circumstances, not surprisingly, is antagonism toward the victim. This is implicit in the disregard for victim life in felony murder, angry killing evolving from an argument, or the loathing that often characterizes slayings in the gangland/juvenile/institutional/sniper category. While the conclusion that antagonistic disregard for the victim is a motivational constant in murder may seem evident, it will prove revealing as we contemplate an explanation for the rate of interracial murder within the black minority that is 16 times as great as the rate of interracial murder by whites.

I would argue that antagonism toward whites is more pervasive among blacks than is the case for whites and their feelings about blacks. That would go a long way toward explaining the lopsided ratio of interracial murderers. There is a danger here of painting too bleak a picture of racial enmity as a dynamic for murder that should be recognized. Black interracial murderers, despite disproportional numbers relative to their white counterparts, amounted to only a very small fraction of the black population during the period of study. I cannot address the remainder of the black population with regard to their racial feelings given the data at hand. Murder is fortunately still an infrequent event, and it is not safe to predicate racial generalizations upon the behavior of what may be unique to individuals who kill. It could be that those blacks who engage in violence toward white victims qualify as an unrepresentative extreme, likely to be driven by racial animosity. Nevertheless, it is only the relative few blacks who engage in egregious lethal violence toward whites who we are trying to understand at this point of the book.

You may recall rape findings reported earlier suggesting that black men who are sexually aggressive toward white women were especially brutal in the treatment of their victims, physically and psychologically; this included the tendency to engage in sodomy as an added source of distress beyond coitus and other indignities. It also was disclosed that black interracial rape deviated from the intraracial pattern found for both black and white offenders. In intraracial rape brutality increased with greater resistance offered by the victim, to some extent representing an increasing show of force to gain contested sexual goals. Black interracial rapists, however, were given to displays of heightened brutality without the provocation of increased victim resistance. This aggravating circumstance seemed to have been noted by the courts, since the most severe sentences in cases of black interracial rape were imposed when the discrepancy was most apparent. It can be inferred from these actual circumstances of rape that the black rapist displayed a greater animosity toward his white victim than was true for either black or white rapists who targeted women of their own race.

The question still remains whether the same excesses of brutality that were apparent in the rape analysis can be found when capital cases involving blacks who murder whites are examined by specific circumstance. I have gone as far as I feel comfortable in going with the general evidence regarding rate of interracial homicides by race on a nationwide basis and the dynamic circumstances of these homicides and inferred motivation without regard to race. Now it is time to inspect some data taken from the study of the death penalty in Georgia and to bring the analysis full-circle back to the dynamics of murder in cases that made it appear that racial prejudice against black offenders was being practiced systematically in its courts. The final questions now become whether aggravating circumstances would be especially apparent in the murders of white victims by black murderers receiving the death penalty and what the motivation of the murderer might have been.

Dynamics of Murder in Death-Penalty Cases by Race of Murderer and Victim

More specific judgments regarding the crime-related behaviors of murderer and victim had been gathered for our 1989 investigation of bias in capital cases within the Georgia courts, although missing information in the files of some death-row inmates limited the number of subjects available for more focused analysis. Murder dynamics will be considered in two ways using these data. The first analysis should be considered preliminary, but it sets the stage for discussing the possible importance of aggravating circumstances in the death-penalty trials of black interracial murderers.

Judges were asked to examine the circumstances of death-penalty murders recorded in prisoner files and to rate the degree of brutality involved in the murder and the amount of provocation offered by the victim. Only cases in which a black or white man had slain a white victim will be considered. These behaviors may be recognized as much the same as those evaluated within the analysis of rape crimes that received attention earlier in the chapter and which contributed to the conclusion that there were ample reasons for the especially severe punishment of the black interracial rapist in the characteristics of the criminal and circumstances of the crime without invoking prejudicial sentencing as the explanation.

The analysis of criminal circumstances for the death-penalty cases in which a white victim was murdered began by exploring the dangerousness of the murderers by race. Two things were apparent. The black interracial murderers presented a far more dangerous picture (index average of 2835) than the white intraracial group (index average of 2220), yet the whites had paradoxically perpetrated more brutal crimes. Some 79% of the murders of whites by whites in capital cases received the maximum brutality rating from the judges despite the comparatively low dangerousness of the white murderers; maximum brutality was observed in 54% of the black interracial murders. That the relationship between dangerousness and brutal treatment of the white victim varied with race of the killer became even clearer when the data were examined in a different way. A positive relation between the two variables was found for blacks; the highest level of dangerousness for the murderer was associated with maximum rated brutality, and dangerousness at less extreme levels was linked to lower levels of brutality in the murder. In other words, black murderers demonstrated the expected relationship between dangerousness and brutal violence. The more pervasive brutality of the white murderers in capital cases failed to show any relationship between dangerousness and excessive cruelty of the homicide. Since there was no precedent for racial differences in index predictability within prior program research, some special circumstance of white intraracial murder in capital cases was sought.

An explanation for these discordant findings may have been found when the white victims of the white murderers turned out to be predominantly women (60%), almost twice the figure found for black murderers (31%). The explanation for this seems simple. Although I have never seen the statistics, I would assume that there is a much greater likelihood that a man and woman in a close relationship, whether marital or not, will be of the same white or black race. Since the analysis considered only white victims, the chances would be greater that domestic strife was more frequently involved in intraracial murders of women by white men and less likely to be part of the interracial murder of a woman by a black man. The emotionally-charged nature of domestic violence could account for the lack of index predictability for the white men who killed a white woman as far as brutality of the act goes. Cognitive deficits and antisocial character flaws, the interactive basis for dangerousness, seem less necessary in explaining cruel excesses of violence when emotions run high and behavioral control becomes tenuous.

The analysis of criminal circumstances also considered the question of whether the brutality displayed by the murderer was related to behavior of the victim that may have provoked the homicide? Provocation by the victim was estimated by adding the ratings on verbal and physical confrontation with the perpetrator as part of the situation culminating in murder.

The evidence regarding victim provocation did reveal one finding that brought the capital murder results in line with the previously considered results of the rape analysis. Black men who victimized whites engaged in brutality that went well beyond any provocation by the victim. In fact, brutality of the black murderer actually was greater when there was less provocation by the white victim; the average brutality rating was almost twice that found for murders when provocation by the victim was on the high side. You may recall that dangerous black interracial rapists engaged in greater brutality than would be expected when victim resistance was low. Now the evidence suggests that dangerous black interracial murderers treat their white victims in a more brutal way when there is less provocation for the killing.

The white intraracial murderers did not demonstrate any relationship between offender brutality and provocation by the victim. They displayed much the same high level of brutality whether the victim provoked aggression or not. The findings for white intraracial rape revealed that white rapists of white women demonstrated brutality in line with victim resistance. When it came to capital murder, however, brutality toward white victims failed to correspond to provocation. It is tempting to believe that this lack of relationship has something to do with the predominance of women as victims and different dynamics of confrontation.

This finally brings us back to the issue of whether aggravating circumstances may have played a part in the disproportionately higher rate of capital-punishment sentences of blacks who had killed whites in the Georgia murder trials studied by the Baldus group. The fact that the black interracial murderer in capital cases had killed the white victim in a particularly inhumane way despite the helplessness implied by low provocation could qualify as a serious aggravating circumstance that makes the grievous act of murder even worse. The further finding that these were very dangerous men by index score, with the high antisociality and cognitive limitations that this requires, makes it likely that additional aggravations that influence jury sentencing decisions could have existed within the criminal circumstances. The conclusion that I would draw from this final analysis is that aggravating circumstances in murder cases involving white victims did contribute to the proportionally high number of black death-penalty convictions.

OVERVIEW OF RACE AND THE DEATH PENALTY

I would be the first to admit that adjudication of the death penalty has been considered from a rather narrow racial perspective. Ethnic identity of the criminal or of the victim could be approached as a criminal circumstance that might influence fairness of sentencing without making it a matter of minority versus majority status. Even if minority racial status were to be chosen for comparison with the white majority, minority groups other than blacks could have been emphasized in the investigation. Even given the advantage of studying the black minority in light of the greater accessibility of information on this racial group within the annual crime reports of the Justice Department, blacks other than in the state of Georgia could have been the object of minority study.

The simple truth of the matter is that the selection of the Georgia black minority to compare with a white majority in order to explore racial issues in capital sentencing was a matter of research opportunity rather than limitation. Baldus had been given access to Georgia prisoner files, and his observations concerning apparent prejudice against blacks who kill whites as far as the death penalty is concerned could not have been congenial to the thinking of those responsible for the state's criminal justice system. As I said earlier in this chapter, the conclusion of the Iowa researchers regarding the lack of justice for Georgia blacks is still being echoed today by those who have an "axe to grind" regarding the barbarous nature of capital punishment in general or the diminished quality of criminal justice in the South. The fact that I had been a consultant within the Georgia criminal justice system for many years prior to my request for access to the records of death-row inmates for yet another examination of death-penalty decisions may have weighed heavily on gaining permission. Yet it must have been discomforting to allow another research team into the criminal archives so soon after the Iowa group's devastating revelations that according to present evidence proved to be so misleading.

The point here is that the research focus in this chapter on the sentencing controversy in Georgia allows an acid test of fairness in administering capital punishment across racial lines. In my opinion at least, the Georgia example addresses the issue of sentencing fairness about as directly as possible by considering whether a deep-South state with a history of racial discrimination toward a particular minority can come to adjudicate in an evenhanded way across racial boundaries when such a critical judgment is at stake. If Georgia can do it, any state should be able to put racial disregard aside.

The conclusion that I would draw from the analysis of capital punishment in Georgia is that the long-assumed bias against blacks who cross racial lines to kill a white victim is more apparent than real. The disproportionately higher rate of death-penalty sentences for black interracial murder can be explained in several ways that have to do with characteristics of the black offender and the circumstances of the crime rather than prejudice in courtroom decisions. Black interracial murderers were especially dangerous when gauged by an independent index and not by their crimes; as such they were vulnerable to excesses of violence found when antisociality and cognitively-flawed behaviors interact. These black offender/white victim murders lacked the mitigating circumstances that might bring a less severe sentence of life imprisonment. These same homicides also involved behaviors of the black offender that went beyond the inhumanity of murder itself; excessive brutality with relatively unprovocative white victims was disclosed, representing an aggravating circumstance that should increase the possibility of a death sentence.

The comparison of racial patterns in homicide cases across the nation disclosed that the chances of being a one-on-one murderer was 6–7 times as great in the black minority as in the white majority over a 20-year period. This figure entered into an even greater disproportionality when the chances that someone in the black minority would claim a victim across racial lines were factored in; the likelihood of black interracial murder was about 16 times as great as white interracial murder. What can be overlooked in this analysis of interracial homicide was the fact that 93–96% of the victims of black lethal violence were black. The overrepresentation of willful killers within the black minority takes a predominant toll of black victims; blacks are paying an extraordinary price for the failure to contain excesses of deadly violence within their ranks.

By putting together the sentencing-rate percentages from the Baldus study and what came to light in the analysis of homicide deterrence effects attributable to the death penalty reported earlier in the book, an approach to reducing black intraracial murder comes to mind. The rate of assigning the death penalty to black murderers in Georgia for killing black victims was found to be 1%, such a low figure that it led some to publicly protest the limited value seemingly placed upon the lives of minority victims. In a different context it was established that states with less effective systems of capital punishment, based upon number and timing of executions, did more poorly as far as deterring homicides. If death-penalty states lean toward leniency in sentencing intraracial minority murderers as suggested, it would follow that this leniency subverts their own capital punishment systems as far as deterrence of black homicide goes. The paucity of capital conviction conveyed by the very low 1% rate of assigning the death penalty in Georgia to blacks convicted of killing other blacks means that executions for black intraracial murder were few and far between. With rare assignment and consummation of the death penalty, there is little to serve as a warning of risk for willful killing of another black.

If the low death-penalty rate for black intraracial murder works against the deterrence value of capital punishment in Georgia, it becomes a matter of interest and importance to understand why the black intraracial murderer so infrequently receives the death penalty. Perhaps the low rate is best explained in terms of the criminal circumstances themselves, that black-on-black murders rarely violate the statutes governing capital punishment. If so, justice dictates that the low death-penalty rate for black intraracial murder remain as it is; let the punishment fit the crime.

There is another possibility, although I have no evidence to support it. Perhaps blacks who killed blacks in Georgia experienced favorable bias as far as capital prosecution and courtroom judgment go. This possibility would be consistent with the patronizing attitude held by whites toward blacks in the South that co-existed historically with the hostile prejudices of both races.

Perhaps the best way to end this chapter is to admit that I may have posed a conundrum for the reader. Why would I reject the possibility that unfavorable bias in the courts against blacks who kill whites systematically elevates their death-penalty rate to an extraordinary 22% of the cases, whereas I am able to accept the possibility that favorable bias can help explain the very low rate of 1% in the more commonplace circumstance where blacks kill blacks? After all, the bias either way could be explained by the same perceived difference in value placed upon a white and a black life. Taking a more valuable white life would be viewed as a more serious offense and more likely to attract the death penalty; taking a less valuable black life would represent a less serious crime by this perception and call for a less harsh punishment.

The difference in my viewpoint regarding these capital punishment sentencing extremes comes down to this. Considerable evidence has been reviewed that provides an alternative explanation for the higher death-penalty rate for black murderers of white victims in Georgia; the assumption of bias, without direct evidence to prove it, is not scientifically viable. On the other hand, I have no evidence in hand that would explain the very low rate of capital punishment for black murderers of black victims, and the possibility of favorable bias remains. I will let someone else tackle that one by looking for evidence of favorable bias in punishing black intraracial murder. It is ironic that we have seen a turnaround in this chapter on racial fairness in adjudicating the death penalty, however. Starting with the assertion of unfavorable treatment of blacks in Georgia if they kill white victims, I have not only challenged that assumption but have ended up allowing for the possibility of just the opposite—favorable treatment of the black if he kills another black. Neither bias would qualify as fair practice.

Chapter Five

Fair Practice in Adjudicating the Death Penalty: The Issue of Gender

It is not difficult to find evidence that suggests women receive biased treatment in American courts, especially when it comes to receiving the death penalty following conviction for murder. I shall review some of this evidence on the pages ahead. What will become clear is that a very different assumption about bias is called for by the evidence than was the case when racial differences in capital punishment sentences were examined by Baldus, discussed in the previous chapter. The seeming bias for women will suggest that they receive favorable treatment from the courts with respect to severity of punishment. This stands in contrast to the assumption regarding race made by the Baldus group with respect to blacks in Georgia. They concluded that unfavorable prejudice was responsible for a disproportionate assignment of the death penalty to blacks under a specific circumstance—when they had killed a white victim. Yet it was found that when the racial sentencing statistics were subjected to alternative interpretation by collecting evidence that went beyond the courtroom decisions to characteristics of the offender and the crime, a compelling case could be made for an explanation other than prejudice.

The question arises whether the statistics forcefully implying that women who willfully kill are being protected in our courts also can find explanation in some way that does not portray our criminal justice systems as being unfairly responsive to an irrelevant factor in adjudicating lethal violence. The challenge of finding an alternative explanation, if one exists, is much the same as was true when racial prejudice was assumed. Systematic judicial bias is not going to be readily evaluated by direct means whether it would prove to be advantageous or disadvantageous to the accused criminal, since it inevitably is going to lack the possibility of immediate verification. Who responsible for decisions in a capital case would choose to confirm an unwillingness or even a hesitancy in finding a person guilty of murder despite the evidence simply because that person is a woman? If found guilty, who would admit the unacceptability of the death penalty for a woman if the circumstances warranted it? Since a direct confirmation or disconfirmation of gender bias at its source is unlikely, research into alternative explanations for disproportional sentencing of women and men comes down to whether evidence can be found that is more compelling than the likelihood of such a blatant display of unfair adjudication.

When we get around to considering explanations other than bias for the gender difference in sentencing for violent crimes in general and in assigning the death penalty in particular, I shall again turn to my own research for answers. Three types of evidence will be brought to bear in judging the basis for the more lenient punishment women receive relative to men. Is this uneven justice to be explained as protective bias of a chauvinist system or will it find more compelling explanation in the criminal conduct of women and the circumstances of their violent crimes?

The first type of evidence will consider whether severity of punishment for female violence fluctuated with cultural revision of the woman's role. Did changes in expectancies for women, changes that should decrease the chances of protective bias in the criminal justice system, make a difference in sentencing pattern? Stay with me here on my reasoning. If there is no change in what appears to be more lenient sentencing for violent women within the justice system even after cultural revision has cleared the way for equal treatment of the two sexes, it would suggest that the leniency is more apparent than real—that the differences in punishment are justified by law and better explained by some unchanging qualities of female violence than in terms of protective bias. Of course, more would be required before protectiveness could be dismissed as an explanation in this type of before-after analysis. Independent evidence would be needed to show that the American system of criminal justice can achieve equal punishment of women and men when the crime is not a violent one. In other words, change toward stiffer sentencing of women in the courts that brings them into line with men must be demonstrated for nonviolent crimes before any lack of change for violent crimes could be attributed to the more benign character of female violence itself.

Evidence of the second kind will involve the construct of criminal dangerousness that was so prominently involved in the analysis of seeming racial bias in assigning the death penalty to black males. The question to be considered is whether dangerousness as a personal attribute of women would demonstrate the same relationships with violent conduct as were found for men. Foremost here would be whether comparisons of female offenders at varying violence-severity levels will result in the differences in criminal dangerousness that were apparent for violent men. It may be recalled that more dangerous male criminals were found to have committed more serious violence, with murder at the severity extreme. This principle of criminal conduct found support time and time again in research with male prisoners. If the same thing is not found when women criminals are considered, especially if it is shown that women who engage in willful killing are not especially dangerous, we would have confirmed that the dynamics of murder by the female cannot be equated to those characterizing male homicide. For one thing, murder by less dangerous individuals would be unlikely to include the egregious behavior that attracts capital prosecution.

The third type of evidence to be considered will have to do more directly with the nature of female violence that results in the death of the victim and whether it can be distinguished from that of the male. Is lethal violence a qualitatively different act for women than it is for men? If so, is there any specific disparity between women and men in the quality of their violent conduct or in criminal circumstance that would help explain the differential punishment received by the two sexes for the nominally same violent crime?

WOMEN AND THE DEATH PENALTY

What is the evidence concerning the capital punishment of women in the United States? Data collected by the Death Penalty Information Center of Southern Methodist University reveal that there have been 566 confirmed executions of women in this country or in preexisting settlements between 1608 and 2002, around 3% of the total number of executions. Capital punishment, then, has been reserved almost exclusively for men for almost 400 years. A more recent compilation following restoration of the death penalty by the Supreme Court points to even greater disproportionality; between 1977 and 2002 the execution of ten women represented but 1.2% of criminals put to death for their capital crimes.

Just considering the wide gender discrepancy in executions lends itself to the conclusion that there is a substantial hesitancy to impose the death penalty upon a woman in our country that borders on total restraint—that there is a bias in our systems of criminal justice protecting females. However, there is even more suggestive evidence available if you follow the statistics through the capital punishment progression. The Death Penalty Information Center reports that women accounted for about 1 in 10 murder arrests following restoration of capital punishment. My own examination of the crime statistics published annually by the Department of Justice between 1977 and 2002 put the gender ratio closer to 1 in 8 murders being committed by a woman when only single-offender/single-victim homicides are considered. These Justice Department figures are based upon evidence collected by the police following investigation of a homicide, the first step in a progression that could result in eventual execution.

Although women account for between 1 in 8 and 1 in 10 murders investigated by the police, the Information Center release tells us that they receive only 1 out of 52 death sentences that result from prosecution as a capital offense. This proportion shrinks further when the number of inmates actually on death row awaiting execution is considered. In the same report period, only 1 in 74 of the inmates on death row was a female. Gender disproportionality reaches its maximum when the number of executions during this period is considered; one woman was put to death for every 88 men executed.

The disproportionality requiring our attention in this chapter, then, goes beyond the discrepant number of executions for men and women that depicts this form of punishment as almost exclusively reserved for males. The gender distinction in lethal violence and its treatment by the legal authorities is obvious from the beginning of the capital punishment progression for murder, continuing to mount from arrest to prosecution to courtroom judgment to containment on death row to actual execution. That women are less given to lethal violence seems clear enough given that police investigation identifies only 9–11% of murderers as female. It is safe to conclude, then, that different gender base rates for homicide exist; women simply do not share the male propensity for killing undeserving victims.

The more critical observation that requires explanation has to do with the diminishing number of women relative to men along the capital punishment progression from 9–11% of the murderers to about 1% of those murderers who are actually executed for their crime. Is this a matter of reluctance to believe that a woman could be responsible for perpetrating the kind of sordid acts that attract the death penalty or to execute a woman even if it is clear that she was responsible for a heinous crime? Either attitude would set the stage for gender bias protecting women. Alternatively, does the distinct quality of female lethal violence or of the circumstances surrounding it make it less likely that her crime will meet the legal specifications for capital murder?

Gender Differences in the Quality of Violent Conduct

The strategy of presentation for the evidence that I shall now review on gender differences in the quality of violence is simple enough. We shall first consider the more general question of whether differences exist between female criminal violence and the violence men commit. If the case for a gender difference in the quality of violence can be made, then the more focused questions of what the specific differences in violent crime might be and whether these should influence the severity of punishment for women and men will be entertained.

Changes in Sentencing for Violent and Nonviolent Crimes Associated with the Women's Movement

The changes in women's rights that have attracted national attention since the early 1970s brought with them greater equity in the workplace and in other social spheres previously favoring men. This shift has been implemented by force of law requiring that men and women be afforded the same opportunity to participate and prosper in our society when behavioral options are not limited by gender biology, sometimes even when they are. There is a dark side to feminist doctrine that has received far less attention than the heralded increments in rights and achievement over the past 30–35 years. If women are to be extended the same rights as men by law in our society, it follows that they should be expected to assume the same responsibilities. Just as there is reason to expect rewards equal to men for meeting these responsibilities, women also should be expected to suffer the same adverse consequences for the failure to do so.

One of the major responsibilities of adults in society is to comply with civil laws that in principle allow people to live together harmoniously. Failure to meet this responsibility in our system of justice is associated with a level of punishment commensurate with the nature of the crime and the circumstances under which the crime occurred. Just as feminist doctrine would have women demand rights equal to men, that doctrine should require that women expect equity in the bad consequences of irresponsibility in general and of crime in particular. This is the dark side of feminism; I have seen little evidence to suggest that women have sought penalties for irresponsibility or punishment for antisocial behavior equal to that of men.

While I would not expect equal opportunity for prison time or the death penalty to become a featured plank in the feminist agenda, equity of consequences should be a goal of those who are responsible for dealing with unacceptable behavior—representatives of the criminal justice system, business, educational settings, the military. Gender equity is now practiced in many quarters. I am prepared to say, however, that equity of punishment was not the general practice within the criminal justice system before the women's movement called attention to gender disparities in achieving more appealing goals.

Studies reported in the 1980s (Heilbrun, 1982; Heilbrun & Heilbrun, 1986) offer me the opportunity to accomplish two things. We can examine the statement that in the past women and men were not punished equally for the same nominal crime using evidence from the 1982 study. Since this investigation did not present a clear answer to the question of whether the feminist movement made a difference as far as equalizing the punishment of men and women, the methodology of the 1986 study was revised enough to answer this question. Of greater importance, this later study will allow us to consider the issue of whether patterns of sentencing before and after the ascendance of feminism in the early 1970s support the conclusion that violent criminality for the woman differs qualitatively from male violence.

The 1982 investigation drew upon the Georgia records of 600-plus female criminals and almost 700 male criminals. The crimes responsible for imprisonment had been committed between 1963–1978 for the women and 1955–1976 for the men. One of the things that attracted my interest was the length of time spent in prison by men and women for the same nominal crime. Actual length of incarceration offered a more promising measure of punishment meted out to the two sexes than the court sentence itself, since time in prison offered greater opportunity for gender bias to show up. Women could be treated more leniently not only in the original sentence but in the timing of release by parole officials. As it turned out, men were punished more severely in terms of prison time for six of the seven crimes studied. The average time that men served in prison beyond that exacted from the woman for the same nominal crimes was 32%-59% higher for manslaughter, murder, and forgery offenses and 103%-107% higher for burglary/theft, robbery, and assault. (Drug offenses resulted in almost identical punishment for men and women).

Examination of the treatment accorded to females and males for crimes committed during the 1960s and 1970s favored one conclusion; women were punished less for their crimes than men. The interpretation of this difference remained uncertain, however, since it could be argued that the same nominal crimes involved circumstances that made the female version merit more lenient punishment. This argument would contend that women spent less time in prison than men for the same offense because of qualitative differences in the crimes and not because of gender bias. One feature of the sentencing pattern puts that argument to rest, however, at least as a major consideration. Impulsivity/premeditation of a crime (to be discussed at greater length later in the chapter) is a circumstance that does influence punishment; spur-of-the-moment crimes tend to be punished less than planned crimes. Yet the gender disparity in punishment prevailed for crimes across the board; women were punished less for crimes that are more impulsive when committed by a woman but were also punished less for other crimes in which women are more planful than men. The more lenient treatment for females was found no matter what criminal impulsivity/premeditation would seem to require. Implications remained the same; women criminals in Georgia enjoyed biased treatment in the criminal justice system for crimes committed in the 1960s and 1970s.

The 1986 study of Georgia felons represented an effort to shed light on the bias implications of the 1982 findings regarding punishment of men and women for the nominally same crimes by refining the methodology. The comparison of female and male punishment for the nominally same crime was compartmentalized relative to the surge of feminism in the early 1970s. Crimes and time in prison for the two sexes that largely preceded the impact of the women's rights movement were compared to crimes and prison time that followed, punishment that would have been subject to influence by the effort to reposition the status of women in our country. Would the advent of feminism bring any change in the treatment of women in our criminal justice system and would the pattern of change hold any implications regarding gender bias in the post-feminism era?

New and even larger samples of female and male prison records were drawn for the 1986 study, and the same crimes were considered except for murder which for some reason was almost unrepresented despite the generous sample of females. The results of comparing men and women on time spent in prison for the same crime before and after feminism arrived on the national scene fall into three categories depending upon gender differences in impulsiveness/premeditation (see pages ahead). Comparative punishment for two nonviolent crimes, forgery and burglary/theft, offenses in which greater female premeditation is found, demonstrated a remarkable change. Before the early 1970s women convicted of committing these crimes spent about half the time in prison that men did; after feminism arrived, time in prison was about equal for the two sexes. These shifts in punishment testify to the willingness of criminal justice officials to finally consider the actual premeditation of nonviolent criminal conduct for women and stop treating women in keeping with a stereotype that routinely portrayed them as more impulsive and less planful than men.

The second category of results also points to an improving appreciation of gender-related criminal dynamics, although the results are not as dramatic. Robbery had been part of the gender-bias problem before the arrival of feminism; women were more premeditated than men in this type of crime but were incarcerated on average only 43% as long for their offense. The punishment for robbery shifted appropriately in the post-feminism era; women were serving more time in prison and men were spending less, although female incarceration time was still only 70% of that spent by males. Women were more planful when it came to drug offenses as well, but at least their punishment was as great as that of male drug offenders both before and after the early 1970s.

To this point the interpretation of the 1986 Heilbrun and Heilbrun results portrays a remarkable improvement in the calibration of punishment extended to women and men for the same nominal crimes, at least as far as making the punishment correspond to degree of criminal intent and planning. Crimes in which women were just as or even more premeditated than men began to attract the same punishment for the female after equal treatment of the sexes became a prevailing social mantra.

The third category of results allows us to examine what happens when the crimes considered in this analysis involve physical violence, criminal behavior that is generally on the impulsive side for both men and women but is especially so for women. Examination of manslaughter and assault cases revealed that women, who were punished less than men for these offenses before the early-1970s, continued to be more leniently treated after. Physical violence for females, the only crimes studied for which greater female impulsivity was found, brought less harsh punishment before and continued to do so after the doctrine of equal treatment of women and men had become widely adopted in the United States.

What can we conclude from these three categories of results bearing upon the punishment handed out to women and men for the same crime before and after equal treatment of the sexes became the legal norm? It seems clear that the courts were paying more attention to the spontaneous or planful characteristics of the crime and less attention to the sex of the criminal, and this held true in every category. Having reached that conclusion, we can return to the issue under consideration in this section—whether gender bias protecting women represents a plausible explanation for the less severe punishment of female violence.

The comparison of punishment extended to women and men for the nominally same crime before and after the early 1970s, considered in light of premeditation and intentionality, affirmed an improved responsiveness to the specific qualities of criminal conduct rather than the sex of the criminal. With crimes involving greater premeditation on the part of the woman, she began to receive punishment equal to the man. At least the change was in that direction. The failure for crimes involving physical violence to demonstrate this shift toward equal punishment over time is best explained by the nature of the criminal behavior—in this analysis the woman's distinct impulsivity when she does engage in physical aggression. Impulsive crimes attract less serious punishment, and this legal precedent would not change from the earlier to the later period; the more limited punishment for women compared to men for physical violence continues because the special quality of female physical aggression dictates that it should.

It could have been argued that the lack of a punishment effect for physically-violent crimes, using the women's movement as the potential cultural pivot, represented the continuation of a chauvinistic leniency toward women in punishing physically-violent crimes by a justice system that was unable to mend its ways. However, finding a shift toward equivalent punishment for several other types of crime in which women are not more impulsive makes it clear that the system was capable of change toward fair treatment by gender that considers the actual nature of female criminal conduct. The impulsive nature of women's physical violence merits less punishment than due men for the same crimes; the planful character of their criminal conduct for other types of crime argues against mitigated punishment.

Applicability of the Dangerousness Model to Female Criminals

A second approach to examining criminality in women and men in a way that may shed additional light on the disproportionality by gender of capital punishment turns our attention once again to the concept of criminal dangerousness. This two-factor construct, as you may recall, reflects the interaction between antisociality and cognitive competence wherein high antisociality and low cognitive competence represent characteristics of the individual that, acting in concert, increase the risk of criminal behavior in general and violent criminality in particular. I already have provided a more complete description of this construct and how it is measured in the previous chapter on racial bias, and an entire book on the subject is available elsewhere (Heilbrun, 1996).

It is important to note as this section on criminal dangerousness begins that validation of the model was carried out almost exclusively using evidence provided by male criminals. Men in the United States are far more likely to be involved in crimes than women, so they were more readily available as research subjects. Some study was made of female criminality and dangerousness, however, and we shall make use of that evidence as the comparison between male and female violence continues.

To briefly summarize what it took our research program on dangerousness years of data collection to confirm—the higher the level of male dangerousness, the greater the harm inflicted upon the victim by his violence. That is not a brash overstatement; consider the following evidence presented in the book relevant to dangerousness, measured independently of the crime, and the penchant for dangerous men to engage in harmful violence:

(1) Men who commit violent crimes are more dangerous than men who commit nonviolent crimes.
(2) Men who start out by committing a nonviolent crime but who are nonetheless identifiable as very dangerous are subsequently more likely to engage in a violent crime.
(3) Men who engage in the most serious form of violence (murder) are more dangerous than those who are responsible for intermediate-level violence

according to parole board tables (rape, robbery) who, in turn, are more dangerous than others who commit what are considered to be the least severe forms of violence (manslaughter, assault, child molestation).

(4) Men who rape women are more dangerous than men who molest children in keeping with the level of harm likely to be suffered by the victim.

(5) Men who rape women in an especially brutal way are more dangerous than rapists who use only enough physical force and psychological intimidation to accomplish their sexual goals.

(6) Men responsible for brutal killings are more dangerous than murderers who are less inclined to engage in excessive brutality.

Perhaps this brief review is enough to make the point that more elevated dangerousness in the male criminal carries with it the threat of greater physical harm to the victim of a crime; the capital punishment investigation added to the list as men who engaged in lethal violence so repugnant as to attract the death penalty were found to be more dangerous than ordinary life-sentence murderers. The fact that incremental risk of physical/psychological harm posed by increases in dangerousness is empirically established so well in men offers a second approach to examining the general nature of female and male violence with an eye toward differences. Will severity of violence perpetrated by women be governed by their criminal dangerousness as has been demonstrated with males? If not, will the difference shed any light on the gender bias issue?

As a case in point, would a comparison of female criminals responsible for violence at different severity levels demonstrate the same disparity in dangerousness as was found when male criminals at these severity levels were considered? If not, it would represent added evidence that violence in women is qualitatively different from male violence, not to be as readily understood in terms of enduring dispositions of the individual like antisociality and cognitive deficit. If, however, dangerousness looks much the same when related to violent conduct in women and men, it would represent a setback for the argument that female violence is qualitatively distinguishable from male violence.

Data collected with Diana Kors in 1991 and later included in my 1996 book on criminal dangerousness provided the information necessary to score dangerousness in a sample of Georgia women sent to prison after 1981, well beyond the arrival of the feminist tide. The subjects had been convicted of violent crimes at three levels of severity for the woman criminal as gauged by intentionality and harm to the victim—murder (high severity); aggravated assault, voluntary manslaughter, cruelty to children, kidnaping, and robbery (intermediate severity); involuntary manslaughter and vehicular homicide (low severity). Comparison of average dangerousness scores across these levels of female violent crime revealed significant variation statistically, but the differences were not systematic nor did they correspond to those found previously with men. Women who engaged in intermediate-level violence were more dangerous than low-severity offenders as dangerousness theory would predict; however, they were also more dangerous than women who murdered. The fact that female murderers were only moderately dangerous relative to other violent women came as a surprise, but it did signal a qualitative gender difference in the disposition toward violence at a level of severity most relevant to the death penalty. Murder for the female, as it turned out, is less amenable to explanation in terms of enduring dispositions toward violence than is the case for the male.

There is a potential problem of interpretation here that I could probably ignore and get away with as far as the reader is concerned. The social sciences like psychology place a premium on positive findings and upon the use of statistics to confirm that a positive finding did not occur by chance. Our analytic procedures are not geared to reveal how confident we should be about a negative result, a failure to find an effect. You will recognize just such a negative result when female murderers were not found to be the most dangerous violent criminals. If that does not make much sense to you, I hope you will take my word on the matter; the failure to find an effect that you are expecting is a problem for interpretation.

It may appear that I have contradicted my cautionary note by calling attention to the only moderate degree of dangerousness in female murderers as a point of interest, since it represents a failure to correspond to the theoretical model as well as to find an effect that was in evidence when male murderers were compared to men committing less severe types of violence. The lack of systematic differences in dangerousness across female violence-severity levels might preferably be interpreted more conservatively as an indication that the model does not sensibly apply to women at all. Fortunately, for sake of clarity, the verdict that the dangerousness model has no meaning for women can be rejected because of additional data we collected. Research with male criminals had established that dangerousness differences not only related meaningfully to victim harm caused by their criminal behavior, but dangerousness also distinguished between convicted felons who more generally conformed to codes of conduct and those who violated codes governing their behavior. More dangerous men proved to be prone to rule violation whether prison regulations, parole conditions, or post-parole civil laws were at issue. Nonconformity to the rules, then, was a commonplace and sensible correlate of the antisocial and cognitively-limited male criminal.

The study of rule conformity in female criminals was included in our investigation by comparing the dangerousness of women who differed in parole outcome, using the same subjects as we did in the violence-level analysis. Those who **succeeded** had conformed to parole conditions well enough to be discharged from parole. Those who **failed** had violated the conditions and had been sent back to prison. An **intermediate** group was continuing on parole when the data were collected, qualifying as neither successful nor failing at the time. This rule-conformity analysis for women provided a clearcut replication of earlier male findings; in fact, the predicted dangerousness score differences for women between parole-outcome groups were even more striking. Consistent with theory and prior male findings, successes had very low dangerousness scores, failures extremely high scores, and intermediate parolees fell in-between. Since we can have some confidence in the applicability of the dangerousness model to the female criminal, the asymmetrical violence-level comparisons for the same women can be taken more seriously. Finding only moderate dangerousness in female murderers, when added to the impulsivity findings for physical violence in women, builds an even stronger case for a difference in the dynamics of violence for the two sexes that could relate to the death penalty. The only moderate danger posed by women who kill would not readily translate into the egregious lethal violence that attracts capital punishment; neither would the highly impulsive nature of female physical aggression.

Specific Attributes of Lethal Violence in Women and Men Relevant to Capital Punishment

The gender comparisons of violent conduct found in female and male criminals that have been discussed to this point have suggested that physically-aggressive violent crimes perpetrated by the two sexes differ in behavioral quality in ways that could make the death penalty less likely for women. I admit, however, that evidence used in order to reach this conclusion has been indirect, depending upon the lack of sentencing changes for post-feminist crimes of impulsive physical violence and the failure of female murderers to show the expected elevation in dangerousness. Now we will turn to somewhat more direct evidence relevant to the question of whether the near-absence of capital punishment for women is better explained in terms of unfair protectionistic bias or in terms of the quality and circumstance of female violence.

Impulsivity-premeditation of Criminal Behavior for Women and Men

Premeditation in the commission of a crime refers to the extent of intent and planning involved prior to the actual commission of the unlawful act. By legal precedent a premeditated crime would be considered a more serious offense than the same act that is committed impulsively. This is reasonably explained by the clearly intentional nature of a premeditated crime, although criminal outcome may go beyond original intent. An impulsive crime, at the other extreme, is one in which the instigation to act in an unlawful way arises near the time of commission or represents an unanticipated elaboration of the original plan of misconduct. In either case, the thought given to the criminal act or to going beyond the original act is limited and likely to be ineffectual.

The distinction between impulsive and premeditated criminal acts seems to be especially important when it comes to violent crimes, probably because in our society the thought of planning, thus intentionally inflicting, physical injury or serious psychological harm is generally considered repugnant. The more impulsive the violence, the less it will be viewed in terms of an intentional violation of this basic value; the less intentional the act, the less serious the punishment merited. Intentionality, then, representing the motivated instigation to act in a particular way, is a vital determinant of how serious an act of violence should be considered and how much punishment should be meted out. For example, responsibility for the death of a victim can result in a number of convictions—murder, voluntary manslaughter, involuntary manslaughter, vehicular homicide, reckless endangerment. As intentionality decreases going down this list, so does severity of punishment.

Results taken from a study I reported in 1982 have already been cited as we examined female and male criminality from the perspective of impulsivity/premeditation involved in their unlawful behavior. Presentation of the actual data is overdue, and consideration of this qualitative dimension in greater detail is in order. The preceding discussion leaves no doubt what the trend of gender comparisons would have to be before the impulsive or premeditated quality of criminal conduct could serve as an alternative to protective bias in explaining the low representation of women in the capital punishment system. Women would not only have to display a more impulsive quality to their physical violence than men, but the impulsivity margin should widen as more serious crimes of violence are considered. Murder, then, should represent the most impulsive expression of violence for a woman and show the greatest difference in this regard from the male if we are to address the gender discrepancy in capital punishment.

Impulsivity/premeditation of a given crime was determined from ratings of the criminal circumstances in a prisoner's file along a four-point scale ranging from "clearly not planned and clearly a spontaneous act" (score = 1) at one extreme to "clearly planned and clearly not a spontaneous act" (score = 4) at the other. The information in the files was gathered at the time of the crime from all available sources by the investigating authorities. More than 600 female criminals were drawn for the sample from Georgia state files with seven crimes represented—murder, manslaughter, and assault as violent crimes involving physical aggression, robbery as a violent crime in which the threat of physical aggression is paramount, and burglary/theft, forgery, and drug offenses as nonviolent offenses. Male files of an almost equal number were drawn from state records, and the same crimes were rated on the four-point scale of impulsivity/premeditation. Table 9 provides the average ratings for both the women and men convicted of the same nominal crimes.

Some general observations are in order concerning the rating in Table 9 before getting to the more specific gender comparisons. Violent crimes that feature physical attack upon the victim are generally more impulsive in character whether you are considering women or men. Robbery, in which threat of attack is typically involved, falls on the premeditated side of the scale for both sexes at an intermediate value. Nonviolent crimes are the most premeditated by far and again this is true for women and men. Any differences between female and male criminals in the impulsivity or premeditation of their offenses make their appearance despite the overall correspondence in pattern across crime categories.

On a more specific note, female crimes involving physical aggression were consistently more impulsive than the same crimes committed by men, and the discrepancy was increasingly apparent as more serious physical violence was considered. The average ratings portray murder by the female as the most impulsive and as 40% more skewed toward the impulsive end of the scale compared to male homicide. This impulsivity differential fell to 28% for manslaughter and 21% for assault. The impulsivity of female murder was so

Table 9.   Impulsivity/premeditation[a] of Crimes Committed by Females and Males

Crime Description	Average Female Rating	Average Male Rating
Violent Crimes Involving Physical Aggression		
Murder	1.50	2.51
Manslaughter	1.67	2.32
Assault	1.95	2.56
Violent Crime Involving Threat of Physical Aggression		
Robbery	3.44	3.16
Nonviolent Crimes Involving No Physical Aggression		
Burglary/Theft	3.56	3.26
Forgery	3.91	3.36
Drug Offenses	3.90	3.25

[a]On a four-point scale ranging from 1.00 at the inpulsive end to 4.00 at the premeditated end.

striking, in fact, that one wonders how the requirement of premeditation for the crime of murder was ever met.

These gender comparisons for physically-violent crime become even more vivid when the remainder of Table 9 is examined, since it becomes clear that the woman who resorts to crime is not consistently, or even generally, more impulsive in her criminal misconduct than the male. Even when it comes to robbery offenses in which physical violence is threatened in order to achieve the criminal goal, the woman's behavior is more calculated than is true for men. The shift to more premeditated criminality of women becomes most apparent for nonviolent offenses in which "spur-of-the-moment" participation was almost unrepresented in our sample. Put in quantitative terms, women were 9% closer to the premeditated extreme of the scale in their robberies than men, 11% closer for burglary/theft, 16% for forgery, and 20% closer to the extreme in their drug offenses.

This evidence clearly suggests that serious female violence involving physical harm to the victim is more likely to erupt spontaneously than is the case for males, and this is especially true when murder is involved. Furthermore, the gender discrepancy in physical violence shows up despite the fact that the male shows some degree of impulsivity relative to other male crimes and despite the female's more premeditated style when committing other types of offenses. Their impulsiveness may be one reason why women are identified by police investigation as responsible for only 13% of the one offender/one victim murders that are committed in the United States; impulsive killing is less likely to be considered murder than a killing planned in advance. If women find it so difficult to contemplate killing another person and to plan the action in advance, how much more difficult must it be for them to premeditate a killing that turns out to be so egregious as to attract capital prosecution?

When you consider the apparent aversion of women to contemplating violent expression in general and killing in particular, their limited exposure to the death penalty becomes less of a mystery. The impulsivity of their violence, especially murder, would have a mitigating influence in courtroom decisions. Added to the infrequency of willful killing by women to begin with, the near-absence of female executions is more readily explained.

Mitigating Circumstances Surrounding Violent Crimes of Women and Men

Having noted that physical violence in women is not only uncommon but more impulsive and less premeditated than comparable conduct in men when it does occur, especially when it is an act of murder, the focus will now shift to the circumstances under which physical violence occurs for further explanation of why so few women are sentenced to die for their lethal violence. Any circumstance that could reasonably be considered a provocation for killing or for some other reason could lessen the stigma of the act becomes of interest at this point. These mitigating factors that make the crime more understandable or otherwise less repugnant would decrease the likelihood of capital punishment for taking a life.

My attention was drawn in a roundabout way to victim gender as a basis for mitigation in killings committed by women. The Justice Department's annual report on crime in the United States reveals a remarkable similarity between homicides perpetrated by women and men over a 26-year period, 1977–2002. Men are the victims of choice for almost everyone. More than 80% of the murders by females over this span of years targeted a male, and about 73% of the male murderers victimized another male. Victims ranged in age from mid-adolescent to adult in virtually every case.

The importance to me of these similar percentages regarding victim gender in trying to distinguish the homicidal behavior of female and male offenders became apparent when heterosexual relationships were factored in as an added variable. The most common prelude to murder according to national statistics is some type of angry confrontation. The fact that women home in on men as murder victims 80% of the time points to the possible importance of emotional fallout from problems within a man/woman relationship in motivating the reluctant female murderer. Men, however, are disinclined to target women with only 27% of their murder victims being females. It followed that the man would be less likely to murder the female partner in a heterosexual relationship riven by strife. This offered a hint that angry confrontation in a heterosexual relationship would be a more important dynamic of murder by a woman than by a man.

The possible relevance of these preliminary observations to mitigation in cases when a woman kills a man with whom she has had a continuing relationship would be as follows. Given the greater strength and aggressiveness likely to be found in the man within an adult heterosexual pair, physical abuse of the partner should be a predominantly male choice of showing displeasure and more likely mode of expressing anger. Prior physical abuse by the male within a heterosexual pair, then, could be a prominent predisposing circumstance of cases in which the man is eventually killed by the woman. Anger, resentment, or fear provoked by the abuse could serve as motivation for the act. To complete the reasoning, for a man to take advantage of his strength and aggressive inclinations to physically abuse a woman is socially unacceptable and can be readily understood as a basis for anger, fear, or resentment. While it probably would not excuse killing the man, prior abuse might very well serve as a mitigating circumstance in determining the woman's punishment for the deed. Killing under mitigating circumstances is not a likely basis for capital punishment. A history of physical abuse suffered at the hands of a female heterosexual partner who is eventually killed by the abused male would not qualify as a likely scenario.

One way to validate this line of reasoning would be to demonstrate the prominence of prior physical abuse by the man in relationships between women who kill and the men who become their victims. The study of criminal dangerousness in women at varying levels of violence severity, reported earlier in this chapter, included evidence that will allow us to examine the proposal that female crimes involving the death of an adult male will include prior physical abuse by the victim as a prominent predisposing circumstance. Either murder or voluntary manslaughter crimes will be considered, since the Department of Justice combines both in their statistics on willful killing. Raters had been instructed to examine the case histories of these female killers for reference to physical mistreatment in the relationship by the male victims. As it turned out, a remarkably high 20 of the 36 cases (56%) revealed a history of prior battering. I am not aware of a reliable figure concerning the prevalence of physical abuse by the man within heterosexual liaisons in general, and I doubt if one is available given the privacy issues involved in obtaining such information. However, it does seem safe to conclude that 1980s women in general were not subject to a 56% rate of battering by men with whom they had continuing relationships.

The fact that physical abuse by the male was commonplace in the heterosexual relationships between women who kill and men who are their victims does not mean that it was necessarily a motivational dynamic in the abused woman's crime. The section on circumstances in a criminal file does not often provide a definitive statement on the conditions motivating the criminal act. However, to the extent that we are ultimately interested in decision by jury in a capital case, a history of prior abuse by the victim could be enough to sway the jurors, mitigate the crime, and limit the punishment. It could be assumed that abuse set the stage for violence without clear evidence that it motivated the violent act itself.

Since the women who suffered abuse before slaying their male tormentor were convicted of serious lethal violence (murder or voluntary manslaughter) despite the mitigating circumstance, one might question how much help to the defense it was? It is worth noting in this regard that the 36 cases considered in the analysis do not include women who have killed their abusers and have not been subject to prosecution, have been tried but found to be innocent of a crime, or have been found guilty of some lesser violation such as involuntary manslaughter. Prior physical abuse has not been fully tested as an influential mitigation in cases of lethal violence by reviewing only convictions for willful killing.

The most important points to remember from this suggestive analysis are that prior physical abuse by the male victim commonly appears in the case history of female homicides and that it would likely qualify as a mitigating circumstance. Although prior abuse by her usual male victim may not spare the woman from stiff punishment, it could at least prevent such cases from being prosecuted successfully as capital offenses. Combine this with the very impulsive character of female murder relative to the male, another possible source of mitigation, and the chances of capital punishment drops even further. Then consider the low base rate of female violence to begin with, and the absolute number of women actually executed in this country would be expected to fall to a very low figure compared to the male figure.

Does Race Matter in Assigning the Death Penalty to Women?

I have gone to some lengths to make the point that the glaring disproportionality in capital punishment between women and men for killing their victims can be explained in large measure by sex differences in the circumstances and nature of their lethal violent behavior. These differences should make it less likely that a woman would receive the death penalty according to law. The assumption of systematic protective bias is not required to explain the disproportionality by gender any more than systematic racial bias was necessary in order to explain the disproportional rate of capital punishment sentences in cases where blacks had murdered white victims in a deep-South state. Judgments either favoring or detrimental to an undeserving offender based upon gender or race may occur but as occasional aberrations and not as systematic bias. No system requiring human participation is perfect, and criminal justice certainly does not prove an exception.

Even though the death sentence is infrequently handed out to women does not mean that it is fairly dispensed by race. It is always possible that closer examination of capital punishment cases by race will reveal some clearer hint of protectionistic bias in decisions reached for women, although I have no evidence from my own research that suggests black women and white women are treated differently. Analyzing bias by race within gender will be my second effort to consider the two variables conjointly, since it represents a complement of sorts to what was reported in the previous chapter when the death penalty was examined by race of the offender and victim but for male murderers only. If anything suggesting bias did show up in this analysis of capital punishment for white and black women, consideration was to be given to alternative explanations.

Actual Numbers of Women by Race Given the Death Penalty

A tally by the Death Penalty Information Center, Southern Methodist University, indicates that 146 women were sentenced to death in the United States from the 1970s until the end of 2002 within 24 state jurisdictions. The tally broke down female offenders into several racial categories, but they fell predominantly into two—white (64%) and black (27%). I shall concern myself with that racial division for purposes of analysis. The 94 death sentences extended to white women were 2–3 times the 39 handed down to black women. A ratio portraying more white than black women sentenced to die over the period of study was apparent in 18 states, an equal number in four states, and only two states reversed this order with a greater number of black women sentenced to death.

These figures might seem to suggest a clear difference by race in assigning the death penalty to women given the rare circumstance when it is the verdict of choice in homicide cases. The sentence was imposed far more frequently on whites than blacks. However, you probably need no reminding that additional information is required before concluding that racial bias is involved in disproportional sentencing counts. Even though there were 2–3 times more capital sentences handed down to white women than to black women, there are a lot more white women in the country to commit homicide that could attract the death penalty. The issue of rate must be considered.

Actual Numbers of Women by Race Engaging in Homicide Offenses—
The Question of Rate

The homicide trends for white and black women offenders plotted between 1975 and 2000 by the Department of Justice Statistics Bureau, combined for present purposes over age categories, are reported in terms of the number of homicide offenses per 100,000 population in the United States, a rate figure. The trend lines seem to indicate a decline in homicide rate for both races over the quarter century, although this is clearer for black females than for white females. Murder rates range over the years from 1.33 to 2.17 per 100,000 population for white women, whereas the range of murder rates is from 6.67 to 20.67 per 100,000 for the black females. Perhaps the most useful homicide rate comparison is between the average for each race over the entire period— 1.75 per 100,000 population for white females and 13.78 per 100,000 for their black counterparts. Black women engaged in homicide offenses at a rate almost eight times that of white women.

Although these average rate figures allow us to compare the homicidal proclivities of black and white women in this country, the actual numbers of homicides committed would be a more useful statistic in making sense out of the actual numbers of death sentences handed down. Unfortunately, for sake of this comparison, I was able to establish actual numbers of homicide offenses by black and white women for only two of the years included in the trend analysis—1978 and 1979. For some reason these needed figures were reported for those years but became unavailable for the remaining years of the analysis given changes in style of presentation within the Justice Department's annual compilation of crime statistics.

In 1978 there were 79% more one-offender/one-victim homicides perpetrated by black females than by white females; in 1979 there were 63% more homicides by black females. For these two years, at least, the far greater rate of 13.78 per 100,000 population for black female homicides compared to 1.75 for white females translates into a substantially greater number of murders despite the limited number of black females in the general population. Given the discrepancy between the actual homicide counts in 1978–1979 and the fact that black-female homicide rates never fell below five times that of white-female homicide rates over the remaining years, it seems safe to conclude that the absolute number of willful killings by white females fell below that of black females in any given year.

Now if you put together the comparison of death-penalty sentences handed out to white women and black women who kill and the comparison of the actual number of homicides that are committed by women of both races, one conclusion seems incontestable. White women are sentenced more harshly when it comes to capital punishment; fewer people are murdered by white women, but they are more frequently given the death penalty than black women. This discrepancy brings us to the third step of this analysis. I will try to cast some light on the question of whether this misalignment is better explained by some characteristic of white female homicide that is more likely to attract the death penalty or represents evidence of bias against white women who kill or favoring the black female murderer.

Revisiting the Dangerousness-versus-Prejudice Controversy in Courtroom Sentencing

The issue of whether the inordinate number of death-penalty sentences given to black men who had killed white victims was to be explained as an example of "southern justice," as Baldus and many others have believed, has been discussed at length. An alternative explanation in terms of the dangerousness of the criminal was considered and proved to be more compelling than courtroom bias. The extreme dangerousness of the black interracial murderer and the circumstances of his violent act go a long way in explaining the egregious excesses that mark death-penalty crimes.

Consideration of dangerousness in violent female criminals failed to provide the same orderly differences between levels of violence that had been found for men. Index scoring procedures failed to provide evidence that black or white women convicted of murder, the most serious violent crime, were especially dangerous. This finding led to a search for some circumstance unique to the dynamics of female murder that might prove capable of instigating willful killing but would not be related to criminal dangerousness. The search, if successful, would help explain why criminal dangerousness was not a critical determinant of murder committed by women.

One such dynamic was discovered and has been reported earlier in this chapter—a history of physical abuse by the male who eventually became the woman's homicide victim. Given the provocation of physical abuse and the anger, resentment, or fear that it must generate, there is less reason to expect character traits such as dangerousness to play a role in the woman's lethal violence directed toward a male, the usual target of female homicide. As it turned out, prior physical abuse by the male victim was evident in a substantial number of cases involving murder by both black and white females.

This leads us to the question of whether dangerousness would emerge as a promising explanation of female violence, especially lethal violence, if the cases involving the provocation of physical abuse by the male victim were ignored. The importance of finding a lawful ordering of violence severity levels by dangerousness of the female criminal when the sample is reduced in this way goes beyond vindication of the theoretical model. If women who kill other types of victims—male non-abusers, women, and children—demonstrate behavioral compliance with the model in keeping with male murderers, dangerousness might then qualify as relevant to explaining the disproportionality of female capital cases by race. In order to qualify as an explanation, however, it would have to be shown that women's homicidal behavior without provocation of physical abuse is governed by the same dangerousness principles as that of men for white women but not black women.

The reworking of dangerousness evidence by omitting willful killing cases involving prior abuse by the male victim resulted in a major realignment of dangerousness scores at the three violence severity levels for white female criminals. The revised tri-level comparison brought white women in line with violent men. In other words, remove physical abuse as a provocation for the white woman's lethal violence and she behaves in keeping with her dangerous predisposition. Those guilty of high-severity violence (murder) attracted an average dangerousness score that was quite high and 20% above the average score for white women committing intermediate-level violence (voluntary manslaughter, aggravated assault/battery, armed robbery, kidnaping). The intermediate-violence group, in turn, had an average dangerousness score that was 30% above that of the white women who had committed low-severity violence (involuntary manslaughter, vehicular homicide). These graphic discrepancies in dangerousness between violence severity levels are consistent with the theoretical model and with results obtained from men, white or black, who commit violent crimes. This correspondence would lead us to expect egregious excesses of violence for some highly dangerous white females who commit murder, unfortunately emulating highly dangerous males.

The same effort at revision by excluding cases involving prior abuse of black women provided a very different picture. There was still no systematic relationship between severity of violence and degree of dangerousness as the theoretical model would require. Intermediate-severity was associated with the highest dangerousness, high-severity violence was next, and low-severity violence was perpetrated by the least dangerous black women, the same as before. Dangerousness simply does not do very well as a predictor of willful killing in black women whether abusive men are counted among their homicide victims or not. Dangerousness only works as a predictor at the low end where deadly violence occurs without intent.

It may occur to the reader that this effort to introduce dangerousness of the criminal into the discussion of possible racial bias in capital sentencing of women is both complicated and unnecessary. Why not just take the fact that white women have received the death penalty 2–3 times as often as black women, even though black females have committed the greater number of homicides, and use this to assume that bias does exist against white women and favoring black women as far as capital punishment goes? We are dealing with such restricted numbers of capital cases that this interpretation would not represent much of a black mark against criminal justice proceedings anyway. If such bias were conceded, meaning that white women are held to some higher standard of conduct than black women or that black women are protected to some extent from the consequences of their violent excesses, it would be a far cry from the twist often given to the treatment of the black minority that casts it as unfair. However, it would have its counterpart in the very low rate of capital punishment sentences given to black men who had murdered black victims.

I, personally, would rather stick with what can be quantified even though the dangerousness analysis was cumbersome at best. The dangerousness counterargument to bias would only require us to believe that the few homicides by white females not provoked by physical abuse by the male victim involve more highly dangerous women who are not only capable of murder but seemingly can be as mean as junkyard dogs in the way they go about it. I do not have a ready explanation for why this anomalous female behavior would be more of a white phenomenon than black; the reader's guess is as good as mine.

Chapter Six

Fair Practice in Adjudicating the Death Penalty: Mental Disorder as a Competence Issue

Whether mental competence of an offender has been fairly considered in capital sentencing and actual consummation of the sentence by execution is even more difficult to submit to empirical investigation than race or gender. In the first place, the qualities of mental disorder are often difficult to pin down. This opens the way to a number of complications as far as adjudicating the death penalty is concerned, not the least of which is determining the extent to which mental disability influenced criminal conduct. Disagreement among experts, dissembling by offenders, strategies of legal prosecution and defense, misunderstanding by lay jurors, etc., can only introduce further ambiguities into trial proceedings involving mental disorder; establishing race or gender of the accused is rarely an issue. The greater uncertainty surrounding mental competence of the offender in any given case makes it that much more difficult for the researcher to establish whether the sentencing outcome is biased or not.

Another related complication that accompanies the issue of mental competence as a mitigating factor in capital punishment is the fact that there are two forms of competence that are commonly distinguished in determining criminal responsibility or, if found guilty of a crime, what severity of sentence should be imposed. Mental disorder covers a wide range of dysfunctional behaviors from less serious character flaws, through anxiety-based neurotic and psychobiological anomalies, to incapacitating psychotic cognitive/mood conditions. Mental disorder not only includes a wide range of disabilities but attracts a substantial amount of diagnostic disagreement among experts regarding symptoms and their meaning. Disordered behavior is not likely to be important to criminal justice proceedings unless it reaches the more disabling end of the spectrum where cognitive impairment of an offender could qualify as a major determinant of the crime or consideration for punishment.

A second type of competence considered in criminal cases is mental retardation, a restriction of intelligence that is serious enough to impair social functioning. Among the higher intellectual processes that will be deficient are those involving reasoning, judgment, decision-making, memory, abstraction, etc. The two types of cognitive impairment will be considered separately following further introductory remarks. Mental disorder and issues of bias will be covered in this chapter, and bias issues relating to mental retardation will be discussed in the next.

The fact that either of two forms of mental incompetence may be considered in determining criminal responsibility and sentencing adds to the complexity of investigating bias. The rules of engaging mental disorder and mental retardation within the justice system sometimes do not coincide, whereas at other times they are treated identically. For example, mental disorder has long received more attention as a basis for exculpation from criminal responsibility; sentences such as "not-guilty by reason of insanity" or "guilty but mentally ill" recognize mental disorder as a determining or contributing factor in criminal conduct or at least as a consideration in the quality of punishment. Mental retardation does not seem to have received as much attention as a mitigating circumstance. On the other hand, execution of offenders who are substantially disordered or retarded mentally has been recognized by the Supreme Court as "cruel and unusual punishment," although this preclusion is said to rarely stand in the way of carrying out a death sentence (Miller & Radelet, 1993).

Another feature of mental impairment that complicates the investigation of bias is that one form of disability varies over time in severity and degree of behavioral impairment whereas the other would be expected to remain fairly constant. Mental disorders do respond to self-help, professional intervention, changes of circumstance, or simply the passage of time so that symptomatic improvement will occur; symptoms may worsen over time and circumstance as well. Accordingly, the question of whether mental disorder can be regarded as relevant to a decision in the justice system in capital cases often requires clarification. Are we to be concerned with mental status at the time of the crime (criminal responsibility)? at the time of the trial (competence for trial)? as execution approaches (competence for execution)? A failure to acknowledge proper time and circumstance could lead to a serious misjudgment regarding the importance of mental disorder.

On the other hand, mental retardation is likely to follow a stable course. More than a modest swing in IQ, which often serves as the defining criterion of this form of mental limitation, would alert the professional to some kind of flaw in test administration. An IQ score, given skill of the tester and a reasonable degree of cooperation from the person being tested, should not demonstrate wild fluctuations. The retarded individual, then, represents a far less complicated picture when it comes to judging extent of prior or future incapacitation. However, as will be elaborated in the next chapter, an overdependence on specific IQ scores to determine mental retardation can be responsible for biased judgment by even modest variations.

I have made the point that studying mental competence of the offender and just adjudication of the death penalty is more complicated since determination of competence requires measurement or at least crude estimation by experts; race and gender do not. In addition, cognitive ineffectiveness as a source of bias can be expected to wax and wane in some cases and at other times it can be expected to remain relatively constant. The problem of establishing mental competence for making important legal decisions is made even greater since these obstacles are compounded. The criminal justice system seems to pay the lion's share of attention to the more abstruse and variable type of incompetence, mental disorder, thereby making it necessary to depend far more often upon less reliable evidence.

Decisions regarding the role of mental disorder in criminal conduct are even more difficult than I have portrayed them. It is the psychological condition of the offender when planning and executing the crime at some earlier time that is relevant to determining criminal responsibility. This requires reinstatement of a past mental condition in determining criminal responsibility at a later trial and a fluctuating condition at that. This adds to the difficulty of diagnosis in many cases and is one reason why presumed experts can differ so much in trial testimony. The failure to recognize past disordered mentation at the time of trial can also help explain the unexpected appearance of mental problems in death-row inmates that raise concerns regarding competence for execution.

Yet another difficulty in establishing the importance of the criminal's mental competence for the adjudication of capital punishment is one shared with both gender and race as potential sources of bias. In order to weigh the question of whether women are protected within our criminal justice system from capital punishment, it proved important to consider not only their infrequent engagement in willful killing but to examine the quality of violence in women as well. Serious female violence by this analysis proved to be convincingly less conducive to imposing the death-penalty, since it was found to be mitigated by greater impulsivity and the provocation of prior physical abuse by the male victim. The rare occasions in which women receive a death sentence for murder and even more infrequent executions that follow indicate that women not only are less inclined to engage in willful killing but that these distinctions in the quality of lethal violence for women have been appreciated. By the same token, the issue of a disproportional number of death-penalty sentences for blacks when the victim was white not only led to consideration of murder rate among blacks but also to the dynamics of black male violence.

In the same vein, the importance of mental competence in adjudicating the death penalty should come into sharper focus if the dynamics of lethal violence for those who are mentally disordered or retarded are more closely examined. There are obstacles to accomplishing this that may be formidable, however. One obstacle already mentioned is reliably specifying the mental status of the offender at some earlier time when the crime was planned and executed. Before juries or other decision-makers can constructively appreciate how mental competence affects violent action, they must be provided reasonably reliable information regarding prior mental status that is relevant to the task. In contrast, if the offender is a woman now, she was a woman then; if the offender is a black male now, he was a black male then.

Once you get past the issue of gaining reliable information regarding past mental status, there is yet another reason why considering mental competence represents a substantial problem in fairly adjudicating violent crimes. Even if a reliable reinstatement of some past psychological condition is available, the manner in which the reinstated aberrant mentation is supposed to have mediated criminal conduct must be specified before its role can be properly weighed. Was the act commanded by hallucinated voices? Was it given unrealistic meaning by delusional fabrication? Was it compelled by an impulse that overwhelmed self-control? Simply acknowledging that an offender was mentally disordered at the time that a crime was committed does not suffice as an explanation for why the crime was committed.

In short, trying to understand the criminal act of a mentally-disordered person may require that we comprehend a different, sometimes bizarre, standard of conduct, a task not made any easier by the infusion of opposing information from legal adversaries. If ordinary displays of violence are often difficult to understand, what can be expected when the idiosyncratic world of the mentally disordered or the simplistic world of the mentally retarded must be considered?

Just because I have emphasized mental disorder as the type of incompetence that complicates fair adjudication of the death penalty does not mean that mental retardation should be overlooked in this regard. Being retarded does tend to be a more stable quality; a finding of retardation now allows you to assume retardation at some earlier point. However, the failure of low-IQ individuals in general to grasp social and physical realities because of deficiencies in their higher mental processes can show considerable variance. The lower the IQ, the greater the deficit in reality testing and in drawing proper inferences regarding their relationship to the environment. To understand lethal violence committed by someone who is mentally retarded, it would be important to consider not only how someone would function without appreciating environmental nuances but also with limited ability to reason, judge, make decisions, resolve conflicts—to make use of information. Most people are not in a position to do this because they have rarely been exposed to those kinds of limitations in themselves or in others; the lower the IQ, the less likely the exposure.

Trying to comprehend the behavior of the mentally retarded and the underlying mental processes can be as puzzling as would be the case for the mentally disordered once you get beyond the simplified routines to which the retardate has become accustomed. However, when determining criminal responsibility is at issue, it is important to make the effort. Just as it is not enough to settle for co-existence of active mental disorder and the crime to relieve the offender of responsibility, it falls short simply to conclude that the retarded perpetrator was disabled mentally at the time a crime was committed. There should be some way to explain the specific way in which limited intelligence resulted in the commission of the crime before the person is relieved of personal responsibility.

A final difference to be considered that sets mental competence apart from race and gender as a source of bias is that the law requires competence to be considered as a possible mitigating or exculpatory factor for criminal conduct and as a basis for decision further along the criminal justice progression. Although neither proved to be a source of systematic bias based upon evidence I collected, openly acknowledging that either race or gender merits consideration as a basis for determining responsibility or punishment would probably have proven an embarrassment to the criminal justice system. The fact that mental competence has been explicitly identified as a possible determinant of legal responsibility and punishment for criminal activities has been the basis for defense in the courts and for subsequent court appeal. The legal ramifications of mental competence have added to the importance of thorough psychological assessment in cases in which disorder is suspected or for an elaborated IQ estimate when retardation is at issue.

Yet even with these refinements comes the opportunity for confusion and unfairness. Experts may be chosen because their views on mental disorder are invariable (Winslade, 1983); opposing counsels may choose different experts because their views accommodate defense or prosecution strategies. Despite the fact that specific IQ scores are adopted to define mental retardation in general or to elucidate levels of retardation, there may not be sufficient appreciation of the negligible difference in functional capabilities of those falling just above or below these fixed cutting points.

MENTAL DISORDER AND COMPETENCE

It might seem contradictory to use the term "bias" in reference to procedures that comply with legal mandates. The 1986 **Ford versus Wainwright** decision of the United States Supreme Court held that the execution of the insane was unconstitutional under the Eighth Amendment. It was ruled that this punishment was "savage and inhuman" in light of our common-law heritage and represented cruel and unusual punishment. Three years later the Supreme Court ruled in the **Penry versus Lynaugh** case that the same Eighth Amendment would likely prohibit execution of profoundly or severely retarded persons who are unable to understand or appreciate the wrongfulness of their actions. Since incompetence of the mentally disordered or mentally retarded has been ruled legally relevant to death-penalty decisions, the question arises how systematic bias would enter into such cases.

The Supreme Court has stipulated that the seriously mentally disordered and mentally retarded should not be held accountable for willful killing, at least to the extent that the death penalty for such crimes should be exacted. Note, however, that the rulings protect the extremes of mental incompetence — "insanity," a psychotic condition in which the person's thinking is going to be seriously out of kilter, and "profound and severe retardation" in which intellectual competence is at its most primitive level. The more obvious problem of bias and challenge to fair adjudication comes when mental competence of an offender is found to be limited, but it is uncertain whether it is to the degree suggested by the Court for consummating the death penalty. A related problem would derive from uncertainties regarding whether and how legal guidelines protecting impaired offenders from execution should be applied to issues of responsibility for the actual crimes.

Two possibilities seem to present themselves. The protective mindset fostered by the Supreme Court decisions regarding execution at the extremes of mental incompetence could promote a lenient bias favoring offenders with less serious limitations. If so, the system may go too far in allowing lesser degrees of mental impairment to serve as a restraint upon execution or to qualify as a mitigating factor in assigning criminal responsibility in cases of murder or other forms of violence. It could work the other way as well. The vast degree of mental incompetence required by the Court to invoke Eighth Amendment protection could set such an extreme standard that lesser mental impairment would not receive sufficient attention as a source of mitigation.

The evidence to be considered in the remainder of this chapter will bear upon mental disorder and the responsibility for criminal behavior. The discussion will approach the issue of fairness in adjudication obliquely, as was true in considering race and gender as sources of possible bias in assigning the death penalty. There was no way for me to determine whether criminal justice was slanted toward leniency or unwarranted accountability in the sentencing for any given case involving mental competence of the offender. What will be at issue is whether the decisions reached more generally within the system regarding punishment for violent criminal conduct suggest undue protectiveness of the impaired offender or unresponsiveness to his limitations.

Legal Insanity of Violent Criminals and Dangerousness— the Initial Study

The court verdict "not-guilty by reason of insanity" (NGRI) relieves individuals from responsibility for otherwise criminal acts because the misconduct can be explained by their mental disorder. Responsibility for a criminal act requires that the person is capable of forming criminal intent and exerting reasonable control over his actions. Thus, those judged to have been mentally disordered at the time their crimes were committed may not be held legally accountable if their mental status rendered them incapable of forming intent to act in a criminal fashion or of exerting control over their impulses to do so.

The NGRI verdict has been the subject of controversy for some time. Its detractors have called for abolishing this legal determination as an unreasonable exemption from responsibility for one's personal actions. Supporters voice a need for understanding and compassion with regard to the mentally disordered which involves recognition that at some level of impairment people may not be responsible for what they do. The acrimony associated with the NGRI verdict, much like the death-penalty controversy, has been difficult to resolve, since positions on the issue often are based more upon emotion than critical analysis. In my opinion at least, this has led to compromise legal positions that attempt to placate both extreme viewpoints. Georgia, for example, has come to feature the "guilty-but-mentally-ill" sentence that requires incarceration commensurate with the crime but recognizes the offender's need for mental-health care while in prison. Punishment for criminal conduct is coupled with compassion for the criminal; both extreme views on the NGRI issue have been considered.

Whatever the fate of the NGRI determination, cases in which the courts have reached this verdict represent a promising source of information regarding fairness of adjudication in cases involving mental disorder. One of the more obvious questions to ask is whether offenders who have been acquitted in NGRI cases because their mental condition was held responsible for their offenses do or do not demonstrate other personal attributes in common with ordinary criminals that could just as readily be held responsible? In other words, is there a reasonable alternative explanation for their criminal conduct? It will come as no surprise that criminal dangerousness appealed to me as just such an alternative. The research question would be whether NGRI acquittees were dangerous enough to explain their violent conduct without taking mental disorder into consideration? If so, fairness of adjudication would require a closer look at personal accountability, since dangerousness does not exempt individuals from responsibility for their actions.

An investigation reported by Heilbrun and Heilbrun in 1989 followed up on the possibility of alternative explanation in NGRI cases by considering the dangerousness of the criminally-insane. Our reasoning went like this. The men who received an NGRI verdict when tried for their violent crimes had not been held accountable for their acts; their mental disorders absolved them from responsibility. Criminal dangerousness as a personal attribute had been verified by a considerable number of studies in our research program as a predictor of rule violation and criminal risk in general and violent criminality in particular (see Heilbrun, 1996). What if those who receive an NGRI verdict in trials of violent offenses prove to be just as dangerous as men held accountable for their violence and punished by imprisonment? This finding should qualify dangerousness as just as viable an explanation for offender violence in NGRI cases as their mental disorders. On the other hand, if NGRI acquittees proved to be less dangerous than their violent counterparts in prison, the argument for mental disorder as responsible for their violent conduct would be strengthened.

Methodology of the Study

The subjects in this study included over 50 male forensic patients obtained from three mental hospitals in Georgia and Florida. Each of these men had committed a violent crime (murder, manslaughter, assault, battery, rape, robbery, kidnaping, terroristic threat) but received an NGRI verdict when tried for his offense. Comparison subjects came from the files of the Georgia prison system; all had been tried for one of the same violent crimes and found to be guilty without any implied role of mental disorder in their offenses. The men in these samples were closely matched for average age (33–35 years) and average education (10–11 years); the forensic sample included 45% white patients and 55% black, whereas the sample from the general prison population was comprised of 64% white prisoners and 36% black.

The formula for criminal dangerousness was quite similar to that used in other studies within the program but not identical. The index included the dimensions of antisociality and intelligence as before, but a third dimension of social introversion/extroversion was added. The new dimension was found to strengthen predictions of dangerous conduct in prison with introversion escalating the risk involved (Heilbrun & Heilbrun, 1985).

Comparison of the NGRI patients who had engaged in violence to violent prison inmates with respect to criminal dangerousness provided a surprising result. It did not turn out that the NGRI acquittees were less dangerous than incarcerated violent prisoners, a finding that would lend strength to the argument that mental incompetence was responsible for their crimes of violence as the sentence requires. Nor did it turn out that the NGRI patients were just as dangerous as ordinary violent criminals, identifying dangerousness as a viable alternative to mental disorder when trying to explain the crimes of the forensic sample. Those who had been legally exempted from responsibility for their crimes proved to be **more** dangerous than men who had committed the same kinds of violent offenses but had been held accountable and sent to prison.

It is difficult to interpret these results as anything but bad tidings for advocates of compassion and understanding for those who suffer from mental disorder. Men whose violent actions were attributed to mental disorder and who received an exemption from responsibility because they were declared legally insane turned out to be especially dangerous in psychological disposition. Their violence could be readily explained by an enduring disposition to harmful behavior without invoking mental incompetence at the time of the crime as an exculpating factor. Keep in mind that the NGRI patients qualified as especially dangerous relative to violent criminals who made up the comparison group, a very high standard of dangerousness. To be substantially more dangerous than men incarcerated for violent crimes suggests a substantial risk of violent criminality in the NGRI patients.

What we have in these results is quite reminiscent of the findings reported by Heilbrun, Foster, and Golden in 1990 regarding the assignment of the death penalty to blacks who have been convicted of murdering white victims. That study considered the possibility of racial bias inherent in the disproportionately high number of capital punishment sentences reached for blacks by the Georgia courts in black-on-white murders. As discussed in Chapter 4, an alternative to unjust and unlawful racial bias was proposed as an explanation for disproportionate sentencing. Perhaps, it was reasoned, the black murderers of white victims were more criminally dangerous and therefore more capable of the inhuman displays that can attract the death penalty than whites who kill other whites. That was what we found. The extraordinary dangerousness of black interracial murderers in capital cases was gauged by comparison with the lofty standard of dangerousness set by other murderers who had received the death penalty. The contention that the Georgia courts had practiced systematic prejudice against blacks was weakened, if not disproved.

Since I would contend that the excessive dangerousness of NGRI patients qualifies this character flaw as the more compelling explanation for their violent conduct than their mental status, what does this say about courtroom bias? The propensity for violence among NGRI acquittees, ignored in determining the dynamics of their crimes and in subsequent court judgments, does seem to suggest an unfair bias protecting mentally-disordered criminals, explicitly encouraged by legal mandate and reinforced by compassion for the mentally ill.

I suppose a caveat offered previously merits repetition here in order to discourage overgeneralization from anything said to this point regarding fairness in adjudicating violent crime. Three possible examples of bias have been discussed, each open to interpretation as resulting from an unfair administration of justice—disproportionality of sentencing suggesting racial prejudice, less severe sentencing of women pointing to gender discrimination, and court verdicts offering protection to dangerous mentally-disordered offenders. The evidence on violent criminality suggests to me that unfair bias is more apparent than real when it comes to race and gender and that sanctioned bias goes too far when legal insanity verdicts are rendered. The caveat then: These pieces of evidence should not be taken to mean that racial prejudice or gender permissiveness never occurred in adjudicating individual cases of violence or that mental disorder should not be considered a satisfactory explanation for violence in others. Even clearcut results from scientific inquiries into human behavior include exceptions to the trend of evidence. Research bearing upon criminal justice is not "rocket science," but it is the best basis we have for drawing conclusions on the subject.

It may have come to your attention that the 1989 investigation by the Heilbruns into the insanity plea and criminal dangerousness as an alternative explanation of the crimes in question dealt with a range of violence extending from murder at one extreme with rape not far behind in public concern, down to robbery and terroristic threat in which the victim is exposed to the lesser psychological effects of menacing communication that only threatens physical harm. The purpose of this NGRI research had nothing to do with the death penalty at the time it was conducted, although it subsequently struck me that the results were potentially relevant to bias in capital sentencing. Evidence that shall be considered next, taken from my research files, is intended to close the conceptual distance between the NGRI results and protective bias in invoking the death penalty.

Dangerousness, Severe Violence, and Brutality of the Crime

The gap between the NGRI evidence and the current topic of fairness in adjudicating the death penalty could be bridged by a hypothetical study in which the mental status of murderers held responsible for their crimes and sentenced to be executed was compared with the mental status of others who were prosecuted for capital offenses but found not-guilty by reason of insanity. Presumably the NGRI acquittees would prove to be more mentally impaired, at least if the sentence is to have meaning. Even this study would miss the mark unless mental status at the time of the murder could be reliably formulated for purposes of scientific comparison.

Actually, the more critical evidence for extrapolating from the NGRI results to death-penalty bias would be a hypothetical comparison of dangerousness in murderers who were prosecuted for a capital offense but were acquitted because they were judged to be legally insane with the dangerousness of others who were held accountable for their crimes and received the death penalty. Do not get your hopes up though. I certainly do not have either kind of evidence in my files, and I would be surprised if such hypothetical studies have ever been conducted.

What was available in way of evidence concerned index-measured dangerousness and the risk of especially brutal displays of violence, and that is where we shall start this empirical odyssey. The question subjected to analysis was whether the level of dangerousness found in the NGRI acquittees, high even for violent criminals, would be associated with the excessive brutality of murders that attract the death penalty. If the same high level of dangerousness is found among men who receive NGRI verdicts and men who engage in more brutal displays of lethal violence and receive the death penalty, we can reach the following conclusion: The high level of dangerousness found in men who were acquitted of violence because they were considered legally insane would render them capable of the excessive violence that attracts capital punishment.

Dangerousness of the Murderer and Brutality of the Murder in Capital Cases

The choice between high dangerousness and mental disorder as explanations of violence perpetrated by men held to be criminally insane and not held responsible for their crimes has been broached as a fairness issue in assigning the death penalty. Since heightened criminal dangerousness has been shown to be a likely determinant of violent crime, it would appear that mental disorder is being assigned undue importance when NGRI verdicts are rendered. Extrapolating to murder cases, NGRI acquittees who have engaged in heinous acts of willful killing could have been heir to unfair decisions that negate the death penalty for murderers who are mentally disturbed. Too many men would not be held responsible for brutally killing a victim when the act is predictable based upon their dangerous character flaws.

The subjects in this follow-up analysis of Georgia capital punishment data included all of those on the state's death row at the time of the Heilbrun, Foster, and Golden (1990) study for whom the necessary file information could be found to derive a score for criminal dangerousness. This sample has been subjected to analysis before but not in its entirety; you may recall that only cases involving white victims were relevant. The crimes committed by these men were rated for cruelty involved in the slaying, with these ratings made on a five-point scale ranging from "no cruelty" (beyond killing the victim) to "excessive cruelty" (often involving torture or other painful or anguishing preludes).

The dangerousness scores for the death-row murderers were separated into three equal-size groupings representing low, intermediate, and high dangerousness in men convicted of this most violent of crimes. Preliminary examination of the cruelty ratings within these levels of dangerousness made it clear that rated cruelty of the crime did not differ at the lower two levels; death-row murderers at intermediate and low levels of dangerousness looked much the same as far as how much cruelty was displayed in killing their victims. Accordingly, I chose to compare the cruelty of the most dangerous murderers with that found for the rest of the death-row sample.

The less dangerous men who were sentenced to die for their lethal violence included 53% who received the highest rating possible, "excessive cruelty." About 32% received the lowest rating, "no cruelty." Even the less dangerous among the murderers on death row had engaged in excessive cruelty toward their victims in over half the cases. However, men in the upper tier of criminal dangerousness made the less-dangerous death-row inmates look constrained by comparison. Some 93% of the high-dangerous group engaged in homicides receiving the highest rated cruelty; not one qualified for the lowest rating. The ultra-dangerous among those convicted of capital murder and sentenced to death had almost invariably disposed of their homicide victims in the most cruel manner conceivable to the judges.

Given these dangerousness/brutality findings for death-row inmates, the risk of repugnant violence in men who are especially dangerous by index score comes into clearer focus. Although it has been a somewhat circuitous route that has been followed, the conclusion that the most dangerous of criminals are capable of the most vicious of violent crimes takes me back to the legal-insanity study and the significance of its results for mental disorder and the death penalty.

Men in the NGRI study were judged by the court to have been so mentally disordered at the time they engaged in some act of violence that they should not be held responsible for their actions. This judgment led to their acquittal and probably a long hospitalization. Yet despite the court view of these NGRI patients as non-criminals, the study found them to be more criminally dangerous than a comparison group of imprisoned violent offenders who set a rather lofty standard of criminal risk in themselves. The point now can be made that dangerousness at the high level found in the NGRI patients not only serves as an alternative explanation for all kinds of violence represented in the sample but that it also poses a more specific risk of deadly violence that is characterized by excessive cruelty toward the victim. This places violence of those considered by the courts to have been legally insane and not responsible for their crimes at the conceptual doorstep of capital punishment by not only qualifying dangerousness as an alternative explanation for their violence but also cautioning us regarding their vulnerability to excessive cruelty should they enter into willful killing. The burden of responsibility for violent conduct among mentally-disordered criminals is at issue here as is the risk of being responsible for a capital crime.

What I am suggesting could readily be construed as a lack of compassion for the mentally disordered, since it challenges the allowances made for their mental condition should they become involved in violent crimes. What I am opposed to is unjustified compassion for mentally-disordered offenders whose violence is not generated by their illness. Unjustified compassion results in unfair adjudication of criminal behavior, since they are not being held accountable for their actions as others are, oftentimes despite being dangerously disposed.

The Limitations of Either-or Thinking in Considering Mental Disorder/Criminal Dangerousness as Alternative Explanations of Violence

I have taken the opportunity to contemplate the results of the NGRI study on several occasions since the original paper was published in 1989, and my thinking on the accountability issue that it addressed has been modified to some extent. The conclusions have been presented to you in much their original form with dangerousness being offered as a viable alternative to mental disorder when incapacity is used to explain violence and eliminate legal responsibility for the act. It was dangerousness **versus** mental disorder. Although weighing these explanations as alternatives seemed then and seems now to be the clearest way to conceptualize the issue given the evidence that was available, it is certainly not the only way that the NGRI results could be interpreted. Fortunately for sake of clear exposition, it will become apparent that my conclusions about mental disorder and sentencing bias will remain the same whether the original or revised interpretation of those results is favored.

The interpretation problem stems from the fact that the NGRI patients were both mentally disordered **and** criminally dangerous. Dangerousness was chosen as the preferred explanation for their violent conduct largely because of the extraordinary level of the index score for the NGRI acquittees when compared to a control group of violent prisoners who were held responsible for their crimes and incarcerated. There was no intention of implying that mental disorder could never be an acceptable explanation for violence, only that it was a less important dynamic relative to dangerousness. Lost in an either-or mode of thought is the real possibility that dangerousness as a character flaw and mental disorder as impaired cognition may coalesce in some men so that the presence of both poses a risk of violence beyond that of either condition existing alone. Consideration of coalescent effects of mental disorder and criminal dangerousness lends itself to an interesting possibility. Serious mental disorders in those who are not predisposed to dangerous behavior may show themselves in any number of deviant behaviors, but violent conduct will not be prominent among them. Serious mental disorders in those who are also criminally disposed introduce an enhanced risk of violence.

These conclusions shed light on the issue of whether mentally-disordered people represent a special threat to society—the risk that they will engage in violent conduct. It would seem that both poles of this controversy, the compassionate defenders of the mentally ill and the ultraconcerned proponents of heightened security, have a point. The mentally disordered without dangerous predispositions need not attract any special concern about their affinity for violence. It is mental disorder in someone who is otherwise dangerously predisposed that can be a problem, and here special concern is warranted since they may mutually contribute to the danger of violence.

The NGRI results that instigated these conclusions about mental disorder and criminal dangerousness as independent yet potentially interactive psychological dispositions that can increase the risk of violence are important enough to call for replication. Do these psychological conditions coalesce in other criminal samples, especially in violent criminals? This question was addressed in preparing my 1996 book on criminal dangerousness by compiling two samples of prisoners from my files for whom the dangerousness index could be computed and for whom additional psychometric information was available to gauge the mental status of the prisoner. Scales from two venerable multiscale questionnaires, the Minnesota Multiphasic Personality Inventory (Hathaway & McKinley, 1951) and the California Psychological Inventory (Gough, 1957), were in the files for evaluating mental status.

One sample of prisoners represented a mixture of violent and nonviolent cases, half of each type. This group, then, had been responsible for crimes far-ranging in seriousness, and the analysis considered the question of whether extreme dangerousness would be associated with disturbed mental status in a fairly routine sample of prisoners. If so, it would argue for the positive correlation of dangerousness and mental disorder for criminals in general rather than for violent criminals in particular as was true for the NGRI sample. One index of mental status combined the scores of four scales from the Minnesota Inventory, each measuring (among other things) a different form of disturbed thought—delusional, obsessive, bizarre, or flighty. This combination of scales has been termed the "psychotic tetrad" (Dahlstrom & Welsh, 1960). A second index took the opposite tack by measuring "effective thought"; scores from two scales of the California Inventory were combined as a gauge of how well a prisoner was able to consider and understand the motivational basis for behavior, his own or that of others. To make a lengthening story shorter, the results of this analysis made it clear that high dangerousness measured by the index and more disturbed/less effective thinking tend to be found together in a mixed sample of violent and nonviolent criminals.

The second sample of prisoners drawn from my files included only violent criminals, men who had committed sex-offenses against adult women (rape/sodomy) or against female children (child molestation). The same indices of disturbed thinking and effective thought were computed along with the dangerousness score, and analysis of their relationship provided the same result as before. Highly dangerous sex-offenders demonstrated the greatest deficit in their quality of thought. With the commonality between these psychological characteristics twice replicated, it seems safe to conclude that men who are very dangerously disposed also tend to suffer in the quality of their thinking, at least if they are known to have committed a crime.

Finding that heightened dangerousness is frequently associated with impaired thinking in men who commit crimes, whether the offense is violent or not and whether they are held responsible or not, is not the ideal way of demonstrating that their coexistence introduces a greater risk to the victims of crime. It would have been better to determine whether individuals who are mentally disordered and criminally dangerous, as determined by independent measurement, are more likely to commit a crime, particularly a violent crime, in the future than individuals who may demonstrate only one or neither of these flaws. Furthermore, it would be important to know whether such dangerous/mentally-disordered men show an increased risk of more grievous harm to the victim should they commit a crime.

Even without empirical proof based upon future prediction, psychological analysis offers a rather convincing corroboration of the added criminal risk provided by coexistence of extraordinary degrees of dangerousness and disordered mental activity. The people described as being both dangerous and disordered are not only antisocial, with a disdain for social regulation and conventional moral imperatives, but also lack the intellectual resources to effectively judge the reasonableness of their criminal intent and how to deal with unforeseen consequences of their criminal actions. Add the distortions, fabrications, and limited reality testing of serious mental disorder to victim risk, and I find it difficult to understand how the psychological picture can be viewed as other than bleak.

I expressed the view several pages back that whether dangerousness and mental disorder were to be treated as alternative explanations of violent crime or as collaborative determinants of violence, the possibility of unfair bias remained. In the original interpretation of the NGRI results it was suggested that excessive criminal dangerousness had been overlooked by the verdict that did not hold the perpetrators of violence responsible for their acts; dangerous criminals would be expected to have some ability to appreciate the harm they are doing. The revised version would allow for both dangerousness and mental disorder to be assigned responsibility for the violence, since both were amply represented in the NGRI sample. Assigning responsibility when both dangerousness and mental disorder are involved requires consideration of how much each contributed to the criminal conduct, and this difficult differentiation still allows for bias to influence judgment. The point is this: As long as criminal dangerousness can be shown to have potentially influenced the expression of violence, independently or collaboratively, the assumption of diminished responsibility for the offender because of mental disorder is vulnerable to protective bias and unfair adjudication.

MENTAL DISORDER AND FAIR ADJUDICATION OF THE DEATH PENALTY—A SUMMARY

Mental disorder as a source of incompetence qualifies as a peculiarly difficult consideration in fairly adjudicating violent criminality in general and lethal violence deserving capital punishment in particular. I have emphasized three things that stand in the way of just sentencing when mental illness enters the picture.

If extremes of cognitive impairment are to be considered as influential determinants of violent behavior, it is necessary to gain a reliable assessment of the mental disorder for any given case. Reliability, understood as agreement among experts, can be a problem. Symptoms of a disorder may be blatant during a florid period, abate to more subtle display as the person shows improvement over time, or even disappear if the condition goes into full remission. This variability contributes to unreliability of diagnosis as the disorder waxes and wanes; different experts may be exposed to different symptoms at different times. That is not the only source of unreliability, however. Clinicians may disagree over the meaning of a symptom even when it is apparent to all. Diagnostic manuals help but are no guarantee of agreement from one expert to the next. The importance of identifying a mental disorder, judging its severity, and deriving implications from these observations for criminal conduct is obvious; if the observations are unreliable, people are unlikely to be considered fairly with respect to their mental condition.

Sentencing for a crime when mental disorder is a consideration depends upon cognitive competence at the time of the offense, not when the accused person is in custody and awaiting trial. This aggravates the problem of reliability even further as assessment of mental disorder requires that the assessor must retrospectively shift the relevant period of observation back in time to reconstruct the mental condition before it can be related to the crime in question. The difficulties of reestablishing psychological status after a passage of time are enormous, especially when the condition is subject to variability and not governed by the usual principles of behavior. This, of course, will depend upon the quality of information available for making the assessment. A man may have escaped from a mental hospital where he had undergone intensive observation just prior to committing a violent act; that would be helpful information. On the other hand, there may only be the circumstances of the crime to work with in reaching conclusions about mental competence. Adding to the inferential dilemma facing this type of assessment is the fact that the accused perpetrator is potentially the best source of information concerning past mental state. A factual report from this source may not be in order, however; as long as treatment for the mentally disabled is perceived as a possible alternative to punishment, the person being assessed may not be motivated by honesty. Current mental status may not even allow cooperative reinstatement of past mental condition.

The evidence on criminal dangerousness of violent NGRI patients added a further complication that became apparent when fair adjudication of violence was considered for the mentally disordered. Dangerousness was found to be even more apparent in men who engaged in violence but were not held responsible because they were considered legally insane at the time of the crime than in inmates who were held responsible for the same range of violence and punished by imprisonment. The NGRI patients qualified as serious risks for harming others, although dangerousness as an alternative explanation was apparently ignored in reaching the verdict that exonerated them. This association of heightened levels of impaired mentation and criminal dangerousness found in the NGRI study was replicated in two further samples of prisoners. One sample included both violent and nonviolent men, and the other was made up of men who were convicted of sexual violence toward women or female children.

Interpretation of the NGRI results originally warned of the potential unfairness of accepting mental disorder as the basis for dismissing responsibility for violent acts when an alternative explanation, criminal dangerousness, would hold the NGRI acquittees responsible for their actions. Revised interpretation embraced the possibility that mental disorder and dangerousness could represent a risk-enhancing combination that led to violence. Either interpretation, however, would require that the contribution of dangerousness be factored into the decision concerning responsibility for the crime in order to diminish the chances of unfair adjudication. Perhaps "guilty but mentally ill" has more merit as a verdict than simply being a compromise between forces of compassion and required responsibility in cases of crimes committed by the mentally disordered.

Chapter Seven

Fair Practice in Adjudicating the Death Penalty: Mental Retardation as a Competence Issue

Consideration of mental retardation as a competence issue in adjudicating criminal behavior might seem like a much less complicated matter compared to mental disorder given the diagnostic pitfalls that have been described for disturbed mentation. There should be less reason for debates over the symptom picture in mental retardation, how these interdependent symptoms combine to form a particular syndrome, and what the implications might be for the antisocial conduct of the retarded person. Perhaps of greatest importance to the adjudication process, little guesswork should be required regarding what the psychological status of the person might have been back when the crime was committed. Whereas mental disorder typically varies in intensity and incapacitating effects over time and situations, mental retardation is a more stable condition. If a person is retarded now, that person was most likely retarded at the time of the crime. Finally, it is at least assumed by some that to establish mental retardation all that is required is the administration of an intelligence measure under standard conditions and comparison of the resulting IQ to an accepted cutting score. Performance below this score, often taken to be an IQ of 70, would point to retardation. There should be less temptation to limit the diagnosis of mental disorder to a single test score.

Despite the seemingly simplified diagnostic requirements, the fair adjudication of criminal offenses involving mentally retarded offenders will turn out to be far more complicated than the picture drawn to this point would lead you to expect. In fact, one of the obstacles to fair treatment within the criminal justice system when limitation of intellectual function becomes involved is the oversimplified manner of dealing with mental retardation that seems to prevail. Resulting errors of commission or omission can result in treatment within the justice system that is too lenient or too harsh. Those who are familiar with the issues of retardation and the law may not be surprised by my selection of obstacles to accurate evaluation and just treatment. However, recognizing problems brought about by oversimplification and correcting them are two different things.

Involvement of Mental Retardation in the Adjudication Process and Possible Problems of Simplification

The Cutting-Score Problem

We commonly encounter the use of a particular score along a continuum of scores as the basis for assigning a person to some category. A certain weight (considered in terms of height) can define an "obese person." A particular score on an ability test may qualify the person for membership in some elite organization. Sometimes cutting-score procedures are part of a more elaborate classification scheme in which scores are employed to assign people or other objects to one of a series of categories that constitute some meaningful progression. That has been the rule with intelligence tests as ranges of IQ scores are designated by particular cutting points along a dimension of intellectual competence. When the intelligence dimension is treated in this way, the IQ scores that designate the range of intellect are to some extent arbitrary, but, nonetheless, the procedure continues to provide useful classification schemes based upon intellectual capability. For example, people by one such scheme would be ordered by IQ into retarded, borderline defective, dull normal, average, bright normal, superior, or very superior categories (Knopf, 1979). Whatever the number of categories to be included in a classification scheme, several rules remain inviolate; the IQ scores to be used to designate a category must remain fixed, must be contiguous but not overlap, and must have values that satisfy some logical or theoretical principle.

Special interests may make it valuable to focus upon a particular IQ range along the intelligence dimension and to introduce a more refined breakdown of category. The manual of the American Association on Mental Deficiency, to illustrate such a refinement, proposed four levels of retardation rather than one— mild (IQ = 52–67), moderate (IQ = 36–51), severe (IQ = 20–35), and profound (IQ = less than 20) (Grossman, 1973). We are told that about 90% of all retardates have IQs that fall in the mild category, perhaps 6% test in the moderate range, and the remaining 4% qualify as severely or profoundly retarded. (These percentage figures will become relevant further along in the chapter.) Reasonably consistent with the more refined AAMD classification scheme, an IQ of 70 has become a popular cutting score for identifying mental retardation within the criminal justice system.

Employing IQ cutting scores to establish categories of intelligence can serve a useful purpose in guiding decisions regarding learning potential and adaptive capabilities as long as it is remembered that these are test scores and variations in individual test performance can occur—that a person's IQ is a reasonably stable but not rigidly fixed figure. Our concern at this point is with the dependence on IQ scores that fall near a cutting point, especially when a critical judgment based upon category is at stake. An example of oversimplification in assessing criminal dynamics would be to accept a person's IQ of 70, the conventional cutting score for retardation, as unqualified evidence for the role of mental retardation in the crime. The most obvious folly associated with this simplifying assumption is that it would follow that a criminal with an IQ of 70 might merit mitigation in sentencing for a crime based upon limited mental competence but another criminal with a 71 IQ would not. Given the suspiciousness concerning the authenticity of test scores in general that exists in some quarters and the variability of the IQ score, such rigid dependence on the meaning of a particular score seems particularly ludicrous.

While this example of naive dependence on a cutting score can be recognized as a parody of classification in forensic assessment and not a commonplace mistake, an actual example will be forthcoming that is reminiscent of such absolute commitment. The fact of the matter is that competent assessment homing in on intellectual competence and criminal responsibility of an offender would only use an intelligence test score as a guide in reaching conclusions and not as a basis for making a retarded/not retarded discrimination. Whether offenders are able to grasp the meaning of participation in a criminal act, can contribute to their own defense, or can understand the punishment that is to be meted out for their crimes not only depends upon level of tested intelligence but must be further evaluated by means of case history information and skilled questioning by the assessor.

The IQ and resulting intelligence category, then, is only part of the retardation picture and should be considered along with other types of information when it comes to fairly adjudicating criminal behavior in the individual case. There may be times, especially for the forensic researcher or scholar, when IQ is the only piece of data you have relevant to mental competence. Conclusions based upon IQ scores alone across sufficient numbers of offenders can be useful as long as it is conservatively noted that the data are imprecise and exceptions are to be expected.

An example at this point of overdependence on an IQ cutting score for defining mental retardation is in order. It will illustrate how competent scholars/practitioners can get caught up in oversimplification and reach biased conclusions in the individual case when (in my opinion, at least) they are emotionally invested in their opposition to the death penalty. I chose an actual professional anecdote to exemplify the cutting-score problem because the consultant who performed the forensic assessment in question was an academic colleague, and I have some first-hand information because of that.

The case in question was that of Jerome Bowden, a 55-year-old black offender, who had been convicted in Columbus, Georgia, of murdering a white woman and sentenced to death. We are told by those who have recounted the circumstances of the trial (Miller & Radelet, 1993; Perske, 1991) that there were several issues bearing upon whether he was responsible for the crime and with his death sentence as a consequence. There was a confession without much corroborating evidence, an alternative suspect, an IQ of 57. Obviously, whatever legal appeals there might have been prior to 1987 had not been successful, since a final last-minute appeal was made for clemency from execution in June of that year based upon the mental retardation of the prisoner. A stay of execution was granted by the Georgia Board of Pardons and Paroles, and an assessment of Bowden's mental competence was scheduled. It is this assessment and its aftermath that were discussed critically by forensic scholars, targeted for criticism by the news media, and even heralded as an issue in a concert tour of celebrities sponsored by Amnesty International. We are told that the Parole Board received hundreds of protest letters from around the world, no doubt the result of this widespread notoriety. The common themes woven into the protests were opposition to capital punishment and compassion for the mentally retarded.

To get to the assessment itself, the prisoner was administered the best individual intelligence test available for adults and received a full-scale IQ of 65. This placed Bowden high in the retarded range according to the classification scheme used by the test and, more specifically, defined his retardation as "mild" within the classification system of the American Association on Mental Deficiency. The prisoner's prior IQ of 57 also fell within the mildly retarded range. The more current IQ of 65 came close to the conventional 70 cutting score, but since it did fall in the retarded range it could have been interpreted as a basis for clemency from execution if it were assumed that the state should not execute anyone who is mentally retarded.

However, assessment went beyond obtaining an IQ. A verbal inquiry considered the prisoner's grasp of the difference between right and wrong, functional cause-and-effect relationships relevant to the crime, and the meaning of execution. This part of the assessment has been generally ignored by critics; the prisoner was found to be capable of comprehending the basic realities essential to his crime and its punishment. When the results of intelligence testing and the verbal inquiry were reported to the Parole Board along with the consultant's conclusions, it was decided that the prisoner was mentally competent enough to understand his situation and why he was to be put to death for his crime. He was returned to a state prison for immediate execution. There may be aspects of Bowden's exposure to the criminal justice system that warrant criticism, but the 1987 assessment of mental competence is not one of them. He was mildly retarded to be sure, but his fundamental cognitive grasp of relevant social realities was judged to be sufficient despite his retardation. Denouncing an assessment that met professional standards as well as the actions of the Parole Board that were legally responsive to its conclusions represent unwarranted criticisms; apparently nothing short of mercy in this case would satisfy those adamantly opposed to the death penalty.

One more comment about the Bowden assessment is in order, since it further elucidates how sentiment on an issue like the death penalty can encourage criticisms that are misinformed, biased, and damaging. While I am mystified how access was gained to a confidential document such as the consultant's report to the Parole Board, the Perske book makes reference to specific statements that reflect unfavorably upon the assessor and the Parole Board when presented out of context. The assessment report, in reflecting on the obtained IQ of 65, is said to have expressed the opinion that it would have taken an IQ of 45 before a reprieve from execution would have been recommended. Perske, in criticizing this statement, suggested that the difference between the obtained IQ of 65 and the hypothetical requirement of a 45 IQ gave the Parole Board too much cushion for their decision regarding whether the prisoner's IQ was high enough to allow the execution to proceed. Bowden, in other words, was made to appear even more capable than his retarded IQ of 65 would indicate simply because it stood in contrast to the lower figure.

Overlooked in this criticism was the Supreme Court ruling (**Penry versus Lynaugh**, 1989) regarding execution of the mentally retarded that prevailed at the time of Perske's book in 1991. The Court held that the "cruel and unusual punishment" stipulation of the Eighth Amendment would likely prohibit the execution of the severely retarded (IQ = 20–35) or profoundly retarded (IQ = less than 20) who would not be able to appreciate the wrongfulness of their actions and why they were being executed for their conduct. The fact is that the prisoner's measured intelligence was 30 IQ points higher than the upper limit for showing leniency; furthermore, Bowden's awareness of the difference between right and wrong and his grasp of why he was being executed had been established to the assessor's satisfaction by the assessment interview. The IQ of 45, proposed by the report as the level of retardation required for the assessor's recommendation of clemency, was on the lenient side, actually above the range stipulated by the Supreme Court as meriting special dispensation from execution. Neither the assessment nor the Parole Board decision violated professional or legal standards as it turns out. Whether moral standards were breached depends upon which side of the death-penalty fence you are on and how tenacious your views happen to be.

The purpose of including the Bowden case was not to "beat the drum" for either side of the death-penalty controversy, however. It was selected to illustrate how dependence on a conventional IQ cutting score for defining retardation in the individual case without being more specific regarding degree or without elaboration by further evidence can open the way to seemingly unwarranted and attitude-driven conclusions about crime and its punishment.

The Overgeneralization Problem

Knopf (1979), in summarizing his discussion of mental retardation, begins by describing it as a heterogeneous condition with "many different patterns of assets and liabilities." This understanding of retardation would lead us to expect not only a lack of uniformity between retardates but also variation within the performance of a retarded individual except perhaps at the severe or profound extremes. Scores, then, representing the cognitive and cognitive-motor skills measured by the intelligence test and other tests selected for assessment will demonstrate some unevenness in their implications with regard to the individual's effectiveness. The same thing would be expected as the adaptive skills of the person are considered by interview; mental retardation may have a more serious impact on some aspects of self-sufficiency and social living than on others.

Given these expectations regarding variable limitations, the challenge of making a helpful assessment of mental competence when a retarded offender comes to the attention of the criminal justice system would be twofold. First, it would be necessary to establish the pattern of relative "assets and liabilities" shown by the offender. Then, it would be necessary to judge which aspects of the pattern are most relevant to the decision that must be reached involving the competence of the offender. If these two goals are satisfied, the way would be open to making a more enlightened statement regarding how offender mental competence bears upon whatever action is being considered. As you might guess, if clinical judgment drew its implications from the IQ alone, it would run a greater risk of being in error. Too much inference is being predicated upon too narrow a band of evidence. No matter how well-regarded the IQ may be as a reliable and valid gauge of intelligence, it remains a summary score that does not in itself reflect shadings of asset and liability. Failure to recognize the narrow base of inference offered by the IQ taken alone increases the risk of overgeneralization—the failure to make proper allowances for the retardate's pattern of psychological assets and liabilities.

I have emphasized the importance of two things in evaluating the competence of the retarded offender—establishing a pattern of relative assets and liabilities from formal measures and instituting less formal inquiry into everyday facets of competence. Both procedures allow improvement over the use of IQ alone in drawing conclusions about the offender and what can and cannot be expected in way of behavior. There is an added complication that makes a broader sampling of information even more important. The type and breadth of information required regarding mental competence of the retarded offender depends somewhat upon the answer to a legal question—competence for what? Some demands of fair treatment within criminal justice systems that hinge upon offender competence would require a more extensive exposition of assets and liabilities than others. If more elaborated information is important to deciding whether an offender's retardation merits special consideration, the problem of overgeneralizing from an IQ score alone becomes even more acute.

Specifying some of the legal situations in which the offender's intellectual competence might warrant close examination should make this last point more readily understood. I will use a hypothetical case in which a killing has been committed by a man thought to be intellectually impaired. An early issue that might call for assessment is whether the offender is competent to stand trial; is he capable of understanding trial proceedings and of assisting his counsel in defending against charges by the prosecution? Assessment would involve an evaluation of the offender's comprehension in general and rudimentary grasp of legal procedures in particular, quality of memory, self-insight, etc.—functions necessary for some collaboration with the defense counsel. A simple IQ score is not going to be enough here unless, perhaps, it points to severe or profound retardation (IQ of 35 or less) and the futility of a formal trial.

Another legal situation in which mental competence of the retarded offender may be subject to evaluation has to do with guilt or innocence and, if guilty, with the question of how much responsibility he should bear for the killing, the issue of mitigation. This seems especially complicated since the criminal act partitions logically into several sequential steps, and the cognitive/social liabilities and assets of the retarded person could vary in importance from one step to the next. Was the offender capable of planning and premeditation in this killing? Was he able to anticipate the legal consequences of the fatal act? Did the violence escalate because the offender was not prepared to deal with the victim's resistance or provocation? Did the offender experience remorse or fear of arrest suggesting an awareness of its seriousness? Without trying to itemize the specific psychological functions that would be important at each of these steps, it should be clear that an IQ number alone is not likely to satisfy the requirements to provide the information required for assigning degrees of responsibility at each stage of lethal violence.

Yet another type of legal situation in which mental retardation could become an issue is competence for execution. Here the question becomes whether the offender can understand why his life is to be taken and whether he has a rudimentary sense of what dying really means. (One anecdote I came across in the literature had the prisoner acknowledge his forthcoming execution that day but follow this by a comment regarding his breakfast the next morning.) Competence for execution was apparently at stake in the Jerome Bowden case that was discussed previously.

There are aspects of decision-making in determining competence for execution that transcend what might appear to be fairly simple inquiries into awareness of what crime and punishment represent and what it means to die. My impression is that actions taken within the justice system near the execution point in the capital punishment progression are driven more by desperation than by enlightened appeal to legal precedent. One reason I say this is that mental retardation profound enough to deny execution should have called for some special dispensation in assigning responsibility to the offender long before consummation of the sentence. If prosecution for a capital offense was the choice, if mitigation was deemed insufficient by the jury to not only reach a guilty verdict for murder but to choose capital punishment as the sentence, and if subsequent appeals of the trial proceedings have not been successful, then the retardate's competence must have been weighed previously and found to satisfy some minimal standard. Raising the issue of competence for execution remains the last bulwark against consummating the sentence, and response to the appeal would probably have as much to do with facing the pressures from those who oppose capital punishment as it does with the psychological status of the offender.

In my opinion the reason the guidelines for carrying out the death penalty for mentally-impaired criminals are blurred by moral debate has as much to do with the protection of society as with protection of the criminal. The Supreme Court, as a final arbiter of legal proceedings, has been asked to rule upon the constitutionality of numerous aspects of the capital punishment system, including the issue of competence for execution. Their rulings in the 1989 **Penry versus Lynaugh** appeal, in which the petitioner possessed an IQ of 54, clearly supported the consideration of mental retardation as a mitigating factor in deciding death-penalty cases. However, the Court rejected the claim that the Eighth Amendment categorically prohibits execution of retarded offenders. It was conceded in the majority opinion though that the execution of those who are profoundly retarded would likely be prohibited as "cruel and unusual punishment" by the Eighth Amendment because they would be unable to understand or appreciate the wrongfulness of their actions.

Keeping in mind the classifications of the retarded offered previously, this Supreme Court ruling would prevent the execution of someone with an IQ under 20, the definition of profound retardation. This "rock-bottom" level of measured intelligence, along with severe retardation (IQs from 20–35), also would seem to qualify for the common-law prohibition against punishing "idiots" for misbehavior that was referenced in the Court's majority report. Yet one could wonder about the reference to severe or even worse retardation and what it has to do with the Penry appeal, since his IQ was well above these levels. Perhaps the answer to that can be found in the opinions handed down by the Supreme Court in the 1986 **Ford versus Wainwright** decision.

At the time of the 1986 appeal no state allowed the death penalty to be exacted if the offender was judged to be insane at the time of the crime and not responsible for his act. In **Ford versus Wainwright**, however, the question raised was whether the prisoner was competent for execution, since the prisoner is said to have become mentally disturbed while on death row. Even though this case hinged on mental disorder rather than retardation, the specific question regarding mental competence posed by the appeal should be relevant to both conditions. Reference to common law in the majority opinion explained the Court's decision that execution could not be carried out if the offender is insane. Three reasons found in common law were given for the ruling: (1) The retribution value for society must be questioned when you execute those who have no comprehension of why they have been singled out for dying; (2) civilized societies feel a natural abhorrence for killing people who have no ability to come to grips with their own conscience or deity; (3) intuitively it appears that nations generally view execution of the insane to be an offense against humanity. The humanitarian quality of these common-law references is undeniable, yet it does seem that the sensibilities of society are being protected here by the prohibition against executing the mentally ill much more than the rights of the mentally-ill offender. By executing someone who is deemed mentally incompetent, society would be denied retribution value, exposed to a natural abhorrence, and complicitous in an inhumane act.

When the majority report in the **Ford versus Wainright** case considered the Court's decision in light of the Eighth Amendment rather than common law, the issue of who was being protected by the Constitution remained. It was conceded that the Court's ruling was intended to protect the dignity of society from the barbarity of mindlessly wreaking vengeance upon a helpless individual. The second aim, seemingly in line with the mandate against cruel and unusual punishment of an offender, was to protect the mentally-incompetent person from fear and pain while awaiting execution without the comfort that comes from understanding why he or she was being put to death. Just how much "comfort" is generated by knowing that you are going to be executed because you killed someone would be an interesting, if heartless, thing to investigate. In fact, there seems to be a prevailing sentiment in legal writing about the death penalty and readiness for execution that the prisoners' awareness regarding what is transpiring represents their immutable right much like a fair trial and appeal based upon legal grievances. Whether being aware of the gruesome realities of capital punishment for the person who is to be executed represents a curse or a blessing is open to debate. Despite the altruistic rationale for requiring lucidity before execution can proceed, it could be argued that it would be more humane to allow the prisoner to experience whatever degree of unreality that mental disorder or mental retardation may allow. However, if retribution is paramount in exacting the death penalty, as common law was said to require, then a lucid offender is what you want.

Discontinuity of Meaning as a Problem

In case you have lost track, we are considering the problems associated with the seemingly simple procedure of using an IQ score to define mental retardation and to establish degrees of intellectual limitation within this broader range of impairment. Belaboring these kinds of problem should not be taken as a repudiation of intelligence testing per se. The problems considered to this point can be magnified by the consumer of psychometric information but kept within reasonable limits by judicious use of testing results. Rigid adherence to a discrete IQ cutting score in the individual case may be convenient for expository emphasis, but it subjects interpretation to the risks introduced by unreliability when the IQ falls near that cutting score. Interpretation of mental competence based upon the IQ score alone without a more extended probe of the assets and limitations of the retarded individual runs the risk of overgeneralizing the extent of impairment from restricted evidence. The risk of overgeneralization from IQ alone is further complicated by the need to distinguish between the patterns of impairment that would be relevant for assessing criminal responsibility, competence for trial participation, or readiness for execution of sentence in capital cases.

Moving on to yet another problem inherent in fairly adjudicating the crimes committed by people of diminished intellect, particularly violence which may be serious enough to attract capital prosecution, we encounter what may be called discontinuity of meaning for IQ scores. I am referring here to the possibility that IQ score differences between people with subnormal intelligence take on a different meaning as far as criminal behavior goes depending upon whether they occur above or below the arbitrary dividing point of 70. If decreasing IQ below 70 assumes one type of meaning that is absent when decreasing IQs between 90 and 71 are considered, it could have implications for criminal justice. The issue comes down to this: Should retardates be treated by the justice system as categorically different from others with subnormal intelligence who do not qualify officially as retarded?

Let me begin clarifying matters by reiterating a point made earlier in this section on the use of IQ in defining mental retardation. The IQ is a continuous score, but for sake of expedience in understanding, communication, and action we treat intelligence level categorically by adopting specific IQ scores that set off ranges of intelligence. Retarded, borderline, dull-normal, normal, bright-normal, superior, and very superior represent elements of one system of classification in which the categories encompass the entire range of IQ scores; profoundly retarded, severely retarded, moderately retarded, and mildly retarded were described previously as another classification system imposed upon continuous IQ scores of 67 or below. Both the intelligence quotient and the two systems of categorization represent human devices introduced as ways of expressing neuropsychological potential as a quantitative score. These score-defined categories derive meaning from differences in behavior that show up in individuals along the intelligence dimension.

Here is where we get to the discontinuity in meaning that may exist. Allowances can be made for degrees of retardation with offenders showing an IQ of 70 or below, especially as far as mitigation of criminal responsibility goes. The further the IQ falls below 70, the less the person should be held accountable for an offense; the correspondence between falling IQ and decreasing responsibility becomes part of score meaning. However, if offender IQ is below normal but above 70, this meaning may be lost; the IQ is not likely to assume mitigating importance as scores above the dividing point decrease in value toward 70. In short, declining IQ scores between 90 and 71 take on a different meaning. But the rejoinder here might be that it is a different interpretive context, since the IQ category of 70 or below includes the "mentally retarded"; diminishing scores mean increasing degrees of retardation. This overlooks the obvious; the 70-or-below categorization is arbitrary, a matter of diagnostic convenience, and not a fact of nature.

Is there a "disconnect" in the meaning of decreasing IQs as far as criminal behavior is concerned when the lower reaches of the intelligence dimension are considered as opposed to the adjacent range of competence somewhat higher on the dimension? Put another way, is lower intelligence treated as a more certain basis for mitigation of criminal conduct as IQs below 70 are considered but lack this meaning when subnormal IQs above that dividing point are considered —IQs 71–90? If so, discontinuity of meaning would present a problem in fairness of adjudication.

My suspicion that decreasing intelligence might assume importance for explaining violent criminal conduct across a broader range of disability than just the mentally retarded is readily explained. Intelligence is one of the two factors included in the index of criminal dangerousness that was a mainstay of my research program into crime and violence. The IQ score was not considered independently but was entered into the quantitative index in combination with an antisociality score in deriving a dangerousness indicator. Dangerousness was studied, then, as an interactive disposition of the individual. Even so, the quantification procedures in deriving the final index score mathematically require that those with lower IQs will be prone to more serious violence, since the success of the index in discriminating between criminals showing differing degrees of violence has been amply demonstrated (Heilbrun, 1996). What has not been emphasized previously is that retardates, defined by IQ score, were rarely represented in the thousands of prisoners that were studied. This means that whatever contribution low intelligence made to the risk of violence severity depended in large measure upon mental limitations of nonretarded criminals with IQs above 70.

This logical analysis of how intelligence has entered into dangerousness index scoring and the prediction of violence puts the issue of discontinuous meaning in a clearer light as far as I am concerned. The courts have helped to ensure that mitigation of violence is considered for the retarded as intelligence decreases and responsibility for criminal action wanes. Dangerousness studies require the assumption that decreasing intelligence in nonretarded men with IQs between 71–90 is associated with increasing risk of serious violence. Should decreasing level of intelligence be taken into consideration by more lenient sentencing guidelines for violent offenders who are subnormal in intelligence but not mentally defective by conventional standards?

Some Empirical Evidence on Limited Intelligence and Fairness in Adjudication

I do not have research results that will allow me to address all of the proposed problems associated with the oversimplified use of intelligence cutting scores in adjudicating responsibility and sentencing for serious criminal violence. It will be possible to examine two questions relating to the discussion with the evidence in hand. Am I correct in assuming that the risk of serious violence increases as level of intelligence drops? Considering only lethal violence, is it true that men with below-normal intelligence who are not retarded by conventional standards fail to receive the advantage of mitigation for their crimes?

Intelligence and Severity of Violent Crime

The relation between intelligence and violence severity was established by ordering the records of about 1100 male criminals found in my files by the seriousness of their violent offenses according to the table of severity maintained by the Georgia Board of Pardons and Paroles. When a criminal had a history of more than one crime, he was assigned to a severity level based upon his most serious offense. Three levels of violence were established for the first analysis—murder with a life sentence; a middle range of violence including rape, voluntary manslaughter, robbery, assault, and battery; and the least severe crimes involving unpremeditated or otherwise mild violence such as involuntary manslaughter, vehicular homicide, or noncontact sexual offenses.

The usual way of reporting IQ comparisons would be in terms of averages, but percentages of men with low, normal, and high intellect offered a more informative way of organizing the results. That way the reader will have a better idea of the numbers of criminals at each violence severity level who can be expected to present some limitation in intelligence. The IPAT Intelligence Test (Cattell & Cattell, 1958), which served as the basis for all IQ scores, has been used for many years in the Georgia prison system as a culture-free estimate of intellect. The percentages reported in Table 10 represent the proportion of men at each crime severity level whose IQ scores fall: (1) below the normal range of intelligence (IQ = 90 or less), including those who are retarded, borderline, or dull-normal; (2) in the normal range (IQ = 91–110); or (3) above the normal range (IQ = 111 or greater), including those who are bright-normal or superior.

Examination of Table 10 suggests an inverse relationship between severity of violent crime and intelligence of the perpetrator, although this is only apparent when the below-normal and above-normal extremes are compared. Reading vertically, men with below-average IQ gravitated toward more serious violence; the percentage of subnormal offenders convicted of murder was more than three times the percentage found guilty of low-severity violence. In contrast, men with above-normal intelligence demonstrated the opposite pattern. The percentage figure for men committing low-severity violence was almost twice that found for murder when criminals with above-normal IQs were considered. The table can be read horizontally as well with the same implication. Murder sentences were handed down slightly more often to criminals with below-normal intelligence than to criminals falling above the normal range. Intermediate-level violence was found 3–4 times more often in the above-normal offenders than in their subnormal counterparts. Low-level violence appeared 5–6 times more frequently among the higher-IQ criminals than among the

Table 10.   Severity of Criminal Offenses and Level of Intelligence

	Percentage at Each Intelligence Level		
Criminal Severity	Below Normal (IQ = 90 or Less)	Normal (IQ = 91–110)	Above Normal (IQ = 111 or More)
High (Murder)	29%	44%	27%
Intermediate (Rape, Assault, etc.)	13%	41%	46%
Low (Involuntary Manslaughter, Vehicular Homicide, etc.)	9%	41%	50%

lower-IQ criminals. Examined either vertically or horizontally, limited intelligence was associated with more serious violence. This was especially obvious when murder was considered.

Another way to analyze the relationship between intelligence and severity of violence was offered by reexamining a different sample of violent men—the death-row sample used to consider racial bias and possible unfair adjudication of the death penalty. This will be partially redundant since IQ was part of the dangerousness index that was central to the earlier analysis, although IQ was not considered independently of antisociality. The death-row sample was split into the same three intelligence levels—below normal (IQ = 90 or less), normal (IQ = 91–110), and above normal (IQ = 111 or greater)—and the percentages falling into those categories were calculated. The results showed below-normal offenders made up 36% of the death-row sample, normal offenders 38%, and above-normal offenders 27%. If we concern ourselves with the extremes, it turned out that men with below-normal intelligence were more frequently represented in the death-row sample of murderers than those with above-normal intellect.

This finding is consistent with those obtained in the preceding analysis in which lower intelligence was associated with more severe violence, especially murder, but there is a difference. Mitigation of violence in some capital cases based upon retarded status of the offender would be expected because of Supreme Court rulings. Mitigation based upon low intelligence would have spared some murderers from a death sentence and inclusion in the death-row sample. Such exclusions would affect the below-normal category of this second analysis, but no one of above-normal intelligence would be similarly exempted. Accordingly, the greater frequency of prisoners on death row with a below-normal IQ was found **despite** the possible counteractive effect of mitigation based upon mental retardation. The distribution of IQs in the capital punishment sample most likely underestimates the contingency between low intelligence and commission of severe violence.

Mitigation of Lethal Violence in Nonretarded Men Having Below-Normal Intelligence

Two types of evidence have been presented supporting the general thesis that more serious violence tends to be perpetrated by less intelligent men. Convicted murderers included slightly more men with below normal than with above-normal intelligence. Less serious levels of violence were committed by criminals who were far more likely to be of above-normal intellect. Another sample of death-row murderers, who can be considered the most violent criminals of all, was made up of more men with below-normal than above-normal intelligence.

These results were obtained despite the counteractive effects of mitigated sentencing for retarded men who committed serious violence; mitigation would have spared them from capital punishment and from inclusion in the below-normal group.

The next question is whether the criminal justice system does or does not consider limited intelligence to be a mitigating factor in adjudicating lethal violence when offender IQ falls above the range conventionally regarded as retarded (IQ = 70 or below). This can certainly be considered a fairness-of-adjudication matter, since it bears upon what happens when the courts confront criminals with "shortcomings" in intelligence, subnormal but not retarded by conventional standards? My supposition has been that little cognizance is taken of offender intelligence in cases of violent crime unless conventionally-defined retardation is at issue; simply being subnormal will not mean much. If so, the implications of IQ variation change at a score of 70. Decreasing scores might call for greater leniency below that point but have little importance in adjudicating cases for those whose IQs fall above this point but who still have below-normal mental competence. Whether shadings of intellectual grasp and criminal responsibility should be treated in a categorically different way within these two ranges of subpar intelligence—retarded as opposed to borderline/dull-normal—would become an issue of discontinuous meaning.

What kind of evidence would bear upon the discontinuity issue? Access to court sentencing deliberations in a substantial number of trials involving violent offenders with IQs that fall short of the normal range might be helpful, although the suggestion is not very practical; such private deliberations are not likely to be made public nor should they be. My approach to studying discontinuity of meaning began by taking the stronger mitigation of lethal violence in retarded men as IQs decreased for granted. This protection is in line with Supreme Court ruling and common law. Attention was turned to whether some weight in adjudicating lethal violence is given to declining intelligence in the range of IQ scores between 71 and 90, subnormal but not retarded. If a mitigation effect is present, it might be expected to show up in the decreasing number of offenders held fully responsible for their lethal violence as intelligence declines. Considered in simple terms, mitigation would require that fewer men of borderline intelligence (IQ = 71–80) who kill should be held fully responsible for the act than would be the case for men with dull-normal intelligence (IQ = 81–90) who kill. Full responsibility, including premeditation and intent, would call for a sentence of murder; accordingly, a sample of men convicted of murder should include fewer men with borderline than dull-normal IQs if lower intelligence has been considered mitigation for the killing.

There could be complicating factors in trying to infer the fact of mitigation from sentencing outcome alone for violent crimes. For one thing, mitigation does not require that the offender be freed from criminal responsibility. It often results in a reduction in severity of the violence for which the offender is held responsible—manslaughter rather than murder, for example. Just how can a researcher distinguish between a sentence that involves mitigation and one that does not without access to courtroom deliberations? This complication did not appear to be important in the current analysis because every subject was convicted of murder with life imprisonment as the sentence. A life sentence is unlikely to represent a drop in severity except in the rare case of capital prosecution that fell short of the death penalty. Very few of the 600–plus murderers in my sample would have received a life term as a mitigated sentence so the "fact of mitigation" could be inferred from the sheer number of murderers serving life sentences in the sample falling within the two IQ groups.

That brings us to the second complication, however. If you use the number of men who are convicted of unmitigated murder as evidence of whether the justice system makes allowance for below-normal but nonretarded intelligence, how can you distinguish between a low murderer count resulting from mitigated sentencing down to a less serious crime and the possibility that the low count in the sample resulted from fewer killings to begin with? Intelligence is generally considered to be represented in the general population by a bell-shaped distribution. A substantial proportion of people have IQs falling in the normal range; lesser numbers have IQs falling on either side—the dull-normal or bright-normal ranges; even fewer people have IQs that would place them still further away from normal—borderline on one side and superior on the other. The smallest numbers would qualify as retarded or very superior.

The point to be taken from this description of IQ distribution is that there are fewer men in the general population with borderline IQs than with dull-normal IQs, and fewer borderline men should lead us to expect a lower murder count. If the comparison between the number of murderers with IQs between 71–80 and IQs between 81–90 turns out showing fewer borderline men with that sentence, the interpretive choice between mitigation and diminished opportunity is not possible; both conclusions depend upon the same result. If the results are in the opposite direction, more murder convictions in what was the smaller original group, the argument that no mitigation was allowed for lower intelligence can be waged with greater confidence. The fact that I have gone to this much trouble in anticipation of results offers a clue as to how the mitigation analysis turned out.

When the IQs of the 600 men convicted of murder were considered, virtually the same number fell in the borderline and dull-normal ranges—10%. Certainly there was nothing in this result to suggest that any mitigation of sentencing based upon limited intelligence occurred, particularly given the more restricted pool of men with borderline intellect that would be expected in the general population.

The implications for mitigation because of subnormal but not retarded intelligence becomes even clearer when the death-row sample of murderers is considered. The men convicted of capital murder and awaiting execution on death row presented IQs of 81–90 in 8% of the cases, but IQs of 71–80 were found in 16% of the sample. This amounts to even stronger counterevidence regarding mitigation of sentencing for men with borderline intellect. Despite the limiting feature of a smaller pool of men in the general population, there proved to be twice the number of borderline men relative to dull-normal that were not only held fully responsible for the act of murder but also for the circumstances that allow capital punishment. Given the evidence from the two murder samples, the conclusion seems clear enough. As crimes under consideration come to involve premeditated/intentional deadly violence, I could find no evidence that limitations in offender intelligence short of retardation serve systematically as mitigation.

The imperfections of using IQ percentage figures in a sample of criminals guilty of lethal violence to infer shadings in courtroom sentencing decisions have been amply considered, although there is at least one more thought on the matter that should receive mention. Differences in the number of murder sentences within a sample could be contingent upon differences in susceptibility to violent criminality at varying IQ levels. The 10% and 16% figures for frequency of borderline murderers in my two samples could be as high as they are relative to the 10% and 8% figures for dull-normal criminals because men with IQs between 71 and 80 are more likely to be homicidal, especially under grievous circumstances, than men in the 81–90 IQ range. This line of reasoning would require that borderline men are so susceptible to lethal violence that it outweighs the fact that there are so few of them in the general population in determining sample numbers.

Whether the frequencies should be interpreted in terms of a greater risk of lethal violence for borderline men or the reluctance to mitigate violence at that level of severity when the perpetrator is not retarded by conventional standards cannot be determined without going beyond the percentages. However, choosing to believe that an IQ between 71 and 80 renders a man that much more dangerous, without even considering the antisociality factor, would imply an alarming view of retarded men as IQ falls to even more restricted levels.

Whatever the final verdict might be with regard to the role of low intelligence, the issue addressed by this discussion remains the same. Any point chosen on the IQ dimension that would allow reduced responsibility for criminal behavior to be assigned introduces the risk of discontinuous meaning. An IQ of 35 or less means, according to the Supreme Court and common law, that the person should not be executed for killing someone. An IQ of 36 should not mean that another person would be eligible for execution. An IQ of 70 means that someone is mentally retarded by convention; an IQ of 71 does not mean that there is no retardation. The problem of discontinuity in meaning being emphasized by these illustrations does not even invoke the added problem of IQ reliability. If scores for a given individual can and probably will change from one intelligence test to the next or from one assessment to the next on the same test, the offender may fall on both sides of a cutting score.

Implications of the Discontinuity Findings

Discontinuity of meaning poses a threat to fairness since it requires the assumption that deficits in intelligence should be considered as mitigation for a crime only if they fall within an arbitrary IQ range. What about limitations that fall above that designated range? If IQs at 70 or below in the retarded range are assigned some weight in determining criminal responsibility, would it not be fair to take borderline IQs of 71–80 into consideration as a mitigating factor or even dull-normal IQs between 81–90? No one whose intelligence falls into these three ranges is likely to have the ability to reason or appreciate the nuances of interpersonal transaction expected of brighter people, although there would be reason to expect an improvement in cognitive capability as you move up from retarded to borderline to dull-normal. As long as limited intelligence merits consideration for greater leniency in holding offenders accountable for their crimes, some greater latitude in acknowledging degrees of impairment above the retardation level would seem to be in order.

The same issue could have been raised when mental disorder was considered as the source of mental incompetence in criminal cases even though no counterpart quantified procedure for specifying degree of mental illness is available that has the general acceptance of the intelligence quotient as a determinant of mental competence. With no quantified indicator of mental disorder you seem to have nothing comparable to an IQ cutting-score problem, overgeneralization from a single IQ score, or abrupt discontinuity in meaning of IQ scores. However, the clinical diagnosis of mental disorder, as it pertains to the adjudication process, does hold at least one parallel to the assessment of mental retardation for purposes of legal decision-making.

A possible parallel to discontinuity problems in determining punishment for crimes committed by those limited in intelligence is evident in the verdicts of "guilty but mentally ill" and "not-guilty by reason of insanity." The former verdict acknowledges the role of mental disorder and presumably assures some form of special consideration while incarcerated. This could, I suppose, be considered a modest mitigation in sentencing. The latter verdict absolves the offender totally from responsibility for committing the criminal act, although the absolved offender may be institutionalized longer in a mental hospital following trial than would have been the case if convicted of the crime.

Being "mentally ill" and being "insane" appear to be categorical descriptions that do not allow for graduated adjudication based upon degrees of mental incompetence. Either a finding of "guilty but almost mentally ill" or "not-guilty by reason of near-insanity" would have an absurd ring to it. Yet diagnostic classification of mental disorders is evolving into an increasingly articulated system where "spectrum disorders," "-oid" suffixes, or reference to some type of disorder as a personality deviation allow for shaded representation of the highly disruptive symptoms of a psychotic condition. The question becomes whether such graduated and less disabling mental conditions can convince a jury that the offender was sufficiently incompetent at the time of the crime to have made a difference in how responsibility should be assigned. If so, the problems presented by discontinuous meaning in decision-making based on IQ would be confronted even though no continuous quantitative scale of mental disorder is involved. Should less serious versions of mental disorder be given some consideration in mitigating the punishment handed down? If adjudication of criminal conduct does not take degrees of incapacitation by mental disorder into account, then the problem of discontinuous meaning would appear to exist for both forms of mental incompetence.

Section Three

PUTTING IT ALL TOGETHER

Chapter Eight

A Verdict on the Death Penalty as a Deterrent to Murder

By this point in the book enough evidence has been reported regarding the death penalty to formulate a comprehensive view of its merits and liabilities as part of the state systems of criminal law in the United States. I have chosen to investigate this controversial topic in stages, and that is how these final two chapters will be organized. First, we shall consider the evidence bearing upon the essential issue facing any jurisdiction that considers including capital punishment as a possible punishment for willful killing. Does providing the threat of execution qualify as a social asset by deterring the act of murder and sparing the lives of people who would otherwise become victims? Deterrence value is the only justifiable basis for adopting capital punishment; individual passion favoring retaliation against the offender as a rationale for the death penalty or concern about taking an offender's life as the basis for rejecting it simply miss the mark.

The final chapter will deal with whether death-penalty statutes can be fairly adjudicated once they are adopted. Reaching just decisions regarding the death penalty is an especially compelling concern because it involves the extreme punishment in which offenders must irreversibly surrender their lives. That being the case it is imperative that the sentence be rendered in keeping with legal precedent and without irrelevant bias. If capital punishment as a deterrent proves of pragmatic value to society, that value would have to be weighed against any evidence of unfairness in the way it is administered before reaching a conclusion regarding its worth.

DETERRENCE VALUE OF THE DEATH PENALTY

There is no doubt what the evidence collected in this investigation has to say about whether having death-penalty statutes in place within a state deters willful killing. It plainly does. Murder rates drop, albeit gradually, when the death penalty is put into effect, and they go up precipitously when the death penalty is compromised as a deterrent or abolished. The changes in rate translate into thousands of victim lives preserved or lost over time and jurisdictions, depending upon whether the murder rate is going down or up. This general conclusion, however, is the point where unequivocal interpretation of the evidence ends for me, and it becomes necessary to consider possible restrictions or modifications. But despite this conservative approach to scientific evidence, I never lose sight of the fact that capital punishment does have social value despite what the outspoken critics of the death penalty would have us believe.

The Research Method

The first place one might look if it were deemed important to challenge the general conclusion that the death penalty is an effective deterrent to willful killing would be the research methodology that produced the evidence, assuming, of course, that the scientific method was employed. Was there something in the planning or procedures used to investigate deterrence value that generated misleading data and a faulty conclusion? Do not think for a moment that all methods of investigation on the subject have equal merit. The references in the literature to the lower murder rates of states without the death penalty are a case in point. That revelation has been the basis for not only challenging the effectiveness of capital punishment as a constraint upon murder but even for proposing that it has a counterproductive effect upon the murder rate. The low murder rates, as it turned out, could be readily understood in terms of population parameters of these states—low density and modest minority representation. The restricted murder rates were undoubtedly the reason for not having the death penalty in the first place and not a consequence of its absence. Other studies invited unreliable results by restricted sampling; too little time was allowed or too few jurisdictions were considered. Sometimes inquiry avoided the pitfalls of scientific methodology entirely by turning to professional experts such as forensic-association presidents or police chiefs for their opinions on capital punishment. We are left to wonder what kind of evidence went into these expert judgments.

The method employed in the present investigation was based upon a psychological principle governing whether something qualifies as a source of inhibition or restraint for a given behavior. Something, say X, is said to have inhibitory potential if the given behavior (Y) increases when X is removed and decreases when X is reinstated. You will recognize the psychological equivalence of inhibition and deterrence here. The criminal paradigm becomes: Deterrence by X (death penalty) has been demonstrated if Y (murder rate) goes up when X is absent and goes down when X is present. It is worth noting that this deterrence paradigm not only satisfies a psychological principle but corresponds to the dictates of logic as well.

The procedures for investigating deterrence using a present/absent paradigm took advantage of a nine-year moratorium/abolishment period for capital punishment nationwide in which the state death-penalty systems were diminished in effectiveness and then rendered inoperative by Supreme Court decisions on constitutionality issues. This provided the research opportunity to examine the influence on murder rate in death-penalty states when capital punishment was immobilized or abolished as an option, and, following the nine-year hiatus, what happened to murder rate when capital punishment was reinstated by the Supreme Court. The fate of states lacking the death penalty was available as a type of control comparison for this inhibition paradigm. Problems with unreliability based upon limited sampling were negligible, since 45 years of murder statistics covering every state in the union were gathered.

Now I suppose if someone were really grouchy about the results of this research, there would be ample opportunity to identify flaws. The deterrence value of the death penalty is not an easy subject to study, nor is naturalistic observation as scientifically rigorous as the contrived conditions of the laboratory. Criticism of methodology should be accompanied, however, by specifying why the proposed flaw provided the particular positive results that were obtained or why the flaw was responsible for the failure to disclose what the critic expected to see. Of course, criticism could be leveled at the interpretation of the evidence and not the method used to collect it; that is a legitimate enterprise. It is fair to ask, however, how much time and effort have been invested by the critic in preparing an alternative to the interpretation that is dismissed.

In my view, the natural course of recent legal history in America offered an exceptional opportunity to study the deterrence value of capital punishment, and the results were undeniably positive. Treating this study as "junk science" would be a mistake.

Differences in Commitment to the Death Penalty and Deterrence Value

I have not been reluctant to use cause-and-effect terminology throughout this book in reference to the relationship between capital punishment and changes in murder rate. The moratorium on executions beginning in 1968 **caused** the murder rate to escalate throughout the country; the escalation was the **effect**. The abolishment of death-penalty statutes as unconstitutional in 1972 **caused** the murder rate to continue its climb; the continued escalation was the **effect**. The reinstatement of revised death-penalty statutes in 1977 **caused** the murder rate to begin its progressive decline; the progressive decline was the **effect**. You get the idea. The possible problem in this presumption of causation is that we rarely have the opportunity to deal with observable cause-and-effect relationships in social science, and this is most certainly the case in studying the deterrence value of the death penalty. Social scientists are usually faced with correlational relationships in their research. That A relates to B in a certain way can be established empirically, but causation remains a matter of conjecture. It could be that A causes an effect on B or that B causes an effect on A. It is even possible that both are responsive to some third variable, C, and there is no cause-and-effect relation between the two correlated variables, A and B.

The fact that the deterrent value of the death penalty was not investigated closely enough to allow observable causation can be put into perspective when you realize that deterrence itself is not even what is examined in research like mine. The successful restraint of an inhibitory process that prevents the individual from acting upon homicidal impulses is an internal, private, and largely inaccessible process that is not feasibly studied scientifically. What can be more readily authenticated and subjected to analysis is the failure of inhibition, nondeterrence. That is what murder rate in states with capital punishment allows us to estimate—how frequently the presence of death-penalty statutes has failed to inhibit acting upon murderous impulses. This nondeterrence count certainly tells us a great deal about deterrence value, but it does not mirror exactly what is going on with respect to psychological inhibition as a private event. For example, awareness of the death penalty and the threat of execution may lend themselves to many occasions in which one individual's impulse to kill is deterred, or we might find that occasions of actual deterrence occur in some people who never experience a failure of deterrence. In either likely case, deterrence value of the death penalty would be underestimated using accessible nondeterrence as the variable of interest.

What this discussion of the literal meaning of murder rate comes down to is that I have continued to refer to evidence of "deterrence" when actually the evidence bears upon a correlate—nondeterrence. In doing so, I have taken a conservative approach to interpreting just how useful the death penalty has been as an inhibitor of willful killing. Nondeterrence of homicide **must** underestimate deterrence value. This observation bears special importance for the murder-rate statistics of the post-abolishment era. The grudging reduction in rate following reinstatement of the death penalty actually underestimates the deterrence value of capital punishment. Nondeterrence went down; deterrence increased even more.

It may seem strange that the inferential character of the deterrence evidence is being belabored—that it is correlational and does not deal directly with cause and effect and that it relies on events signaling nondeterrence as a way of drawing inferences about the deterrence process. Such admissions are not standard practice among those who concern themselves with deterrence and the death penalty, and they extend special priority to any evidence regarding the deterrence value of the death penalty that is less inferential. Actually, such evidence was reported in which the interpretive options were considerably narrowed. Please recall the rationale and results of the analysis of execution numbers in a death-penalty state as related to murder rate.

Capital punishment can be considered a system that begins with the circumstances of a homicide and its investigation by the police, progresses into how the crime is to be prosecuted, then involves jury trial and sentencing, merges into a lengthy period of incarceration on death row with the opportunity for filing appeals, and culminates in the execution of the prisoner if final appeals fail. Since the function of capital punishment as a system (as opposed to its effects) is to execute offenders who are guilty of violating death-penalty statutes, it is possible to estimate the effectiveness of a system by the number and pattern of the executions. Those states that have legalized capital punishment vary widely in commitment to their own systems; this is shown by the number of times they actually carry out an execution, the spacing of the executions that are consummated, and whether executions increase or decrease over time. As greater numbers of offenders are executed, as shorter intervals of time pass between executions, and as the tempo of executions increases rather than lags, public awareness of the state's commitment to capital punishment becomes more likely. With greater awareness that capital punishment exists as a legal option and that it is taken seriously by the state would come an enhanced potential for deterrence.

These three parameters of effectiveness were combined into a single index based upon execution figures between 1977 and 2002, and murder rates were determined for each death-penalty state for the final eight years, 1995–2002. States that had the most effective systems—the most executions overall, increasing commitment over time in terms of number, the least spacing between executions—demonstrated the greatest containment of homicides compared to their own 1958–1967 baselines. Willful killing had been brought down to a level 14% below the early standard in states with the most effective systems. States with less commitment to their systems of capital punishment according to the index score remained 39% above their baseline murder rates. States without capital punishment were included in the analysis of murder rate for sake of comparison; they displayed a rate 53% above their 1958–1967 standards. Even questionable commitment to a capital punishment system resulted in better deterrence than no death penalty at all. Counterproposals in explaining these constraint differences were examined and found lacking.

Changes in murder rate reported as percentages can make it clear that greater commitment to implementing capital punishment systems, measured in terms of execution frequency and pattern, is associated with better deterrence of murder. Perhaps I can lend emphasis to this conclusion by providing the social cost/benefit in actual lives represented by these percentage figures. The death-penalty states that qualified as most effective experienced a decline in murder rate from pre-moratorium baseline years (1958–1967) that converted into a hypothetical savings of over 15,000 lives over an eight-year period (1995–2002). On the other hand, the remainder of the death-penalty states that showed up as far less effective in implementing their systems found their murder rates still well above the early standard. This inability to return to the baseline rate cost these states an aggregate of over 24,000 lives in those same eight years.

This analysis of deterrence based upon comparisons between death-penalty states that differ in frequency and patterning of execution should be less vulnerable to dismissal or reinterpretation even among the most committed opponents of capital punishment. The execution data that defined effectiveness were collected from all states in the union having death-penalty statutes for more than a quarter century, and murder rate as an effect was tracked over an eight-year period, then compared to an appropriate baseline period of ten years for each state. Reliability of the results would be difficult to challenge. The problem of inferential distance from deterrence as a private experience is decreased, since the state's commitment to the death penalty as the key variable represents a threat tied directly to that experience.

The conclusion from the overall results comparing death-penalty states to abolitionist states is consistent with the conclusion drawn previously for the major analysis in my investigation of deterrence, that the death penalty has a general constraining effect upon willful killing. No surprise there, since comparing 1995–2002 rates to baseline is a redundant feature of the two analyses. Most importantly, this analysis demonstrated that when capital punishment assumed a more evident and ominous presence within a state as a possible sentencing outcome, murder rate was even more successfully contained. This result corresponds to the dictates of logic and common sense. If a system works generally in achieving a desired goal, a more effective version of that system should work even better. Put in different terms, if the presence of death-penalty statutes decreases the probability of willful killing, heightened awareness of the system and the perception that imposing the death penalty is a serious commitment should add to the constraint. It never hurts to have logic and common sense on your side when offering an interpretation of evidence.

The message from the primary analysis of deterrence was that the threat of execution for willfully killing another person contributes to the suppression of murderous conduct. The message from the secondary analysis of execution numbers goes beyond that, however, to specify that the threat varies with how seriously the state takes its own death-penalty system. As barbarian as it may sound, the more offenders who are executed after due deliberation, the greater the public good as far as sparing the lives of potential victims. This may continue to sound repugnant to those who maintain their strong opposition to the death penalty despite its apparent deterrence effects. Murderers who are executed for their crimes have substance—a name, a face, a family—but potential victims spared by deterrence remain an abstraction. The palpable qualities of the person to be executed may compel compassion for the known individual. The reassurance that the execution contributes to a system that stands to spare the lives of a far greater number of unknown and unknowable people might not have that ready emotional appeal. However, demonstrated deterrence value of capital punishment, especially if a serious commitment is made by the state, has a way of making such compassion a luxury that can be ill afforded if the lives of society members are to be safeguarded by law when personal conscience fails.

The Mechanics of Death-penalty Deterrence to Murder

Having placed sufficient emphasis on the interpretation of deterrence evidence and the conclusion that capital punishment does have an inhibiting effect upon willful killing, we can now move on to the question of behavioral mechanics. How does threat register with the individual in such a way and to such an extent that the risk of intentionally acting upon lethal impulse is reduced? I have to admit that my views on this matter came into much sharper focus as the investigation continued, progressing from some diffuse skepticism regarding the restraining effect, based upon little scientific evidence, to the view that explanation must be possible since states can deter murder to some degree by adopting a death-penalty system, even more if they commit to it. The skepticism probably stemmed in large measure from years of forensic assessment in which I saw more than my share of prisoners who (1) had not been restrained from killing despite residing in a state that featured the death-penalty and (2) were not particularly bright considered as a whole.

These observations coalesced, it would seem, into a supposition that capital punishment statutes were not wrong if their intent was to discourage lethal violence but were doomed to inconsequential deterrence effects because potential murderers would fail to cognitively grasp the added risk offered by the death penalty.

I can address the behavioral mechanics of deterrence more thoughtfully now that the new evidence has been reported pointing to the value of capital punishment as a constraint upon murder. Positive evidence in the face of all that others have said about why the death penalty does not work as a deterrent makes it especially important to explain how an increment in restraint can be expected even though a crime bears a heavy imprint of emotion, self-deception, moral deficit, or simple ignorance. It is true that any capital punishment system will be limited in its impact on the individual by a paucity of intelligent reasoning that would include a failure to consider the risk involved in committing a homicide. Even so, it takes only a small percentage of cases in which the threat of execution does succeed in restraining a lethal impulse to convert into massive benefits to society over states and time. The burden of explanation for why homicide is not more frequently encountered in our nation need not require that deterrence by the death penalty play a predominant role; most people would not murder as a matter of conscience.

The mechanics of deterrence afforded by capital punishment for the individual experiencing a lethal impulse, as far as I can discern, depend principally upon the operation of three interdependent psychological factors: (1) awareness that the death penalty exists, (2) if aware, the risk assigned to attracting this sentence, and (3) the fear generated by the presumed risk. The first two of these factors, degree of awareness and assigned risk, should increase with the commitment shown by the state to its system of capital punishment. Commitment, as perceived by the individual, can be gauged by frequency (and pattern) of executions within the state. Consider that between 1977 and 2003 there were five states that executed from between 57 and 313 offenders for capital crime, whereas five death-penalty states at the other extreme engaged in only one execution. There should be little doubt that awareness of the death penalty and subjective risk of attracting this punishment would be greater in these highly-committed states than in states that have consummated only one execution in 27 years.

The fear generated by perceived risk of execution as the third necessary ingredient of deterrence in a death-penalty state is another matter. Some individuals, such as those described as psychopaths, will not respond to risk in the same emotional way as others; most people would experience some degree of dread if they seriously considered the possibility of lethal punishment. Since withdrawal from or avoidance of the source are commonplace responses to fear, this might seem to be a promising place to turn in improving constraint of willful killing—the greater the fear generated by perceived risk, the stronger the constraint. However, there is not much to be done to augment the fear factor within our systems of law beyond the possibility of execution in a state that vigorously pursues the death penalty. Less humane forms of execution that might increase fear of being caught and punished have been eliminated as "cruel and unusual"—hanging, firing squad, electrocution, gas chamber—and replaced by lethal injection. Besides, the manner of execution is more likely to touch upon the concerns of those who oppose the death penalty than to influence restraint of impulse. That people who murder may be required to sacrifice their lives rather than how they will die may be all that will register given the less-than-rational character of homicidal thought.

Expecting fear generated by perceived risk to make a contribution to deterrence must be further qualified by the fact that withdrawal/avoidance responses to the source of this disturbing emotion can just as readily result in relinquishing the thought of being placed at-risk as in surrendering the impulse to kill. One nearly-universal cognitive proclivity is to stop thinking about distressing things and being executed certainly qualifies as distressing. Human versatility being what it is, there are several other cognitive defenses against fear that can be brought to bear if simple evasion fails. Rationalization, for example, allows the individual to assume that he will not be caught . . . . convicted . . . . given the death penalty . . . . executed (pick one) . . . . if he kills somebody.

I will admit that the trio of psychological factors—awareness of the death penalty, perception of risk, experience of fear—offers but a skeletal explanation of how deterrence works. This explanation can be amplified a bit by recalling that evidence in the present investigation led me to propose that a psychological climate of concern over homicide as a crime exists in some states more than others . This concern, fostered by an elevated murder rate, helps to explain why states come to adopt death-penalty statutes in the first place and sustain a greater commitment to these statutes once they are in place. Dissatisfaction with willful killing would not only encourage adoption of the death penalty as a deterrent but would represent a prevailing attitude that could affect the diligence of criminal investigation, the vigor of prosecution, jury decision-making, and resolve of state officials in exacting the death penalty. One by-product of a climate of concern regarding lethal violence would be more frequent and vivid reminders that killing is a targeted crime and one that may bring execution in its wake. This would provide a social environment within the state in which the basis for deterrence is more firmly planted; people will more likely be aware of the death penalty and the risk involved if they kill.

It makes psychological sense that states which adopt capital punishment and maintain some degree of commitment to its requirements do so because of a generalized concern over murder as a societal problem. But short of yet another poll, what kind of evidence can be brought to bear that would substantiate the notion that a "generalized concern" is likely to exist in death-penalty states? Surprisingly, the evidence from the present investigation comes from the murder-rate trends for states that did not allow capital punishment. An initially puzzling feature of the trend analyses was the fact that the moratorium/abolishment periods for the death penalty had the same releasing effect upon one-on-one homicides in states that did not have capital punishment as they did for states that had their death-penalty systems immobilized, then abolished. Murder rates climbed quickly in both state categories once executions were withheld and then ruled unconstitutional. By the same token, murder rates dropped, gradually but steadily, in death-penalty states once their systems were restored to constitutional favor, and a diminished version of the same effect was observed in abolitionist states. The overall impression generated by these trends is that bringing the murder rate down by reinstating the death penalty was a more formidable undertaking than bringing about an increased murder rate by abolishing it.

The conundrum presented by these results is why murder rate should be influenced at all by changes in the legal status of the death penalty nationally when a state does not have the death penalty. My interpretation of this generalized effect would be that there was a more lenient view of intentional killing conveyed nationally by the temporary demise of capital punishment, since the responsible Supreme Court decisions could be taken to mean that murder was in some cases being dealt with too harshly without due concern for the cruel and unusual treatment of the offender. This perception could have filtered into every state no matter what its punishment history. Similarly, restoration of the death penalty by the Supreme Court could have brought with it an increment in perceived aversion to willful killing that could affect states even though they chose not to adopt execution as a punishment. These proposed referred effects would not only explain whatever changes in murder rate that were found for abolitionist states in the trend analysis but also testify further to the importance of the death penalty. Every state seems dependent upon capital punishment as a deterrent to murder whether it is adopted as law or not, since it extends a value judgment on lethal violence available to all.

Variation Among States in the Problem Posed by Lethal Violence

The short answer to why there is variation among states in crimes of murder would seem to be that some states have more people in them, that sheer number of people makes it more likely that problems associated with social living will arise, and that there are emergent problems brought on by overcrowding in a high-population state. This short answer is not so much wrong as incomplete because of the way that willful killing was measured in the investigation. Information on the incidence of murder was taken from annual reports published by the Department of Justice, and the chosen way of reporting these data was in terms of rate, not absolute count. Murder statistics, given in terms of frequency per 100,000 inhabitants, allow one state to be compared directly with another when murder is considered as a social problem, since population size is factored out when rate is used. However, removing population count arithmetically from the comparison of states does not mean that it should be ignored as a factor in explaining the differences in murder rate that arise from the comparisons. The sheer volume of people in a state can help explain lethal violence even though population size is arithmetically removed from murder-rate comparisons. Densely-populated states experience a greater homicide problem than other states that are more sparsely populated and these populous states are more likely to include the death penalty as a possible punishment for murder as a way of stemming the tide of lethal violence.

Minority representation in a state (black, Hispanic, Asian, native American, etc.), as measured by percentage of total state population, also was considered, and two interesting features of this 1995–2002 analysis came to light. First, the 25 states with larger populations by the 2000 census count, with a mean of over 9,000,000 people, had an average minority representation of 21%; the remaining states with smaller populations, averaging under 2,000,000 people, featured a 15% mean minority representation. When population density and minority representation are considered together, this difference in percentages translates into about seven times the actual number of minority citizens in more populated states than in less populated. The second feature brought out in the analysis was that states with a higher minority representation by percentage experienced a murder rate that was twice that found in states with lower minority representation.

An attempt to disentangle the possible effects upon murder rate of the two correlated parameters, population size and minority representation, suggested that minority representation was the clearer determinant. States having the highest murder rates during the 1995–2002 period had an average population under 7,000,000, but states with intermediate murder rates were even larger, averaging over 8,000,000 people. It was not until the low murder-rate states were considered that the expected relationship between population size and problem status became evident; states with the lowest murder rates averaged less than 2,000,000 people. In contrast to this curvilinear relationship, the linkage between murder rate and minority representation was direct and clearcut. States with the highest murder rates had a minority representation of 27%; those with intermediate murder rates included a 17% minority population; states with the lowest murder rates were 9% minority.

There was agreement, then, between the two population parameters only to the extent that the coalition of low population and low minority representation in a state was associated with a restricted rate of willful killing. These also are the usual population characteristics of states that do not subscribe to capital punishment, lending support to my conclusion that states tend to ignore the death penalty because murder represents a less compelling social problem. Finding that abolitionist states are likely to have distinctive population features that seem to limit the problem of willful killing when compared to retentionist states makes it unnecessary to accept the illogical or unwieldy alternatives that (1) the absence of the death penalty serves as a source of deterrence or (2) the presence of the death penalty offers a model of willful killing.

What remains to be answered more definitively, as well as can be done with correlational data anyhow, is whether increased minority representation is simply coincidental to escalating murder rate or whether the two variables are functionally related—one leading to the other. The analysis of murder rate X minority representation that was just considered provides a start. The third of the states having the most serious homicide problems had an average murder rate 3–4 times that of the lowest tier of states having the least serious problems. At the same time, these troubled states had a minority representation that was three times that of the low-tier states. Coincidence or functional linkage?

It was possible by using information from the Justice Department's annual publication of crime statistics to derive separate counts of one-on-one murders committed by someone from the white majority or by someone from any one of the recognized minorities. Annual murder counts perpetrated by the white majority and the combined minority populations for the period 1976–2002 were computed on a national basis. These murder counts were then considered in combination with estimates of their respective population numbers according to the United States census, making it possible to calculate a rough probability figure conveying the odds nationwide that a majority or minority member would be identified following police investigation as a one-on-one murderer. This "murderer rate" was fairly stable over the 27-year period for whites, varying from 2 per 100,000 to 4 per 100,000 nationally. Within the minorities the rate showed more yearly variability, ranging between 8 per 100,000 to 20 per 100,000. Although there was a substantial decrease in minority probability around the mid-1990s, it was evident throughout the entire period of analysis that the chances of someone in a minority group within the United States engaging in willful killing were appreciably greater than found in the white majority.

The crime statistics along with the census reports did not permit calculation of probabilities for discrete minority groups except for blacks. Independent consideration left no doubt that the murderer rate in the black minority was quite high, but we are left uninformed regarding the specific rates for the remaining racial minorities. Even so, one basis for problems in lethal violence that could motivate death-penalty legislation and continuing commitment to a system of capital punishment, perhaps **the** basis, has been identified. The combination of a high general population count in a state that includes a substantial minority representation is a social recipe for an elevated murder rate; conversely, a low number in the general population and a small minority representation in a state bodes well for a restricted murder rate. A large general population and an intermediate minority representation would be associated with a rate of murder falling in-between.

The prominent role of minority representation in considering murderer characteristics and murder rate in the United States and the escalating numbers of minority members nationally make it clear why maintaining capital punishment as an effective deterrent is important. A more constructive long-term view might be that we should improve our efforts to modify the conditions that foster lethal violence in the minorities as well as in the majority white population. However, I find it difficult to be optimistic about attempts to curb murder by benevolent strategies alone. Not only should the states sustain capital punishment systems as a legal deterrent to murder, remembering what happened between 1968 and 1976 when the death penalty was effectively shelved, but the systems should be taken seriously enough by the state to qualify as a credible threat. As long as minorities remain a substantial part of the problem, disparities in the assignment of the death penalty, like those disclosed by the Baldus group in Georgia, should be expected.

Even given the evidence from this investigation that demonstrates that capital punishment deters willful killing, quite persuasive evidence in my opinion, will this contribute to the resolution of the death-penalty controversy? Quite possibly not, since those who fervently oppose state-sanctioned execution can always find some basis for rejecting the death penalty as a form of punishment even if deterrence claims are granted. Arguments against capital punishment, found in the largely oppositional literature on the subject, include those that seem unrelated to a humanistic concern for the criminal being executed. For examples, it has been opposed because of the extraordinary expense of a capital trial and the danger of irreversible error. Criticism on economic grounds maintains that a murder trial in which the prosecution is seeking the death penalty is overly expensive, perhaps costing more than keeping an offender in prison for life. The major problem with this argument is that it seems to conflict with other oppositionist concerns. Contending that capital trials are too costly because of their length and comprehensiveness runs counter to the other favored argument that these trials may not allow sufficient consideration and substantiation of details to warrant the death penalty if the offender is found guilty. Arguments in opposition to the death penalty bearing upon comprehensiveness of the trial cannot have it both ways. Is it to be too elaborate deliberation or too little deliberation? Perhaps the critics of capital punishment need to heed each other's criticisms.

Concerns about irreversible error in investigating or litigating a capital case are not without substance; mistakes cannot be rectified as far as the executed prisoner is concerned. Yet the relatively few cases in which such critical errors have been documented hardly merit scrapping the death penalty with its demonstrated deterrence value. Perhaps a way could be found to limit human error in death-penalty cases beyond comprehensive trials and the lengthy period of appeal on death row. For example, speaking as a psychologist I see no reason why the degree of certainty required in a capital case cannot be increased before the death penalty is decreed. Jurors in criminal cases are instructed to reach a specified level of certainty before assuming guilt on the part of a defendant. Why not have a somewhat more articulated set of options available to the jury in a capital case when the death penalty is conceivably at stake? The standard of "beyond a reasonable doubt" might be enough for a murder conviction in a noncapital case that would bring a life term in prison with parole possibilities or even life without parole. A standard of "near certainty" of guilt might be required before capital punishment could be considered in a sentencing phase.

If the lay juror's ability to discriminate between a personal judgment of guilt that is "beyond a reasonable doubt" and one that reaches "near certainty" seems open to question, it should be remembered that we are already dealing with a very subjective discrimination in the present procedure for establishing guilt in the American courts. The difference between a judgment that does and does not exceed "reasonable doubt" is probably no more nor less mysterious to the individual juror than would be a distinction between "beyond a reasonable doubt" and "near certainty." There are, perhaps, nuances of law being overlooked here, but the point remains the same. Mistakes in death-penalty sentencing could be reduced if greater certainty of guilt were required. It is popularly understood that such differences already exist between decisions reached in criminal cases as opposed to civil cases—the O.J. Simpson trials are recent reminders of that fact.

Chapter Nine

Fairness in Adjudicating the Death Penalty

I have emphasized the point, probably more than necessary, that it is not enough to establish whether the death penalty serves as a deterrent to murder. Although deterrence represents the basic consideration in judging the merits of capital punishment, it also is of critical importance to determine whether the death penalty can be fairly adjudicated. The case for fairness has at its core the repugnance due any abuse of power in the judicial system, and this is never more important than when a human life is at stake—when proceedings may include the possibility of the death sentence. Has this extreme form of punishment been dispensed without being systematically influenced by bias? Individual judgments that are related to determination of guilt and punishment but are based upon factors unrelated to the crime illustrate one type of bias; a second type of bias would involve considering factors that are related to the crime but in a way that would be inconsistent with fairness. Systematic bias, as I am using the term, refers to a pattern of influence across individuals and not to an isolated case.

A fairly rendered version of justice demands that the offender not only is accurately judged as guilty or innocent and, if guilty, receive the punishment due the crime, but it also requires that evenhanded impartiality is shown for all individuals committing the same crime. If capital punishment were found to deter willful killing but also found to be associated with unfair assignment of the death penalty, some revision in the system would be in order. Of course, if it had turned out that capital punishment had no deterrence value, the problem of unfairness could be obviated by dispensing with executions; there would be no sound reason why society should perpetuate the death-penalty if no legitimate social gain could be shown.

The Issue of Race in Adjudicating the Death Penalty

It was not surprising to encounter race as a source of prejudice in death-penalty sentencing, since racial enmity is a fact-of-life in the United States despite our expressed pride in a diverse ethnic make-up. Racial identity offers a way of categorizing people; sometimes it is by choice of those who are categorized and sometimes it is not. With categorization based upon distinguishable features or behavior comes the opportunity to do what people are prone to do—allow themselves to deal with their own insecurities by maintaining prejudicial attitudes toward another race. As it turns out, categorization of people can be based upon any number of attributes besides race, and the attitudes that are fostered or reflected may be positive or negative. In fact, it became evident in considering categories of people and possible contamination of fair adjudication that suspected bias could be either prejudicial or beneficial to the criminal.

Race, Interracial Murder, and Capital Punishment

The disproportionately high assignment of the death penalty when a black offender murdered a white victim became the focus for examining race as a fairness issue in adjudication. The setting for investigating possible racial bias against blacks was Georgia, early 1980s, a "deep-South" state with the death penalty and a history of racial prejudice and discrimination. The investigators were from Iowa, a Midwestern state not noted for racial enmity and without a tradition of capital punishment. Georgia featured a relatively large black minority population; Iowa had one of the smallest black minorities in the country. Georgia was a fairly large state in terms of total population; Iowa had about half the number of residents. Georgia was contending with a relatively high murder rate, the sixth highest in the country; Iowa had a low rate, about one-fifth as high. In short, Baldus and his group arrived in Georgia much like Alice in Wonderland as far as cultural history, legal tradition, and problems with lethal violence were concerned. I have no idea whether these background dissimilarities and exposure to different values had an influence on the choice of conclusions from the Baldus research evidence, and a choice there was. What they found in way of empirical evidence was that blacks who killed whites received the death penalty in a disproportionately high number of cases relative to whites who killed white victims or blacks who killed blacks. What they concluded based upon this evidence was that the Georgia courts took a prejudiced view of blacks murdering someone from the white majority and were more likely to assign the death penalty for these crimes.

The damage from what I believe to be a mistaken conclusion by the Baldus group regarding prejudicial sentencing is most evident in the ready ammunition it provided to those who wished to have a convenient reference to support their opposition to capital punishment. By citing the Baldus study and the Supreme Court's subsequent endorsement of its conclusion within the written opinions appended to **McCleskey versus Kemp**, it became possible to make a case against both racial discrimination and state-sanctioned execution. My own program of research on dangerousness as a personal attribute of the criminal had confirmed the higher risk of serious violence and the more harmful treatment of the victim for highly dangerous men. When black murderers sentenced to die for killing a white victim were studied, they were found to be more dangerous than white murderers who had received the death penalty given the same criminal circumstances. That black interracial murderers received the death penalty in disproportionate numbers was a matter of fact, but that this disproportionality could have resulted from the characteristics of the black offenders rather than prejudice in dispensing criminal justice has not attracted much attention. The black men who had targeted white victims were especially dangerous, even by the lofty standards of death-penalty murderers. Criminal dangerousness of the black interracial offenders proved capable of explaining the disproportionate sentencing.

It was possible to go beyond the death-row sample in order to shed further light on whether blacks were receiving excessive sentences for violent crimes against whites in Georgia and, if so, whether the more severe sentencing could be better explained as racial prejudice or as justified by criminal dynamics. An independent study considered the circumstances of another serious violent crime, rape, to determine whether punishment differences varied according to the race of the rapist and victim and, if so, whether racial parallels could be found to the death-penalty cases involving murder. Given more severe sentencing for black interracial rape, the critical question would be whether dangerousness would qualify as an alternative explanation for the greater punishment.

There was to be one important addition to this analysis though; the circumstances of the crimes would be examined directly to determine whether sentencing severity mirrored brutality of the sexual act as it should. Dangerousness of the rapist should be apparent not only as a characteristic of the rapist but also in the brutality of the rape. Racial prejudice would be clearly suggested in punishing this serious breach of southern tradition if the sentences handed down to black men who raped white women were more severe even though the black rapist was no more dangerous nor more brutal than the white intraracial rapist. Dangerousness of the black rapist would be the reasonable explanation if black interracial rapists were not only more dangerous but more brutal and the punishment fitted the crime.

The results of the rape analysis were helpful in clarifying the meaning of the death-penalty findings. The same racial discrepancies were apparent in

the rape patterns as were observed with capital murder cases. Blacks were frequently involved in sexual aggression against white women, but whites so infrequently raped black women that in my sample the pattern could not even
be studied. Another similarity was found in the especially high dangerousness
of the black interracial rapist compared to intraracial rapists—blacks who target black women and whites who rape white women. The similarities to the
death-penalty study continued in the more severe sentencing handed out to
the black interracial rapist—longer prison terms in this analysis rather than
more frequent death sentences. The criminal picture was set for yet another
debate concerning the seemingly harsher treatment of blacks in the Georgia
courts who have sexually violated white women—racial bias or the justified
consequence of more dangerous dispositions?

Consideration of criminal circumstances for the rape crimes provided an answer that was clearly in line with greater criminal dangerousness as the paramount factor determining the punishment of black violence against white victims in the Georgia courts. Black rapists were more brutal than their white
counterparts in the treatment of white victims and far more likely to further de-
mean the women by forcing them to submit to sodomy. Harsher sentencing for
the black interracial rapists was legitimate considering their criminal conduct;
the more brutal criminal conduct, in turn, was in line with their excessive criminal dangerousness. There proved to be no need to invoke racial prejudice as an
explanation for harsher punishment even though the rape of a white woman by
a black man represents a clearcut violation of southern racial tradition. The co-
alescence of results for the death-sentence and rape analyses lends confidence
to the choice of dangerousness over racial bias as an explanation for more severe punishment of black violence toward white victims in the south.

The investigations of capital punishment and rape sentencing with respect
to one minority in one state and involving only white victims qualify as relevant to the issue of fair adjudication of the death penalty by race but do not
represent a comprehensive look at whether diverse racial minorities are being
accorded fair treatment on a national scale. I did not have access to statistics
that would tell me about the numbers of minority and majority murderers that
are being held on death row in states embracing capital punishment, although
such numbers may well exist in some accessible document or another. What
would almost certainly not be available anywhere would be scientific data on
a national scale revealing the measured criminal dangerousness of death-row
inmates by race, on the one hand, and the analysis of actual violent conduct
and subsequent sentencing by race on the other. Without one or preferably
both of these, there would be little basis for mounting a serious challenge to
an assumption of racial bias should disproportional sentencing be found as a
national trend.

In the meantime, the use of Georgia data represents a rather stringent test of the preferable alternative given its history of minority discrimination. Blacks were not subject to prejudicial treatment when they engaged in violence against whites; they deserved the harsher sentencing that they received.

Implications of the Murderer Rate for Fair Adjudication by Race

Probability estimates regarding willful killing among racial minorities, considered together, and for the white majority received our attention earlier and could prove relevant to the issue of fairness in adjudicating the death penalty. The so-called "murderer rate" was formulated on a national level, so there should be no concern about restricted sampling involving one minority in one state. This rate was calculated by starting with the number of homicides in a year attributed countrywide by the police to anyone categorized as belonging to a racial minority or to the white majority and then dividing by the number of people falling in the minority/majority categories by census count. Over the 27 years that were analyzed, 1976–2002, the year-by-year superiority in numbers of whites over minorities combined in the United States population ranged between 6:1 and 4:1. Even though there were many times more whites than racial minorities combined, the actual number of homicides attributed to minority members was higher in 25 of the 27 years than the white homicide counts, sometimes by as much as 40% higher. Minorities engaged in willful killing against a range of victims at a clip far surpassing the rate found in the white majority, and this proved true across the entire nation.

This more prevalent display of homicidal behavior found in racial minorities opens the way to a more general observation regarding death-penalty sentences handed down to minorities and whites than the Georgia-based study allowed. Murders are being committed by minorities well beyond what would be expected based on their national representation, about 18% of the population as the 20th century ended and the 21st century began. Simple arithmetic and common sense would dictate that since the number of murders committed by minorities is way out of proportion to their national presence compared to whites, the number of capital convictions for minorities should also be disproportionately high. This reasoning would only require the same fraction of murder cases perpetrated by a minority would be successfully prosecuted as a capital case as would be found in murder by a white. A disproportional number of murder cases for minorities translates into a disproportional number of capital cases. Since what evidence I have collected would suggest a greater degree of dangerousness in minorities and a greater expectation of harm to their victims, this common-sense observation turns out to be on the conservative side. The quantity of minority homicide is not only disproportionately high, but the quality of this lethal violence is more likely to invoke capital punishment. The death penalty is overdetermined for minorities based upon offender characteristics and criminal circumstances.

Some might feel that having concentrated this much upon the proclivity for willful killing among minority groups that an investigator should endeavor to provide some explanation for this commitment to excesses of violence. It would not be difficult to speculate about social conditions that foster homicide, but I will leave that to the sociologists or social psychologists. My interest remains with improved understanding of the death penalty as a constraint upon killing and whether this form of punishment has been fairly administered. Perhaps one comment is in order regarding interracial violence. The enmity of minorities toward the white majority because of perceived or real social injustices and economic disparities could add motivational impetus to their violence against whites. "Hate crimes" are not committed exclusively by whites, although popular usage of the term can give that impression. "Hate" based upon racial identity, to the extent that it enters into the serious violence of murder and rape, would appear to be a far more commonplace emotional commodity in interracial crimes when minority men victimized white victims, at least in the case of black minority violence.

I have concluded that the capital punishment system does not adjudicate unjustly as far as racial bias is concerned and that appearances to the contrary can be explained by characteristics of the criminal and other crime-related factors. It cannot hurt to reiterate the disclaimer that goes with that conclusion, however, since it would be far too easy to reject this interpretation of the evidence by overextending its implications. The reference here is to systematic bias that permeates a criminal justice system and not to an occasional lapse in fair adjudication that would prove an exception to the rule. I am no Pollyanna who would believe that complex judgments having critical implications for others are likely to be free of any subjective irrelevancies such as racial bias; deciding guilt or innocence and severity of punishment in a murder trial would be cases in point. However, I would expect legal judgments that are blatantly racist to be rare and just as likely to benefit those who are accused of a crime as to work against them.

The Issue of Gender in Adjudicating the Death Penalty

One thing that stands out quite clearly in death-sentence statistics for this country is that this penalty for heinous murder is rarely exacted for a woman. Over a 26-year period beginning with the restoration of the death penalty in 1977 and going through 2002, the number of women sentenced to be executed represented only 2% of the number of men who received a capital punishment sentence. When it came to actually carrying out the execution over the same period, the seeming reluctance to impose the death penalty on a woman was even more apparent. The number of women executed amounted to only about 1% of the men who suffered that fate.

Since capital punishment is so rarely imposed upon women, the possibility of gender bias in the sentencing becomes an issue—that given criminal circumstances that call for capital punishment, adult females are routinely spared the death penalty for murder, whereas men are unfairly required to face this ultimate punishment. The counterproposal would be that these discrepancies result from the fact that violence is less frequently observed in women, and it is qualitatively different from male violence when it does occur. Female violence by this accounting is not only less common compared to men but is more restrained when it does occur. Both would contribute to the infrequency of death-penalty verdicts for women. The pattern of evidence, as it turned out, favored the counterproposition that the paucity of women on death-row and their rare execution had much more to do with the nature of female violence in general and killing in particular than with a failure to curb bias involving a chauvinistic protection of women from harm.

The evidence on the subject of gender bias in capital punishment begins with the relatively uncomplicated observation that there are far fewer violent crimes committed by women than men in this country as gauged by prison population counts. However, taken alone this is an especially precarious basis for addressing the issue of gender bias. The number of women and men who end up in prison convicted of a violent crime confounds gender bias and criminal proclivities so that the ratio does not go far in deciding the issue. The limited number of women in prison for committing a violent act could result from protective attitudes that influence investigation, prosecution, or courtroom sentencing when a woman is suspected of a violent crime. Restricted numbers of incarcerated women relative to men, on the other hand, could just as well mean that they less often engage in the kinds of violent misconduct that get people into prisons.

Fortunately, there proved to be several avenues of evidence bearing upon the uncertain meaning of the vast difference in number of female and male murder convictions and in the number of death-penalty sentences that result. None proved to be critical in itself, but the implication common to every analysis was the same. They all favored the conclusion that women rarely attract the death penalty because they do not deserve it according to the laws governing crime, not because of protective gender bias.

Sex-role Differentiation and Its Influence on Willful Killing

Actually, developing an alternative to gender bias as an explanation for the seeming reluctance to execute women who have committed murder should begin back a step from their criminal conduct. We should first consider the traditional socialization process that molds female personality as it may be distinguished from male personality—the sex roles. Although it can be readily observed that female sex-role development has been under revision for over 30 years in the United States, some traditional distinctions between males and females have not disappeared. Among these is the female unwillingness to engage in physical aggression that seeks to impose bodily harm. As a general rule, women will not engage in physical violence unless seriously provoked. Cultural accommodation to this sex-role expectation for women can still be observed, although the distinction is certainly eroding. Efforts are still made to prevent intentional insertion of military women into active combat situations; sports are still restricted by gender with those involving aggressive physical contact being reserved largely for male participation.

On the other hand, police forces and other protective agencies are incorporating females into roles requiring the use of physical force if called for and exposing them to the risk of physical violence. A trend showing women filling roles and engaging in activities previously reserved for males would still not contradict a more general observation; involvement in a physically-aggressive act is more alien to the culturally-based character of a woman than a man. This psychological restraint on engaging in physical aggression goes a long way in explaining the lower rate of criminal violence for women and the corresponding sparseness of women in prison convicted of violent crimes relative to men. Focusing on murder as a violent extreme, the fewer occasions in which women have engaged in willful killing automatically translate into a reduced number of capital convictions.

Indirect Evidence Bearing upon Gender Differences in Murder Rate and Capital Punishment

The drastic difference in death sentences handed out to the two sexes, one woman for every fifty men, is so extreme that it encouraged continued exploration into actual crime and punishment factors before the importance of gender bias in capital sentencing could be seriously downgraded. This led me to consider two types of evidence bearing upon the female murderer and her act of lethal violence that could cast additional light upon the subject. The first type included lines of evidence that have indirect bearing on whether gender bias is involved in capital punishment. The second type of evidence was more direct, since it considered the circumstances surrounding the actual criminal behavior of the woman who kills and whether this would have an effect on imposing the death penalty.

One piece of indirect evidence came from examining the impact of the feminist movement in the United States upon the sentencing patterns for women and men as it surged nationally in the early 1970s. Given that the movement was about equalizing the expectations for the two sexes, it follows that this emphasis would show up in the courtroom with more equitable sentencing for the same nominal crimes. Men clearly had been subjected to harsher treatment in terms of prison time before the arrival of feminism turned things around and punishment by gender tended to equalize. This depended, however, upon how physical aggression factored into the crime. Nonviolent offenses began to attract much the same punishment for women and men; time in prison became less discrepant for violent crimes as long as physical violence was only threatened (robbery) or at least did not have lethal consequences (assault). These changes serve as evidence that gender bias favoring the female had been operative before feminist influence and that treatment of the two sexes moved toward equality of sentencing in the courts after the protective lid came off.

But what happened when the crime involved lethal physical aggression (manslaughter in this analysis) as far as sentencing was concerned? There was no change in the discrepant amount of punishment for women and men as a consequence of the women's movement; women received more lenient sentences both before and after its arrival. The implication here, although indirect, is that there is something intrinsic to the circumstances of killing by a female that defied the trend toward equal punishment and precluded a change in the radical sentencing discrepancy between women and men. Even when modified cultural expectations encouraged equal punishment for the two sexes in the justice system and that effect had shown up for other crimes, killing by a woman called for more lenient sentencing. The case for gender bias that favors women who engage in lethal violence would be weakened should anything intrinsic to criminal circumstance be identified that would explain the sentencing imbalance. The singular reluctance of the justice system to punish women who kill as much as men would suggest that such a difference in circumstance does set female killing apart from that of the male. This difference may be even more apparent if you extrapolate from less vicious manslaughter crimes to homicidal behavior.

A second piece of evidence, again indirect, bearing upon the lack of correspondence between sentencing for lethal violence committed by women and men came from the study of criminal dangerousness in women. A substantial amount of research with men had confirmed a linear relationship between level of dangerousness as a personal characteristic of the criminal and severity of violence perpetrated by the offender with murder at the extreme. Increasing dangerousness not only was associated with more severe types of violent crime for men but also with more brutal treatment of the victim within particular violence categories—rape and murder.

When the same measure of criminal dangerousness was introduced into a study of female violent criminals separated by crime-severity levels, the linear relationship observed in male offenders was not apparent. This resulted from the failure of women at the most severe level of violence, those convicted of murder, to qualify as particularly dangerous on the independent measure as had been found with men. Male murderers, then, were found to be exceedingly dangerous even by violent criminal standards, whereas female murderers were lacking in dangerousness using comparable standards for women. This inconsistency serves as a further reminder that the circumstances under which women kill are distinguishable from those surrounding the homicidal behavior of men. The difference implied by the dangerousness evidence resides in the lower expectation of excessive violence for women who murder in contrast to male murderers. Again we have an indirect piece of evidence that would help explain less punishment in general for women who kill, especially less occasion for the death penalty. It is not only that women are less predisposed by character to engage in physically-aggressive crimes that have lethal consequences, but their violence would lack the brutal excesses found in men when they do kill. Gender bias is not necessary to explain the appearance of more lenient treatment.

Direct Evidence Bearing Upon Gender Differences in Murder Rate and Capital Punishmen

The empirical probes of female violence discussed to this point also provided additional data relating more directly to the specific circumstances of the crimes that had been committed. The question became whether the explanation for the remarkably lower number of death-penalty sentences for women than for men could be taken beyond the less frequent indulgence in lethal violence shown by women to differences in the circumstances under which murder is perpetrated by the two sexes. Specifically, are female homicides more likely to include circumstances prescribed by the criminal code as mitigating in nature? If so, the rate of capital sentencing for murder by a woman would be decreased.

One study on sentencing female and male criminals that we considered previously compared their punishment for committing the same nominal crimes—murder, manslaughter, assault, robbery, burglary/theft, forgery and drug offenses. Part of the procedures involved examination of the criminal circumstances in each offender's file and judging the degree to which the offense was impulsive or was planned. The results were clear. Crimes that entailed physical aggression toward the victim (murder, manslaughter, assault) were more impulsive for both sexes than crimes that only threatened such violence (robbery) or did not involve violence at all (burglary/theft, forgery, drug offenses). However, the impulsiveness of the female offender who engaged in physical attack was far more apparent than for her male counterpart.

This extraordinary impulsiveness of female criminals did not extend to robbery or nonviolent offenses; in fact, women who engaged in crimes lacking physical aggression did so in a very premeditated way, more planful than was true for men.

The isolation of physically-aggressive crimes, especially murder, as examples of extraordinary impulsiveness in female criminality is important to explaining the low death-penalty count for women. Impulsivity of a violent act means that there is a lack of premeditation; lack of premeditation signals limitation on intent; and unintentionality serves as a mitigating circumstance. This source of mitigation would be important in determining whether a killing is to be considered involuntary manslaughter, voluntary manslaughter, or murder and whether a murder should bring incarceration or capital punishment. The chances of the death-penalty option being exercised for spontaneous killing is probably close to zero.

The second mitigating criminal circumstance that would contribute to the scarcity of death-penalty sentences for women came to light in the course of analyzing female violence as it related to criminal dangerousness. The random sample of cases involving women murderers usually had adult males as the victim; furthermore, in over half of the cases in which the murderer was female and the victim was male, a history of physical abuse by the man was in evidence. Prior abuse by the victim might well be viewed as provocation for the murder and as a mitigating factor, since it would make the act of killing more understandable in terms of justified retaliation or self-protection.

You might be tempted to question the importance of prior abuse by the male victim as a mitigating factor in female killing, since the women in this study having such a history received a life sentence for murder despite the abuse. More critical numbers, however, required to demonstrate mitigation quantitatively were not available—the number of women with a history of abuse by the victim whose convictions for lethal violence were reduced from murder to manslaughter or not convicted of a crime at all. The most critical numbers for present purposes would be the number of women who did not have to face capital prosecution for a killing with abuse as a circumstance, or if they did, were not given the death penalty. I have little doubt that these numbers would demonstrate the importance of prior abuse by the male victim as a source of mitigation for women who kill.

There you have it—an amalgam of factors that have indirect and more direct bearing on why such a low number of women receive the death penalty for taking a life. Socialization practices restrict the woman's engagement in physical aggression in the first place. Criminal dangerousness plays a more elusive role in willful killing for women. Female lethal violence is especially impulsive and often can be explained as being provoked by abuse, both qualifying as possible mitigating circumstances when it comes to sentencing. It is uncertain whether these and other factors not investigated fully account for the disproportionality of capital sentencing by gender, although it seems clear enough that the lack of balance between women and men cannot be explained by rampant chivalry in the contemporary criminal justice system.

The Issue of Mental Competence in Adjudicating the Death Penalty

The verdict of evidence and reasoning regarding race and gender came out much the same as far as fairness in assigning the death penalty was concerned. The racial disproportionality in capital punishment between minority groups and the white majority as well as the disproportionality in capital sentencing between men and women can be explained to a large extent by differences in offender characteristics or in criminal circumstances without introducing race or gender as sources of systematic bias. The dispensing of justice emerged as generally fair, as a response to crime-related factors rather than irrelevant attitudes toward the criminal.

When mental competence of the offender was investigated as it influences the enforcement of capital punishment statutes, it was a different matter. The effort to integrate compassion for mental incompetence as a handicap with the basic expectation that individual adults are responsible for their own behavior has not as yet been successfully achieved. Consequently, an uneven, therefore unfair, administration of justice has ensued. Irregularities in allowance for mental incompetence can be found in the legal process whether disorder or retardation is being considered. The two types of mental impairment are understandably treated diagnostically as distinct conditions, each presenting its own brand of symptoms, antecedents, and prognostic implications. However, there are surprisingly similar problems inherent in the attempt to take the two types of mental incompetence into consideration in adjudicating crimes of violence and the death penalty.

Mental disorder is most clearly recognized as an exculpatory factor in determining criminal responsibility for violence in the not-guilty-by-reason-of-insanity (NGRI) verdict. This judgment involves the assumption that the offender's mental disorder at the time of the crime was responsible for the act because it made it impossible to distinguish right from wrong, created an irresistible impulse, or provided some other compelling basis for criminal conduct.

Lost in the assumption that a disordered mental condition can be held responsible for a violent act is the possibility that offenders may harbor a disposition toward criminal action that is independent of their mental disorders and that the crime occurred because they were criminally disposed, not because they were mentally disordered. Criminal dangerousness, a complex psychological factor involving an interaction between limited cognitive competence and antisocial values, represents just such a disposition. Closer examination of men who had not been held responsible by the courts for varied crimes of violence when acquitted by an NGRI verdict, revealed especially high scores on an index of criminal dangerousness. Their risk scores were actually higher than those obtained from prisoners found guilty of the same crimes of violence and sent to prison. Accordingly, the men not held responsible for their violence because of mental disorder presented a more serious risk of criminal violence than men who were deemed responsible for their actions. The evidence was rounded out by showing that excessive dangerousness, at a level comparable to that found in NGRI violent offenders, was associated with criminal risk that went beyond a greater chance of violent conduct in general. That level of dangerousness was found in men who had committed the most severe forms of violence, rape and murder, and had done so with excessive displays of brutality. These NGRI acquittees would not be chosen to make the case for the benign character of mentally-disordered men.

Relevance to the death penalty can be seen in a hypothetical murder case where mental disorder is being considered as a mitigating circumstance. If criminal dangerousness as an alternative dynamic qualifies as high enough, the basis for judgment would become more complicated. The chances that the offender is criminally disposed and should be held responsible for violent conduct must be weighed against the incapacitating possibilities of mental disorder. The problem lies in judging the extent to which the person should answer for the crime given the effects of mental disorder that might mitigate responsibility for violent conduct, on the one hand, and criminal dispositions that argue for individual responsibility on the other. To automatically ignore dangerousness in such cases would offer an unfair advantage to dangerous mentally-disordered offenders.

There is a third possibility that makes the diagnostic situation even more complicated. Both criminal dangerousness and mental disorder could act in concert to promote violence; assigning priority to one set of dynamics or the other might be impossible because they are confounded. The deviant thinking of the disorder in this third possibility would feed into the limited thought capabilities of the dangerous individual to put the person's antisocial character into a fearsome cognitive context.

The possibility of unrecognized alternative dynamics in criminal behavior also exists when mental retardation is considered as a mitigating factor, although I did not present evidence to that effect. Dangerousness in the mentally retarded depends entirely upon whether the person is antisocial given the way it is measured; the cognitive limitations contributing to dangerousness are present by definition, since a low IQ is required for establishing mental retardation. Accordingly, any adjudication of serious violence by a mentally-retarded offender should consider antisocial values as a possible determinant. If the offender is antisocial, the potential for dangerous criminality emerges as a risk factor rather than limited ability to appreciate the nuances of social and physical reality inherent in mental retardation.

Another set of problems in considering mental incompetence as a mitigating circumstance in adjudicating criminal punishment was discussed in the context of mental retardation, but analogous complications exist for mental disorder as well. These problems follow from the fact that mental retardation represents a marked limitation of intellectual abilities along with associated social disabilities. Conclusions about retarded status are based to a large extent upon intelligence test scores, and therein reside the problems. Fixed scores are selected as points on an IQ continuum that define who is retarded and who is not or, if retarded, what the level of retardation is. Once such cutting scores are adopted, there seems to be a tendency to take the arbitrary score too literally. This lends itself to the problem of assigning different meanings to scores on each side of a fixed point even though the scores are close in value. Unwarranted dichotomies may result such as "retarded" versus "not retarded" even though the score difference is trivial. The most unfavorable consequence of overdependence on a cutting score as far as fairness of adjudication is concerned is that limited intelligence outside of the retarded range may have contributed to criminal activity but would be ignored rather than given some modulated weight in determining punishment because the person is not "retarded." Simply because an IQ score falls above a cutting point does not mean that limitations in intelligence did not play a role in criminal conduct; deficits in borderline and dull-normal individuals could merit examination without bending the concept of mitigation out of shape.

There is an analogous problem in considering mental disorder as mitigation in that a given disorder may be treated diagnostically as a fixed category when in fact the defining symptoms can be expected to vary in intensity, when all defining symptoms are not evident from one case to the next, or even when the symptoms vary from one observation to the next for the same individual. In short, disorders not only differ from one another in how much they incapacitate someone but any given disorder can be observed in "all shapes and sizes," on a continuum of sorts.

There is no fixed-point temptation in diagnosing mental disorder, since continuous test scores are not likely to be a paramount consideration in reaching diagnostic conclusions. There is, however, a similar problem because of the subjectivity of the diagnostic process upon which degree of incapacity is to be judged. Much the same symptom patterns, varying principally in degree of incapacitation, may characterize graduated versions of the same-sounding disorder. For example, someone could be diagnosed as an acute schizophrenic, as a chronic schizophrenic, as an incipient schizophrenic, as a schizophrenic in remission, as suffering from a schizophrenic spectrum disorder, as schizoid, as a schizophrenic personality disorder, or perhaps, other variations on a symptomatic theme that have eluded me. Where on this progression of incapacity should the line be drawn for the purposes of mitigation if justice is to prevail?

Yet another problem inherent in determining the mitigation value of mental incompetence derives from the requirement that the cognitive limitation in question must be assumed to have influenced the commission of the criminal act to be considered by the court. Two difficulties have to be surmounted in order to reach a valid conclusion. The first of these is that retroactive analysis of the accused offender's psychological condition at the time the crime was committed will be required, and diagnosis based upon inferences about past behavior is more difficult than reaching diagnostic conclusions about current condition based upon present observations. The more distant the time of the criminal act, the greater the difficulty. The requirement of retroactive diagnosis presents a greater problem when mental disorder is being considered rather than mental retardation, since retardation is a less variable condition than mental disorder.

The second difficulty inherent in determining the importance of cognitive limitation in the commission of a crime is that it is necessary to establish whether the mental condition had a bearing on the criminal conduct in question. It is not enough to conclude by retroactive inquiry that the offender was mentally disordered or retarded at the time of the crime. The assessment must establish the extent to which the offender's cognitive impairment was responsible for the criminal act, a formidable challenge in some cases. Someone could be experiencing auditory hallucinations during the period that a crime occurred but that does not mean that voices commanded the execution of the crime; they actually could have been cautioning restraint. A person could have been mentally retarded when the crime was committed, but that does not preclude simplistic recognition that a bullet fired from a pistol can kill and that killing is a forbidden act.

Perhaps enough has been said, pro or con, about fairness in adjudicating the death penalty as far as possible sources of bias are concerned to allow a summary statement about the performance of the criminal justice systems in that regard. The evidence suggests that neither race nor gender represents an important source of systematic bias in capital punishment decisions, appearances to the contrary. Mental incompetence, as mitigation for violent conduct or exemption from execution, does seem more vulnerable to bias because of the inherent limitations of diagnosis and more formidable obstacles to understanding how cognitive limitations influence violent acts. Some improvement is possible, but problems are not likely to be fully eliminated. All in all, there is no basis for bypassing the pragmatic value of the death penalty as a deterrent because of imperfect adjudication of capital punishment systems; imperfection is a trademark of human systems.

References

Adler, F. (1975). *Sisters in crime.* New York: McGraw-Hill.

Armstrong, G. (1977). Females under law—protected but unequal. *Crime and Delinquency, 23,* 109–120.

The Atlanta Journal and Constitution (1988, June 11). Clergy: Toughen sentences in black-on-black crime.

Bailey, W.E. (1990). Murder, capital punishment, and television: Execution publicity and homicide rates. *American Sociological Review, 55,* 631–633.

Baldus, D.C., Pulaski, C., & Woodworth, G. (1983). Comparative review of death sentences: An empirical study of the Georgia experience. *Journal of Criminal Law and Criminology, 74,* 661–753.

Bowers, W.J. (1988). The effect of executions is brutalization, not deterrence. In K.C. Haas & J.A. Inciardi (Eds.), *Challenging capital punishment: legal and social science approaches.* Newbury Park, CA: Sage.

Cattell, R.B., & Cattell, A.K.S. (1958). IPAT Culture Free Intelligence Test. Champaign, IL: Institute of Personality and Ability Testing.

Chesney-Lind, M. (1977). Judicial paternalism and the female status offender. *Crime and Delinquency, 23,* 121–130.

Cohen, R. (2004, November 18). Death penalty: The American way. *The Atlanta Journal and Constitution.*

Dahlstrom, W.G., & Welsh, G.S. (1960). *An MMPI handbook: A guide to use in clinical practice and research.* Minneapolis: University of Minnesota Press.

Erlich, I. (1975). The deterrent effect of capital punishment: A question of life and death. *American Economic Review, 68,* 397–417.

Gough, H.G. (1957). *Manual for the California Psychological Inventory.* Palo Alto, CA: Consulting Psychologists Press.

Grossman, H.J. (Ed.) (1973). *Manual on terminology and classification in mental retardation: 1973 revision.* Washington, D.C.: American Association on Mental Deficiency.

Hathaway, S.R., & McKinley, J.C. (1951). *Manual for the Minnesota Multiphasic Personality Inventory* (Rev. ed.). Minneapolis: University of Minnesota Press.

Heilbrun, A.B. (1979). Psychopathy and violent crime. *Journal of Consulting and Clinical Psychology, 50,* 546–557.

Heilbrun, A.B. (1982). Female criminals: Behavior and treatment within the criminal justice system, *Criminal Justice and Behavior, 9,* 341–351.

Heilbrun, A.B. (1990). Differentiation of death-row murderers and life-sentence murderers by antisociality and intelligence measures. *Journal of Personality Assessment, 54,* 617–627.

Heilbrun, A.B. (1996). *Criminal dangerousness and the risk of violence.* Lanham, MD.: University Press of America.

Heilbrun, A.B., Foster, A., & Golden, J. (1990). The death sentence in Georgia, 1974–1987. Criminal justice or racial injustice? *Criminal Justice and Behavior, 16,* 139–154.

Heilbrun, A.B., & Heilbrun, M.R. (1985). Psychopathy and dangerousness: comparison, integration and extension of two psychopathic typologies. *British Journal of Clinical Psychology, 24,* 181–195.

Heilbrun, A.B., & Heilbrun, M.R. (1986). The treatment of women within the criminal justice system: an inquiry into the social impact of the women's rights movement. *Psychology of Women Quarterly, 10,* 240–251.

Heilbrun, A.B., & Heilbrun, M.R. (1989). Dangerousness and legal insanity. *The Journal of Psychiatry and Law,* Special reprint (Spring).

Katz, J.L. (1987, July 5). Death penalty data dispute racial bias claims. *The Atlanta Journal and Constitution.*

Klein, L.R., Forst, B., & Filatov, V. (1978). The deterrent effect of capital punishment: An assessment of the estimates. In A. Blumstein, J. Cohen, & D. Nagin (Eds.), *Deterrence and incapacitation: estimating the effects of criminal sanctions on crime rates.* Washington, D.C.: National Academy of Sciences.

Knopf, I.J. (1979). *Childhood psychopathology: A developmental approach.* Englewood Cliffs, NJ: Prentice-Hall.

Layson, S. (1983). Homicide and deterrence: Another view of the Canadian time-series evidence. *Canadian Journal of Economics, 16,* 52–73.

Miller, K.S., & Radelet, M.L. (1993). *Executing the mentally ill: The criminal justice system and the case of Alvin Ford.* Newbury Park, CA: Sage.

Perske, R. (1991). *Unequal justice? What can happen when persons with retardation or other developmental disabilities encounter the criminal justice system.* Nashville: Abingdon Press.

Pollak, O. (1950). *The criminology of women.* Philadelphia: University of Pennsylvania Press.

Sellin, T. (1959). *The death penalty.* Philadelphia: American Law Institute.

Smart, C. (1977). *The contemporary woman and crime.* London: Routledge & Kegan Paul.

Vila, B., & Morris, C. (1997). *Capital punishment in the United States: A documentary history.* Westport, CT: Greenwood Press.

Winslade, W.J. (1983). *The insanity plea: The uses and abuses of the insanity defense.* New York: Charles Scribner's Sons.

Wolpin, K. (1978). Capital punishment and homicide in England: A summary of results. *American Economic Review, 68,* 422–427.